Religion, Order, and Law

RELIGION, ORDER, AND LAW

A Study in Pre-Revolutionary England

by DAVID LITTLE

OXFORD
BASIL BLACKWELL
1970

CONTENTS

Acknowledgments

It is perhaps only the Calvinist who can genuinely appreciate the logic by which authors feel compelled to give credit to others for whatever is worth while in their books and to take full responsibility on themselves for whatever failings there are. That common practice comes about as close to illustrating Calvin's "paradoxical" doctrines of grace and sin as anything I know. My debts of gratitude for the grace of others are very great. Correspondingly, those who have so generously aided me bear no guilt for the depravities of this volume.

The study began as a dissertation under the wise and stimulating tutelage of Professor James Luther Adams of Harvard Divinity School. Professor Adams first introduced me to Max Weber and the importance of the questions Weber was raising about the relation of religion and society. Furthermore, he whetted my interest in the law, and particularly in the law of corporations. It was because of his initial encouragement that this entire project came into being. His continuing counsel and guidance on the content and construction of the essay, and his painstaking reading and rereading of the manuscript, simply put me deeper in his debt.

This project attempts to relate materials which are usually treated independently of one another by different disciplines. It is not unpresumptuous to undertake such a study, and whatever success it may achieve is the result of the supererogatory labors of three men who supervised parts of my work during the dissertation stage. The chapter on the common law is the fruit of continuing correspondence and conversation with Professor Harold J. Berman of the Harvard Law School. Likewise, it was through the stimulation and criticism derived from several years' association with Professor Paul L. Lehmann, now of Union Theological Seminary, that the chapter on Calvin was produced. Thirdly, Professor Talcott Parsons of the Department of Social Relations at Harvard University has been of immense help. His general framework of analysis, as well as the specific suggestions and comments he has made, have been invaluable. Ever since the ideas expressed here

i

began to germinate, Professor Parsons has given me encouragement and direction.

At certain points, I have considerably altered the manuscript from its original form as a doctoral dissertation. Whether they know it or not several people, by reading and commenting on the manuscript or by conversing with me about the issues involved, have assisted me greatly in refining and clarifying the argument. I owe particular thanks to Professor Robert N. Bellah of the University of California at Berkeley, to Professor Jaroslav Pelikan of Yale University, and to Professors J. H. Hexter and David D. Hall of the Department of History at Yale University. I also wish to thank the various students at Harvard and Yale who, either consciously or unconsciously, helped to develop and improve the thoughts expressed here.

My appreciation also to Professor Ross Kilpatrick of the Department of Classics at Yale University and to his wife, Susan, for their invaluable assistance in translating the Latin and French passages in the chapter on Calvin. Moreover, I wish to thank those who have assisted with the typing of the manuscript at various stages in its life: Mrs. Judy Becker, Mrs. Madeline Clee, and my secretary at Yale Divinity School, Mrs. Helen Kent.

I should like to acknowledge the Corporation and the Committee on General Scholarships of Harvard University for awarding me the Kennedy Travelling Fellowship for 1961-62. It made possible an enriching year of research in Germany and England and provided an opportunity for preparing this study in its form as a dissertation. While in Europe, the staff of the Evangelische Akademie at Arnoldshain, Hessen und Nassau, were good enough to accommodate my family and me during a seven-month stay. Moreover, I am grateful to Professor Dietrich von Oppen of the Seminar für Sozialethik at Marburg University. He very kindly made it possible for me to combine work on the dissertation with a most fruitful association with him.

Finally, the debt of gratitude I owe my wife, Priscilla, is inexpressible. Her encouragement and cheerful support during the process of research and writing were indispensable. It is to her, and to our son, Jonathan, who helped us both keep our sanity, that I gratefully dedicate this book.

DAVID LITTLE

Hamden, Connecticut, 1968

Preface

In this book David Little shows us what it is to work originally and creatively in a great scholarly tradition. No mind in twentieth-century social thought is richer or more various than that of Max Weber. Nowhere was his insight deeper or his argument more complex than in the famous case of the Protestant ethic. Unfortunately, much of the work ostensibly testing or criticizing Weber's hypothesis has been unenlightening either through failure to comprehend the relevant issues or failure to present new evidence or both. Few have combined a mastery of Weberian dialectic with control of the primary sources, which alone would allow a real advance in the discussion. Merton's work concerning the relation of Protestantism and science and Benjamin Nelson's on usury were notable exceptions. More recently the remarkable book of Michael Walzer, *The Revolution of the Saints,* and now the present volume make it possible to hope that a new level of understanding of these complex issues is being attained.

This book is in no sense simply a defense of Weber. As in the case of Walzer, what we are given is a major revision of Weber's thinking. But what makes these revisions so impressive is that they are not based on casual misreading or stubborn preconception, as so many of the transient "refutations" of Weber have been. Rather they begin with the closest reading of the relevant Weberian texts and a wide comprehension of their place in the entire Weberian corpus. Both Little and Walzer, for example, use Weber's notion of patrimonialism to give structural solidity to the traditional forms of thought and action against which Protestantism was reacting. But whereas Walzer then goes on to

iii

illuminate the implications of radical Protestantism for political ideology and organization much more richly than Weber did, Little proceeds to recast the whole theological basis of Weber's argument.

For long, many have thought Weber's socio-psychological argument concerning the significance of anxiety about salvation in motivating economic action too slender a peg on which to hang such weighty social consequences. Indeed the larger context of Weber's sociology of religion, with its stress on the significance of prophetic religion generally and its special capacity to provide the basis for the rationalization of the whole of life, placed the Protestant ethic problem in a much broader framework. But Weber himself never returned to the sources of Protestant theology to work out the implications of this broader view. It is precisely that broader view which David Little has given us in this book. Without denying the significance of salvation anxiety, he has nonetheless shown that the new contribution of Protestantism lay above all in a new conception of order—of the meaning of personal existence in relation to God, and consequently of the meaning of all social relations and activities. Not only does he reinterpret Calvin's theology in this framework, but he traces the continuity of Calvin's insights through Elizabethan English Calvinists to the period of later seventeenth-century thought, which Weber takes as the classical expression of the Protestant ethic. It is perhaps worth noting that Walzer, too, stresses the continuity of Calvinism through this same period, though by concentrating on political ideology Walzer sees less clearly than Little its underlying theological basis.

Finally, Little applies his insights to the field of law, only fitfully related before to the Protestant ethic discussion. Here, above all, a new conception of order should have important resonances. Without pressing the argument for mechanical "influences," Little nonetheless subtly demonstrates the congruity between the legal revolution associated with the name of Coke and the new conceptions of voluntaristic action and of differentiated spheres of social life emerging from Protestant thought. It is clear from this discussion and elsewhere that Little is not arguing for some emanationist view of ideal causation. Rather he shows how ambiguously and ambivalently many of the new ideas worked out when applied to conflicting interests in intransigent contexts. But where circumstances allowed, the new ideas led to the development of new modes of ordering social relations, modes sharply contrasting to traditional patrimonial forms.

It is impossible here to refer to more than a few of the suggestive implications of the present book. Unlike some of the sensational volumes on "the Weber thesis," this one will be with us for years to come, providing valuable lines of inquiry for future ·investigators to follow through. The significant thing about this book is that in it Weber has found a successor capable not only of holding the line against errant nonsense, but of recasting fundamental features of the argument in the face of new evidence and new theoretical insight. In so doing, Mr. Little has provided us with a high standard for future work in this field.

ROBERT N. BELLAH

Berkeley, California
September 1968

Religion, Order, and Law

PART I.
INTRODUCTION

1. The Problem

Sixty years ago Max Weber published his famous study, *The Protestant Ethic and the Spirit of Capitalism*. In it, as is commonly known, he argued that there was more than a casual or coincidental association between Calvinistic Puritanism and the dramatic social changes of seventeenth-century England. Something in this energetic religious movement made an indispensable contribution to the emergence of modern society. If the "spirit" or "ethos" of that age was becoming secular, was turning toward the things of this world, if it embodied a vigorous concern for economic enterprise, the explanation lay not in the withering away of religious interest but in the development of a new kind of religious motivation. The rise of modern industrial society in England must be understood not only as an economic or social movement but as a religious movement as well.

The Protestant Ethic, of course, did not stand alone. It was part of a much wider comparative endeavor which yielded the brilliant studies of China, India, and ancient Israel. On the basis of all this massive work, Weber sought to develop a theory of religion and society that would account for the independent formative place that religion appeared to him to occupy in the generation and establishment of patterns of social action.

Weber's provocative conclusions in these matters have stimulated a prodigious amount of sociological, historical, and religious inquiry, and they have ignited heated and extensive scholarly controversy that gives no evidence of abating. As we shall see, Weber's theoretical endeavors in the sociology of religion have been attacked, redefined, and defended

1

from an impressive number of angles.

There are particularly two related lines of criticism of *The Protestant Ethic* that set the stage for our reflections on Weber's work.[1] First, different scholars have argued that Weber was wrong in singling out Calvinist Puritanism, or "ascetic Protestantism," as he called it, as a peculiar source of legitimation for modern industrial society. To begin with, they contend that in fact there was nothing very special about the "spirit of capitalism" in seventeenth-century England. To the extent that it existed there, it existed in many other parts of post-medieval Europe as well. Consequently, something other than English Puritanism must account for the emergence of that spirit.

Furthermore, even if it could be demonstrated that seventeenth-century England was unique in the way Weber alleged, he was wrong, they argue, in perceiving any kind of affinity between ascetic Protestantism and the spirit of capitalism. There is a wide gulf separating Calvin's views on economic and social order and those of the Puritans Weber discussed. In contrast to some of the Puritan ideas, Calvin's beliefs could hardly be said to foster an independent spirit in anything, let alone economic affairs. If there are any hints in Calvin's thought of support for modern rational forms of social and economic order, they must be attributed to extraneous influences.

Second, there is a popular assertion that not only was English Puritanism sharply distinct from Calvin's attitudes, but that Puritanism itself represented either no consistent or no positive outlook on questions of social and economic order. Several kinds of argument come to the same conclusion. Puritanism may be seen as a diverse phenomenon about which all generalizations are suspect. Or it may be seen as basically a religious movement, which is for the most part either irrelevant to social affairs or, at least, indistinguishable in such affairs from other religious persuasions like Anglicanism. Finally, Puritanism may be viewed as a coherent movement whose chief effect was to encourage an atomistic individualism in society and thereby to undermine, rather than to promote, any conception of social order at all.

How does Weber's approach stand up in the light of these serious criticisms? Has Weber's work been dispensed with altogether? Need we move now in paths quite different from his? Or are there perhaps suggestions in the method he used and, at least, in some of his conclusions that with further exploration and refinement can be of service to

1. See Bibliographical Essay A, "Representative Literature Critical of *The Protestant Ethic*," for details.

contemporary work?

In order to answer these questions, it is necessary to examine the relation of religion and the rise of modern industrial society more narrowly than Weber did, and to utilize more systematically and somewhat more elaborately some of the methodological suggestions he himself made. Specifically, attention must be given to Weber's underlying contention that a deep conflict pervaded seventeenth-century English society, a conflict between what he called a "traditionalistic" social order and a "legal-rational" (or modern industrial) one. In the most general terms, Weber understood as traditionalistic those societies in which one institution, whether religious or political or familial, dominates all the others on the authority of the past. By legal-rational order, he meant those societies in which the various institutions have achieved a relative degree of independence and autonomy on the authority of "functionally specific" or "rational" norms. Was Weber right in thinking that it was the tension between these two patterns or types of order that characterized the strains not only in political, legal, and economic institutions, but also in the religious institutions and outlooks of the period?

In *The Protestant Ethic,* Weber argued his case for the congeniality of ascetic Protestantism and modern capitalism by leaping hastily, as many of his critics have charged, from a study of Calvin (1509-64) to a study of the Puritan Richard Baxter (1615-91). He thus ignored the formative stages of Puritanism in the late sixteenth century, a period when the historical continuities between Geneva and England were often immediate and direct. With Weber's fundamental hypothesis in mind, we shall investigate the possible similarities in point of view between Calvin and two representative Puritans of the late sixteenth century, Thomas Cartwright and William Perkins. Cartwright is chosen for obvious reasons: he was certainly the intellectual leader of the Elizabethan Presbyterians, and he undertook most energetically to enunciate and defend their cause. Perkins is selected because he was one of the outstanding theologians of the sixteenth century, and his copious writings, while of great influence at the time, have largely been neglected by recent scholarship.

First, we shall try to discern the degree to which Calvin's own theological and moral thought manifests the characteristics of Weber's legal-rational type of order. And we shall try to ascertain whether, as Weber implied but never methodically showed, much of Calvin's thought can in fact be organized around these characteristics. In other words, does

Calvin provide a basis for a conception of social order in which various institutions attain a degree of mutual independence on the basis of delimitable functions? Second, these same questions will be put to Cartwright and Perkins in order to assess their similarity with Calvin and to evaluate their contribution to the rise of legal-rational order in England.

Not only did Weber neglect the formative years of Puritanism, he also failed to deal in any systematic way with the Anglican opponents of Puritanism. Hints of his conclusions about Anglicanism can be found scattered through *The Protestant Ethic* and elsewhere, but he nowhere substantiated his conviction that Anglicanism supplied a theological justification for a traditionalistic pattern of order. This is another of the gaps in Weber's study we hope to fill. Accordingly, the views of Calvin, Cartwright, and Perkins will be compared with those of two outstanding Anglicans of the late sixteenth century, Archbishop John Whitgift and Richard Hooker. The voluminous debates between Whitgift and Cartwright, and the extension and refinement of the debates by Hooker, make such a comparison natural. These debates epitomize the central issues in the religious life of Elizabethan and early Stuart England. Neither the "official Anglican" position (as I shall refer to it) nor the Puritan position can accurately be understood apart from the other. Indeed, a full appreciation of the heart of Puritan thought is impossible without an examination of the Anglicanism against which it was reacting. Furthermore, Anglicanism deserves to be treated in its own right so as to grasp the novelty of the theological point of view it introduced.

Finally, before one can try to relate the religious divergences to strains in the social order, as Weber did, it is necessary to know whether the strains actually do conform to Weber's typology of order. Can the social tensions present in pre-Revolutionary England be adequately understood as tensions between "traditionalism" and "legal-rationality"?

In order to make this question more manageable and also to be more precise than Weber in answering it, our investigations will be limited to some of the legal strains and controversies of the time, particularly those surrounding the control and character of corporations. Given our interests, this is a natural area of inquiry. Weber himself had a good deal to say in *The General Economic History* about the significance of changes in corporation and monopoly law for the rise of modern capitalism. What is more, a lively debate has developed since the publication of *The Protestant Ethic* as to whether the legal decisions on corporations up to 1623 (the Statute of Monopolies) revealed a bias in favor of modern rational capitalism on the part of certain leading lawyers such as Sir Edward Coke.[2]

Until recently, there has been a rather uniform tendency among scholars to view Coke and his colleagues as the innovating proponents of free-market capitalism and the instruments of the "first industrial revolution." This view has now been challenged with the argument that the lawyers were actually traditionalists who rendered judgments more according to the conventions of the past than to the innovations of the future.

It will be our task to determine whether either of these views is completely correct, or whether the legal decisions and statutes on corporations do not manifest precisely the strain between traditionalism and legal-rationality that we have come to look for in the religious controversies of the time. Having answered that question, we shall be in a position to compare the religious and legal outlooks of the period.

2. See Bibliographical Essay B, "The Question of Economic Requlation in Pre-Revolutionary England."

2. Religion, Order, and Law
and the Thought of Max Weber

THE PROBLEM OF ORDER

Weber's interest in studying religion and society centers in what may be called the problem of order. He gives us a hint of the nature of this problem in *The Theory of Social and Economic Organization:* "Conduct, especially social conduct, and quite particularly a social relationship, can be oriented on the part of the actors toward their *idea* of the existence of a *legitimate order.*"[1] Human social action, Weber believed, is fundamentally ordered action; it is organized in keeping with rules and patterns that are reasonably coherent and consistent. The coherent and consistent character of human action is the basis for the creation of patterns of social expectation, or of institutions. In simple terms, societies are systems of ordered or structured action.

More than this, however, a human action system inevitably places a claim upon the participants, that it should be held by them as "legitimate"[2] or as desirable. Societies never demand of their members mere submission to established institutional patterns; they always attempt to "legitimate" or justify their patterns in the name of some higher set of values and beliefs. The foundations of any society are eventually asserted to be in harmony with the ultimate structure of things, and,

1. *Theory of Social and Economic Organization*, trans. A. M. Henderson and Talcott Parsons (New York, 1947), 124; referred to hereafter as *Theory*. This particular translation, which seems more accurate, is taken from *Max Weber on Law in Economy and Society*, ed. and trans. Edward Shils and Max Rheinstein (New York, 1967), 3.
2. The term "legitimacy" for Weber means more than simply a sacred rubber stamp applied to an already existing social order. For Weber, the process of legitimation itself helps to shape a social order.

consequently, to be "right." Such assertions, according to Weber, fall within the realm of belief and therefore of religion,[3] because it is religious beliefs that characteristically symbolize the ultimate "structure of things," the ultimate meaning and purpose of human life and action. Insofar as legitimacy is an ingredient of social life, the question of religion is thus necessarily raised.

The matter of a "legitimate order," however, is not only related to the structure of social relations—to the reasonably coherent patterns of institutional rules and regulations that every society must in one way or another develop. It is also related to another essential element or dimension of social life, the authority to command by which any society is ruled or "ordered." Weber called this the "imperative control" (Herrschaft)[4] of a group. No social order can exist without the designation of centers of authority which have the power[5] to give and enforce orders.

But again, an authority, like a societal structure, involves the notion of legitimation. Just as a society will attempt to justify its "rightness" on the basis of a higher set of beliefs and symbols, so an authority— whether it be a king, a religious leader, or a parliament—will inevitably seek to validate its right to command by reference to some higher set of loyalties. This is because authority requires acknowledgment on the part of the governed; it strives for acceptance, not simply submission. As Weber puts it: "In general, it should be kept clearly in mind that the basis of every system of authority, and correspondingly of every kind of willingness to obey, is a *belief*, a belief by virtue of which persons exercising authority are lent prestige."[6]

From Weber's point of view, then, every society is faced with the process of arranging itself in such a way that its institutional structures and its patterns of authority fit into an ultimate frame of meaning that commands the loyalty of its members. This is, in a word, the problem of order.

Religion is a legitimating agent in social life for Weber because, as

3. See "Social Psychology of the World Religions," in H. H. Gerth and C. Wright Mills (eds.), *From Max Weber* (New York, 1958), 270 ff., and *The Protestant Ethic and the Spirit of Capitalism,* trans. Talcott Parsons (New York, 1958).
4. Weber defines *Herrschaft* as "the probability that a command with a given specific content will be obeyed by a given group of persons" (*Theory*, 152).
5. " 'Power' (*Macht*) is the probability that one actor within a social relationship will be in a position to carry out his own will despite resistance, regardless of the basis on which this probability rests" (*Theory*, 152).
6. *Theory*, 382.

pointed out, it seeks to provide an ultimate framework within which man's total experience and behavior can fit together coherently or "rightly." As he puts it, there is a demand implied in religious belief, "that the world order in its totality is, could, and should somehow be a meaningful 'cosmos.' "[7] In the sense that a general in the army both possesses the highest or most ultimate command (or authority) and is at the same time responsible for the whole army, religion, in Weber's view, handles the problem of "general" order. It supplies the final authority for action and, at the same time, binds together all the various aspects of society into a coherent pattern. "Wherever the direction of the *whole way of life* has been methodically rationalized [or systematized], it has been profoundly determined by the ultimate values toward which this rationalization has been oriented. These values and points of view were thus *religiously* conditioned."[8]

This is a very important point in Weber's methodology. It helps explain why he undertook such general studies of the relation of religion and society in China, India, ancient Israel, and so on. He wishes to emphasize that it is impossible to understand one very salient characteristic of religion without investigating the conceptions and expressions of a society's whole way of life. How are the imperatives and organizational patterns of economic action related to familial, political, and stratification patterns and on what ultimate basis is the particular configuration of relations justified? Religious symbols and language deal with these questions; so they must be analyzed.

Moreover, this point further helps to explain why Weber's three famous ideal types[9] of "order" (or authority)—traditional, charismatic,

---

7. "Social Psychology of the World Religions," 281.
8. *Ibid.*, 286, 287.
9. As Parsons points out in *Structure of Social Action* (Glencoe, 1949), "the only positive characterization of the ideal type that Weber gives is that it is a construction of elements abstracted from the concrete, and put together to form a unified conceptual pattern" (603). For Weber, in other words, the ideal type is a one-sided accentuation upon certain data, for purposes of study and comparison. It is a method by which certain facts are grouped together under general headings and related to what are understood as "leading motifs" or characteristics. Terms like "bureaucracy," and historical categories like Renaissance, Reformation and Middle Ages are examples of what Weber has in mind. A type is "ideal" in the sense that because it is one-sided it is necessarily artificial; it does not concentrate on everything that happened, only selected aspects. For Weber's own treatment of this subject, see " 'Objectivity' in Social Science and Social Policy," *Methodology of the Social Sciences*, trans. E. A. Shils and H. A. Finch (Glencoe, 1949), 90 ff.

and legal-rational—were invariably treated in connection with an analysis of religion. These three fundamental types of social order, according to Weber, are respectively legitimated, and sometimes initiated, by appropriate kinds of religious symbols and patterns of behavior. To discuss categories of general social order and authority is to discuss at some point the system of symbolism that undergirds and gives them ultimate validity. In fact, any sociologist who is concerned to understand society in general as a complete system of action necessarily involves himself, according to Weber, in an examination of religious phenomena.

Weber undertook his empirical study of the relation of religion to the problem of order because of his abiding fascination with the emergence of the legal-rational type of order in the modern West.[10] In keeping with his fundamental theoretical interests, he felt constrained to uncover the belief patterns that legitimated and stimulated the development of an industrialized, bureaucratized, secularized way of life. The institutional arrangements, the "chains of command," characteristic of modern life are, Weber argued, substantively and consistently different from those patterns that in one form or another have dominated most world cultures. His conclusions on this point are succinctly summarized in the following passage:

> In legal [-rational] authority, submission does not rest upon the belief and devotion to charismatically gifted persons, like prophets and heroes, or upon sacred tradition, or upon piety toward a personal lord and master who is defined by an ordered tradition, or upon piety toward the possible incumbents of office fiefs and office prebends who are legitimized in their own right through privilege and conferment. Rather, submission under legal [-rational] authority is based upon an impersonal bond to the generally defined and functional "duty of office." The official duty—like the corresponding right to exercise authority: the "jurisdictional competency"—is fixed by rationally established norms, by enactments, decrees, and regulations, in such a manner that the legitimacy of the authority becomes the legality of the general rule, which is purposely thought out, enacted, and announced with formal correctness.[11]

Weber initially attacked the problem of legal-rational order by way of an analysis of "rational capitalism," something that designated strik-

---

10. *The Protestant Ethic,* 26. See Reinhard Bendix, *Max Weber: An Intellectual Portrait* (New York, 1960), 71 ff.
11. "Social Psychology of the World Religions," 299.

ingly, he felt, the patterns of modern social organization and action.[12]
Rational capitalism is above all characterized, he believed, by modes of
calculation and behavior that are specifically and systematically
"oriented, by deliberate planning, to economic ends."[13] That means
that the authority and duties of the economic office are carefully distinguished from the authority and duties of other offices (e.g., military,
political, or familial offices) and that they are closely defined in terms
of their jurisdictional competency.[14]

> Rational industrial organization, attuned to a regular market, and
> neither to political nor irrationally speculative opportunities for
> profit, is not . . . the only peculiarity of Western capitalism. The
> modern rational organization of capitalistic enterprise would not
> have been possible without two other important factors in its devel-
> opment: the separation of business from the household, which com-
> pletely dominates modern economic life, and closely connected with
> it, rational book-keeping. . . . The development of capitalistic asso-
> ciations with their own accounts is also found in the Far East, the
> Near East and in antiquity. But compared to the modern independ-
> ence of business enterprises, those are only small beginnings.[15]

Of fundamental importance, then, in the emergence of economic
rationality (indeed, of legal-rationality in general) is the *differentiation*
of economic action from the immediate and detailed imperative control
of noneconomic interests and institutions.[16] Such a step makes

12. As Parsons says rightly in his Introduction to *Theory*, "'Capitalism,' in the
    sense in which Weber meant it, must be regarded not as a form of economic
    organization alone, but as the distinctive pattern of a whole society" (79).
    Herbert Luethy makes the same point in an otherwise debatable essay, "Once
    Again: Calvinism and Capitalism," *Encounter*, XXII, 1 (January 1964), 28.
13. *Theory*, 158.
14. The same process of specialization applies, of course, to noneconomic occupa-
    tions as well.
15. *The Protestant Ethic*, 21-22.
16. A very interesting statement of this matter is found in Karl Polanyi, *The Great
    Transformation* (Boston, 1957): "A self-regulating market demands nothing
    less than the institutional separation of society into an economic and political
    sphere. . . . No society can exist without a system of some kind which ensures
    order in the production and distribution of goods. But that does not imply
    the existence of separate economic institutions; normally, the economic is
    merely a function of the social, in which it is contained. Neither under tribal,
    nor feudal, nor mercantile conditions was there . . . a separate economic sys-
    tem in society." And Polanyi makes a point which was also important to
    Weber, as we shall see: "A market economy can exist only in a market
    society" (71).

possible "the specialization of autocephalous and antonomous units in a market economy" whose activity is controlled only indirectly by a set of formal regulations and procedures.[17]

Weber believed that this pattern of institutional differentiation entailed at least five decisive consequences for the "spirit of capitalism"— a term which he understood to mean rational capitalism as a whole way of life:[18]

(1) To render economic action relatively autonomous is, as we have pointed out, to make economic rationality possible. According to Professor Parsons, Weber had two specific things in mind here:

a) Tradition is radically devalued—nothing is sacred merely because it has become traditionally accepted and established, everything must be tested anew in terms of a universalistic [impersonal] standard . . .

b) The systematization of conduct according to rational norms. No single act can stand by itself or be valued on its own merits alone, but only in terms of its bearing on a whole system of rational conduct. [19]

(2) The radical devaluation of tradition implies an important distinction between past and future, between old and new, so that economic action is no longer bound by the stereotypical patterns of the past but is oriented toward the future in terms of continuous growth, movement, advancement. Acccording to Weber, this sort of long-range, future-oriented calculation demands above all a high degree of disci-

17. *Theory*, 229. Weber frequently contrasted "formal" rationality—so much a part of modern society—with arbitrary or "substantive" rationality. The latter subordinates concern for creating objective "rules of the game" to the fancies of a ruler or the oracles of a priest. Bendix correctly summarizes Weber's view: "Patriarchal and theocratic powers are primarily interested in substantive rationality. They approach all legal questions from the viewpoint of political expediency or substantive justice and hence disregard any limitations on their actions that might arise from requirements of formal procedure or logical consistency," from *Max Weber*, 394-395. Cf. "Social Psychology of the World Religions," 298, and *Max Weber on Law in Economy and Society*, 63.

18. The notion of "spirit" (*Geist*), which is admittedly very slippery and which has caused so much trouble in the controversy over *The Protestant Ethic*, designates for Weber the idea of ultimate commitment. That is, the salient characteristics of rational capitalism constitute a meaningful and purposeful way of life in which people come to believe. In other words, wherever one finds the characteristics of rational capitalism commanding the moral loyalty of people, there one may discover the "spirit of capitalism."

19. *Theory*, 80.

pline. It demands the self-conscious systematization of economic activity in such a way that immediate gratifications are deferred (by means of plowing back profits, investing, saving, etc.). "Unlimited greed for gain is not in the least identical with capitalism, and is still less its spirit. Capitalism may even be identical with the restraint, or at least a rational tempering, of this irrational impulse."[20] The demand for self-conscious discipline entails, then, a process of *reordering* economic activity in keeping with differentiated ends and purposes.

(3) To differentiate economic action from other sorts of action, such as familial, military, and political, and to regulate it acccording to impersonal standards, is to make room for independent, voluntary activity. As Weber says, "adventurous and speculative trading capitalism and all sorts of politically determined capitalisms are possible" without a system of formalized, impersonal rules, but not "rational enterprise under individual initiative . . ."[21] Modern rational capitalism presupposes "the rational organization of free labor,"[22] which "in formal terms," as Weber says, "is *purely voluntary*."[23] Such a system implies considerable elbow room for mobility, self-initiative, and individual achievement on the basis of universalistic critieria (e.g., merit), since it does not unalterably fix the individual's occupation, and the way in which the occupation is conducted, with reference to noneconomic, "irrational" considerations.

(4) To rationalize behavior in the modern sense is to base social relationships upon universal or open criteria, rather than upon particular or closed criteria. "The 'objective' discharge of business," says Weber, "primarily means a discharge of business according to *calculable rules* and 'without regard for persons.' 'Without regard for persons' is . . . the watchword of the 'market' and, in general, of all pursuits of naked economic interest."[24]

> A social relationship . . . will be spoken of as "open" to outsiders if and in so far as participation in the mutually oriented social action relevant to its subjective meaning is, according to its system of order, not denied to anyone who wishes to participate and who is actually in a position to do so. A relationship will, on the other hand, be called "closed" against outsiders so far as, according to its subjective meaning and the binding rules of its order, participation of certain

20. *The Protestant Ethic*, 17; cf. 60.
21. *The Protestant Ethic*, 25.
22. *The Protestant Ethic*, 24.
23. *The Theory*, 279; italics added.
24. "Bureaucracy," in *From Max Weber*, 215.

persons is excluded, limited, or subjected to conditions.[25]

In strictly economic terms, Weber firmly believed that a distinctive characteristic of rational capitalism is its universalistic or "mass" orientation. "The unfolding of the modern form of capitalism as an economic system is connected with the development of mass purchasing power for industrial products,"[26] power which, in turn, depends on the development of a mass market.[27] This is, of course, simply an extension of the notion that economic rationality is defined in terms of open-ended, impersonal, nonpreferential standards.

(5) It follows from the foregoing that tasks will be functionally specialized and that they will be allotted on the basis of functional standards. In other words, emphasis will be placed on the useful or instrumental or "efficient"[28] character of a task in attaining economic goals, as well as the technical capacity of an individual to perform it. As Weber remarks, "the specialization of function . . . is crucial to the modern development of the organization of labor."[29]

Now Weber's contention here is twofold: first, he suggests that the five characteristics of the spirit of rational capitalism come to typify the patterns of a complex, differentiated social order, one that allows for relatively autonomous and independent realms of authority and action. That is, Weber is not concerned exclusively with economic behavior, but rather with the development of a broad set of institutional patterns, of which economic activity represents one aspect. Second, he suggests that these characteristics become articles of belief as well as designations of behavior. They come to have normative significance for the participants; they become part of a general, legitimate scheme of meaning. The problem of order, as described above, is no less a problem for an emerging rational capital society than it is for any other type of society. *The Protestant Ethic and the Spirit of Capitalism* was written to suggest that some of the characteristics of the spirit of capitalism are contained in the theological symbols and beliefs that could initially solve—or at least give some direction to—the crisis of order which attends the development of modern industrial society.

25. *Theory*, 139.
26. *Grundriss der Sozialokonomik*. III. Abteilung: *Wirtschaft und Gesellschaft*, referred to hereafter as *WuG (Tübingen, 1925)*, 746. The translation is mine. Cf. *Theory*, 279-280.
27. *WuG*, 742.
28. *Theory*, 161.
29. *Ibid*, 226.

The theological key to the affinity between ascetic Protestantism and the spirit of rational capitalism Weber found in the notion of a supramundane God, one who is both author of the world and at the same time clearly independent or differentiated from the world. He is engaged in a continous process of reordering the world in keeping with his transcendent will and purpose. Consequently, the salvation of man consists in active response to God's "call" to participate in this reordering process as a divine instrument. Weber believed that this set of theological and ethical beliefs inspired a vigorous desire for methodical, systematic mastery over one's vocational life, in order to bring it in line with God's will:

> An unbroken unity integrating in systematic fashion an ethic of vocation in the world with assurance of religious salvation was the unique creation of ascetic Protestantism alone. Furthermore, only in the Protestant ethic of vocation does the world, despite all its crea-turely imperfections, possess unique and religious significance as the object through which one fulfills his duties by rational behavior according to the will of an absolutely transcendental god.[30]

> [Puritanism] alone created the religious motivations for seeking sal-vation primarily through immersion in one's worldly vocation. This Protestant stress was upon the methodically rationalized fulfillment of one's vocational responsibility. . . . The inner-worldly asceticism of Protestantism first produced a capitalistic state, although uninten-tionally, for it opened the way to a career in business, especially for the most devout and ethically rigorous people.[31]

Though Weber never developed very systematically the connections between Puritanism and all five characteristics of the spirit of capitalism, the suggestions are there. Obviously, he believed that the crucial dis-tinction between past and future, old and new, is present in the Puritan system, thereby giving solid support to the devaluation of tradition and making possible a disciplined resystematization of conduct in keeping with long-range, future-oriented goals. Furthermore, status is no longer determined by tradition, but rather by the clear manifestation of volun-tary, independent achievement. Vocational activity is not circumscribed by convention, kinship attachment, or arbitrary favoritism, but is characterized by general rules of conduct set down "without regard for persons."[32] Finally, the Puritan's specialized functional or instrumental

---

30. *Sociology of Religion*, trans. Ephraim Fischoff (Boston, 1963), 182.
31. *Ibid.*, 220.
32. *Religion of China* (Glencoe, 1951), 237.

role in the world becomes of great religious importance in serving the will of God.

It is through this association with Puritanism, Weber argued, that rational capitalism as a way of life—as a general system of legitimate, meaningful order with a distinctive set of institutional norms—became established.

As we have pointed out, Weber wished to compare and contrast the legal-rational or rational-capitalist pattern of order, together with its particular legitimating beliefs, with the other types of order, traditional and charismatic. By means of his comparative method, or "method of difference," he set out to show that, alongside other conditions, the role of religion as a legitimating agent is of central importance to the shape and direction a given social order takes.

In formal terms, Weber understands "traditionalistic order" as a category that is polar to legal-rationality. As he defines it, "a system of imperative coordination ['authority'] will be called 'traditional' if legitimacy is claimed for it and believed in on the basis that the sanctity of the order and the attendant powers of control as they have been handed down from the past 'have always existed.' "[33] Though "traditionalism" is a rich term with many important refinements, it was classically expressed, Weber believed, in China and India, and was legitimated respectively by Confucianism and Hinduism. In both societies, the political, economic, familial, and religious institutions—in short, the patterns of institutional order—were all collectively determined by ancient conventions, by the old order. Despite certain inclinations to the contrary, particularly in China,[34] both societies were closed virtually from top to bottom. Status and occupation were ascribed according to blood relations, family connections, and arbitrary political favoritism. Economic and political activity were all directly interwoven with family and religious life, as exemplified most singularly in the Hindu caste system.[35]

33. *Theory*, 341; *WuG*, 130: "Traditional soll eine Herrschaft heissen, wenn ihre *Legitimität* sich stützt und geglaubt wird auf Grund der Heiligkeit *altüberkommener ('von jeher bestehender') Ordnungen und Herrengewalten.*"
34. Weber, of course, treated with a good deal of sophistication the rational bureaucratic tendencies manifest throughout the history of Confucian China. Nevertheless, he indicated that because of religious, political, and other circumstances these tendencies never issued in a consistently differentiated, impersonal social pattern. Clan and patrimonial considerations were far too strong. See *Religion of China*, VI.
35. See *Religion of India* (Glencoe, 1958). Cf. *Sociology of Religion*, 42.

Consequently, the legitimate patterns of order manifested in both cases opposed the development of independent, rational action.

> The first and fundamental effect of [traditionalistic] religious views upon economic activity was generally stereotyping. The alteration of any practice which is somehow executed under the protection of supernatural forces may affect the interests of spirits and gods. To the natural uncertainties and resistances of every innovator, religion thus adds powerful impediments of its own. The sacred is the uniquely unalterable.[36]

Theological and ritual conceptions in both Confucianism and Hinduism militated against a "social-revolutionary ethic" that would have encouraged institutional differentiation and the emergence of the spirit of capitalism. As religions of the old order *par excellence,* Confucianism and Hinduism fairly consistently resisted all five of the characteristics of this spirit mentioned above.

There is one refinement Weber makes of the category "traditional order" that is especially relevant to our investigations. "Where authority is primarily oriented to tradition but in its exercise makes the claim of full personal powers [of the ruler], it will be called 'patrimonial authority.' "[37] Within this subtype the ruling authority is normally chosen "traditionalistically" (for example, with reference to a traditional family lineage), but it develops a nontraditional discretionary sphere of personal powers. The nontraditional element is not, however, rationalized in impersonal terms, but consists only in an extreme development of the sphere of arbitrary will and grace.

Patrimonial authority, Weber argues, often encourages certain kinds of capitalism, but it is always opposed to the rise of rational capitalism. As a result of the range of discretionary powers invested in patrimonial authority, it is sometimes possible to ignore or substantially to depart from the rigid conventionalism of traditionalistic societies, and to some degree to innovate in politics or economics. Consequently, certain forms of "politically oriented capitalism" (or mercantilism) are possible under the patrimonial control of an Elizabeth or a James in England, of a Louis XIII or XIV in France. However, that which distinguishes rational capitalism from politically oriented capitalism is, as we would expect, the matter of differentiation. Patrimonialism invariably subsumes economic activity under political control and direction. It pre-

36. *Sociology of Religion,* 9.
37. *Theory,* 347.

vents the sort of independent rational economic calculation that is so
much a part of the spirit of capitalism; instead it subjects economic
prospects to political calculation, to questions of national defense, of
the aggrandizement of the crown, and the like. In short, patrimonialism
leads to what Weber calls "fiscal capitalism":

> The essence of mercantilism consists in carrying the point of view of
> capitalistic industry into politics. . . . The purpose is to strengthen
> the hand of the government in its external relations. Hence mer-
> cantilism signifies the development of the state as a political
> power . . .[38]

Weber points out that politically oriented capitalism inspires and, to
a certain degree, cultivates an *Unternehmungsgeist*[39] (an entrepreneurial spirit), but not the independent entrepreneurial spirit implicit in rational capitalism. "The mercantilistic regulations of the State
might develop industries, but not, or certainly not alone, the spirit of
capitalism; where they assumed a despotic, authoritarian character,
they to a large extent directly hindered it."[40] As Weber indicates again
and again, politically oriented capitalism is wedded to a monopolistic
economic policy that is based on arbitrary favoritism. That is, monopolistic control of industries is granted by the crown on the basis of
political considerations, considerations that usually are, from the point
of view of economic efficiency, quite irrational. Speaking of the patrimonialism of England and France in the seventeenth century, Weber
writes:

> In practice, the mercantilism of the Stuarts was primarily oriented
> along fiscal lines; new industries were allowed to import only on the
> basis of a royal monopoly concession and were to be kept under the
> permanent control of the king with a view to fiscal exploitation.
> Similar, although not so consistent, was the policy of Colbert in
> France. He aimed at an artificial promotion of industries, supported
> by monopolies . . .[41]

The distinction, then, between patrimonial capitalism and rational
capitalism is absolutely central to Weber's whole analysis: "It follows

38. *General Economic History*, trans. Frank H. Knight (New York, 1961),
    255-256.
39. *WuG*, 744.
40. *The Protestant Ethic*, 152.
41. *General Economic History*, 257. Cf. 213, though Weber is incorrect when he
    asserts that "these industrial monopolies established for fiscal purposes broke
    down almost without exception after the triumph of Parliament." See also
    Theory, 318.

that the [rational] capitalistic development was not an outgrowth of national mercantilism ... "[42] In the profound struggle and contention over precisely this patrimonial authority and order in seventeenth-century England, Weber saw the opposition of these two types of economic organization:

> Here ... irrational and rational capitalism faced each other in conflict, that is, capitalism in the field of fiscal and colonial privileges and public monopolies, and capitalism oriented in relation to market opportunities which were developed from within by business interests themselves on the basis of saleable services.[43]

Now we must remember that patrimonialism is for Weber a pattern of general order, a way of life. Like any other order it requires religious legitimacy that, in turn, entails certain general institutional norms and directives. So far as England is concerned, Weber found the legitimating agent in the form of Anglicanism, which, as a politically oriented religion, was characteristically inclined toward the "organic" hierarchical social system implicit in patrimonialism. Weber argued that the "ideal of patrimonial states is the 'national father,' " a notion grounded in "the authoritarian relationship between father and children."[44] He further argued that Anglicanism encouraged this sort of arbitrary paternalism by associating itself almost inseparably with the State and by justifying the crown's preferential monopolistic policy.[45] Again, the point to be emphasized is the consistent lack of any basis for differentiated order in Anglicanism, of any leverage for prying certain spheres of action loose from patrimonial domination. There is nothing in Anglicanism that undercuts the traditionally ascribed status and political system or the general allegiance to the old order. On the contrary, Anglicanism vigorously resisted any attempt to do such things.

It was Calvinistic Puritanism, Weber believed, that provided the requisite antitraditional impulse in seventeenth-century England so absent in Anglicanism. The system of belief and action briefly referred to above contained a crucial ingredient in face of the English Establish-

---

42. *General Economic History*, 258.
43. *General Economic History*, 258.
44. *WuG*, 751. The translation is mine.
45. See *Protestant Ethic*, 179; *General Economic History*, 257. In this connection Weber writes: "So in der Neuzeit in England unter dem Regime der Stuarts in ihrem Kampf gegen die autoritätsfeindlichen Mächte des puritanischen Bürgertums und der halbfeudalen Honoratiorenschichten: die Laudsche christliche Sozialpolitik war teils kirchlich, teils patrimonial motiviert," *WuG*, 751. William Laud served as Archbishop of Canterbury until 1645.

ment: a religious basis for the devaluation of political patrimonialism. "Puritan denominations [were, in part, motivated by] ... the theoretical insight that the political apparatus of force could not possibly provide a place for purely religious virtues, whether uncompromising rational ethics or acosmistic fraternalism. This is one source of the affinity between inner-worldly asceticism and the advocacy of the minimization of state control ..."[46] Weber also believed that English Puritanism allied itself with the rising bourgeosie over against the paternalistic favoritism of the crown and the system of politically oriented capitalism that the crown supported.[47]

In England the royal and Anglican policy was broken down by the Puritans under the Long Parliament. Their struggle with the king was pursued for decades under the war cry "down with the monopolies"

46. *Sociology of Religion,* 227.
47. Throughout his investigations, Weber was deeply interested in the relation between religion and social class, an interest certainly stimulated by Marx. "The kind of empirical state of bliss or experience of rebirth that is sought after as the supreme value by a religion has obviously and necessarily varied according to the character of the stratum which was foremost in adopting it. ... These [class] tendencies have not by themselves determined the psychological character of religion; they have, however, exerted a very lasting influence upon it" ("Social Psychology of the World Religions," 279). This association is indicated again and again, for example in *Sociology of Religion,* 92-97. Accordingly, it was the affinities between Puritanism, the capitalist spirit, and the middle class that were particularly intriguing for Weber. He claimed it was Puritanism which "favored the development of a rational bourgeois economic life; it was the most important, and above all the only consistent influence in the development of that life." Indeed, according to Weber, it is difficult to distinguish Puritanism from the burgeoning bourgeoisie: "With great regularity we find the most genuine adherents of Puritanism among the classes which were rising from a lowly status, the small bourgeois and farmers ... " (*Protestant Ethic,* 174; cf. Bendix, *op. cit.,* 78-79).

At many points, Weber writes as though an independent, self-conscious, Puritan-dominated middle class were clearly established during the seventeenth century in England. The same has been assumed and even more fully developed by authors like R. H. Tawney and Christopher Hill. However, serious questions have recently been raised about the degree to which an independent middle class had emerged by the seventeenth century. By his very persuasive study, "The Myth of the Middle Class in Tudor England" (*Reappraisals in History* [New York, 1963], 71-116), Professor J. H. Hexter has made it difficult to speak unambiguously about the middle class in sixteenth- and seventeenth-century England. He does not, of course, deny that "an assertive, self-confident, politically alert, overwhelmingly rich" middle class does indeed emerge in England, but he postpones the emergence until the nineteenth century (114). His conclusions strongly qualify Weber's too easy which were granted in part to foreigners and in part to courtiers, while the colonies were placed in the hands of royal favorites. The small entrepreneur class which in the meantime had grown up . . . enlisted against the royal monopoly policy, and the Long Parliament deprived monopolists of the suffrage. The extraordinary obstinacy with which the economic spirit of the English people has striven against trusts and monopolies is expressed in these Puritan struggles.[48]

The two types of general order discussed so far, legal-rationality and traditionalism (including patrimonialism), both stand in contrast to Weber's pivotal third type: charismatic order.[49] Charismatism is a sort

assumptions about the historical point at which the middle class "takes over."

Nevertheless, Hexter himself, in a very significant portion of the essay, counts the "Calvinist revolts" as one of the two basic conditions which made "the consolidation and activation of a middle class" possible (114). He argues that Calvinism "undermined the hierarchical structures" which militated against the rise of the middle class. As he says, "the Calvinist fellowship did not attack the hierarchical idea, but it spiritually transcended it and practically minimized it" (115). Though, unfortunately, Hexter does not develop these ideas, he confirms precisely the affinities Weber saw between Calvinist Puritanism and the middle class, however much one may want to modify Weber's judgment as to when the middle class actually came into its own.

It ought to be noted, incidentally, that in several places Weber explicitly argues against a simple historical identification of rational capitalism and the mere existence of a middle class. "For the bourgeois as a class existed prior to the development of the peculiar modern form of capitalism . . . " (*Protestant Ethic*, 24). Furthermore, he refuses to explain inner-worldly ascetic religion as simply the result or the function of the middle class: "The mere existence of artisans and middle-class people has never sufficed to generate an ethical religion, even of the most general type" (*Sociology of Religion*, 99; cf. 115). These are important qualifications to bear in mind.

48. *General Economic History*, 257. "Calvinism opposed organic social organiza-tion in the fiscal-monopolistic form which it assumed in Anglicanism under the Stuarts, especially in the conceptions of Laud, this alliance of Church and State with the monopolists on the basis of a Christian-social ethical founda-tion. Its leaders were universally among the most passionate opponents of this type of politically-privileged commercial, putting-out, and colonial capitalism. Over against it they placed the individualistic motives of rational legal acquisi-tion by virtue of one's own ability and initiative" (*Protestant Ethic*, 179; cf. fn. 12, 213, and fn. 110, 282).

49. "The term 'charisma' will be applied to a certain quality of an individual per-sonality by virtue of which he is set apart from ordinary men and treated as endowed with supernatural, superhuman, or at least specifically exceptional powers or qualities" (*Theory*, 358). Weber's understanding of "charisma" is far too individualistic. It needs to be broadened and refined so as to include

of marginal or transitional category between the two polar types. In short, some form of charisma is required in order to move from traditionalism to legal-rationality. "In traditionally stereotyped periods, charisma is the greatest revolutionary force.... It may ... result in a radical alteration of the central system of attitudes and directions of action with a completely new orientation of all attitudes toward the different problems and structures of the 'world.' "[50] Weber felt that in periods of radical social change the question of legitimacy, of ultimate authority for action, becomes particularly intense because many of the old sources of justification are consciously challenged. Consequently, charismatic order manifests in a peculiarly acute way a preoccupation with religious questions.

In one way or another the absolute sanctity of the conventional order is broken by a charismatic "prophet," who opposes his message to "what you have heard of old." He thereby makes room for a conception of a new order. Figures like Jesus and Buddha mark two historical examples of the "charismatic breakthrough," each representing two further subtypes within Weber's general category: "ethical" and "exemplary" prophecy. The first, illustrated by Jesus, demands a substantial reordering of one's life here and now in keeping with a coming eschatological transformation of the entire world. It calls for a congregational manifestation of the new order, oriented toward "conversion" and "overcoming (or mastering) the world." The second is a more passive, world-rejecting form found, for example, in Buddha. Here, if anything, the ideal of withdrawal from action is cultivated.[51]

In other words, charismatic order can move in one of at least two directions: either toward a general institutional restructuring, or toward a withdrawal from and indifference to the world. It can encourage the sort of reordering necessary for the emergence of legal-rationality, or it can devalue the traditional order but in effect tolerate it and more or less legitimate it through indifference. "In its pure form charismatic authority may be said to exist only in the process of originating. It cannot remain stable, but becomes either traditionalized or rationalized, or a combination of both."[52]

The two types of charismatic prophecy provided the basis for

groups and institutions as well as persons. For a development of this point, see Edward A. Shils, "Charisma, Status and Order," *American Sociological Review*, XXX (April 1965).

50. *Theory*, 363.
51. See *Sociology of Religion*, 55-56.
52. *Theory*, 364.

Weber's famous distinction between this-worldly and other-worldly asceticism. He contended that ancient Judaism, as the forerunner of Christianity, provided the theological and social context for the development of ethical prophecy and this-worldly asceticism. For the Hebrew prophets, "the sacredness of a new revelation opposed that of tradition."[53] Particularly in Jeremiah and Isaiah, the identity of Israel's faith with her traditional ethnic, legal, and political institutions is broken in favor of a consistently transcendent supramundane God, who is "making all things new" and calling into question the established rituals of Israel.[54]

The main point is that charismatic ethical prophecy entails a broad reordering or a resystematization of institutional life. It entails a rationalization of life based on innovation, change, adaptation, rather than on the absolutely unalterable patterns of the past. In this way, Weber believed, ethically prophetic charisma serves to legitimate at least the possibility of a "modern rational breakthrough."[55]

Weber systematically investigates the relation of religion and society then because, as we have tried to indicate, the problem of order is for him a question of meaning and purpose (of ultimate legitimation), as well as of institutional organization and coordination. He develops his typology of order in relation to an analysis of religious systems of belief and action precisely to demonstrate how this is so.

53. *Sociology of Religion,* 66.
54. See esp. *Ancient Judaism* (Glencoe, 1952), 11, 12; also *Sociology of Religion,* 66.
55. Weber understood Judaism, however, as a consistently ambiguous movement in relation to the rise of a legal-rational society. On the one hand, because of its prophetism, its supramundane monotheism, and its opposition to magic and orgiastic practices, Judaism fostered a resystematization of social life in keeping with the transcendent will and purpose of Yahweh. On the other hand, it strenuously retained its status as an ethnically defined "pariah people," or "a distinctive hereditary social group lacking autonomous political organization and characterized by prohibitions against commensality and intermarriage originally founded upon magical, tabooistic and ritual injunctions" (*Sociology of Religion,* 109). As he writes, "The methodical control of life was limited in Judaism by the absence of the distinctively ascetic motivation characteristic of Puritans and by the continued presence of Jewish internal morality's traditionalism, which in principle remained unbroken" (*ibid.,* 259). Or, "the separation of economic in-group and out-group ethic has remained permanently significant for the religious evaluation of economic activity. Rational economic activity on the basis of formal legality never could and never has been religiously valued in the manner characteristic of Puritanism" (*Ancient Judaism,* 343); see Benjamin Nelson, *The Idea of Usury* (Princeton, N.J., 1949) for an important elaboration of Weber's insight here.

THEOLOGY AND ORDER

Weber contended that the analysis of the relation between religion and society required an attention to the theological affirmations of given communions. But his own way of proceeding in *The Protestant Ethic* is inadequate, in part because he did not develop some of his suggestive ideas about religion and order. In *The Protestant Ethic,* Weber employs what we might call a method of doctrinal selectivity by which he abstracts certain concepts from Calvin's theology, such as "calling," "the sovereignty of God," "predestination," and so on, and implies that they are representative of Calvinism. He then traces the fortunes of these doctrines in Puritan thinking in order to demonstrate the coherence between Calvinism and Puritanism. With all its value as a beginning,[56] such an approach misses the forest for the trees. These concepts are merely part of a wider framework of thought, a framework that must be grasped in its entirety and complexity before the real pattern of Calvinism can be seen and its implications for social life understood.

In place of Weber's somewhat intuitive method, we need a more comprehensive, systematic theory for analyzing theological ideas in relation to social behavior. The possibilities for such a theory reside, I believe, in Weber's own treatment of what I have called the problem of order, though he himself never pursued these possibilities. It will be remembered that Weber was interested in the two dimensions of the word "order"—the dimension of structure and the dimension of authority or command—as they stand in relation to the question of religious legitimation. Now, while Weber examined social institutions for these two dimensions of order, he never similarly examined theological and ethical language. In the subsequent exposition here, I wish to contend that one very fruitful way of understanding the relation between religion and society is to demonstrate how theological discourse constitutes in its own peculiar fashion a reflection upon the two sides of order—structure and command. In other words, one of the functions of theology is to try to solve the problem of order by means of the development and elaboration of symbolic categories.[57]

---

56. With more humility than many of his critics, Weber accentuates the "provisional character of these studies": "They are destined to be superseded in a much more important sense than this can be said, as it can be, of all scientific work" (*The Protestcnt Ethic,* 28).
57. The assumption is that the problem of order will be handled in some way or

Kenneth Burke, in his book *The Rhetoric of Religion*,[58] has made a substantial contribution to this sort of analysis, and he supplements very helpfully some of Weber's initial insights. For Burke, theological language is inevitably concerned with certain "families of terms," which are internally interconnected by their own logic. One such family is the *order-disorder-obedience-disobedience* configuration:

> Our task, then, is to examine the term "Order," by asking what cluster of ideas is "tautologically" present in the idea of Order. Such a cycle of terms follows no one sequence. That is, we may say either that the idea of Disorder is implicit in the idea of Order, or that the idea of Order is implicit in the idea of Disorder. Or we might say that the idea of Order implies the ideas of Obedience and Disobedience, or that either of them implies the other, or that either or both imply the idea of an Order, etc.[59]

The point is that the very notion of order implies and involves the other three terms and, moreover, that insofar as theology deals with the problem of order, it will be constrained to handle all four terms in some sequence or other.

Turning to the Genesis account of creation to illustrate what he means, Burke shows that the "Word of God" involves the polar terms "order" and "disorder."[60] God speaks his Word of order (command), and the world comes into order (structured coherence) out of disorder ("the earth was without form"). Creation is order in both senses. In the second place, God's act involves man's act. Adam (meaning "man") is he who may *decide* regarding God's order (command). It is this characteristic of responsibility which defines the nature of man.[61] Consequently, obedience and disobedience are implied in God's Word. Finally, the perfect coherence of God's universe is thrown into partial discord by the disobedience of Adam, reflecting the way in which the term "disobedience" refers back to "order." Had Adam been obedient to God's command, the coherence of the universe would have been maintained. The very disobedience of Adam and the subsequent social and natural disorder involve the need for the restoration of order and

other by all religious systems, that all systems will develop in their own symbolic categories a pattern of order. My preliminary examinations of primitive, as well as Confucian and Hindu, religious symbols is quite heartening in this respect.

58. (Boston, 1961).
59. *Ibid.*, 182.
60. *Ibid.*, 174 ff.
61. *Ibid.*, 187.

the achievement of obedience.

Burke is suggesting that the first three chapters of Genesis arrange and interpret in a particular way the constituents of order, namely, the two senses of "order" (command and structure) as well as "disorder," "obedience," and "disobedience." In short, the symbolic categories of Genesis handle these different terms and their interrelationships. Thus the account can be understood not as a series of stories strung together arbitrarily, but as a consistent religious response to the problem of order in its major dimensions. Yahweh is identified as the legitimate source of order, or the ultimate authority over the world. The capacity for acknowledging or not acknowledging final authority (obedience and disobedience) is located in man, and the reason for the disruption of the true order is linked to man's disregard for authority. Diagrammatically, what we amy call the anatomy of order looks like this:

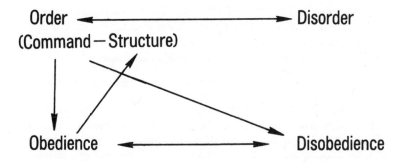

Although Burke discovers a variety of families of terms in religious discourse, we shall attempt to show that the order-disorder-obedience-disobedience configuration, already examined briefly, is particularly appropriate for an analysis of the divergences between Calvinist Puritanism and Anglicanism. If Burke is right, these terms should, in each system, fall into a definite consistent pattern. In short, they should form what we may call a discrete pattern of order in relation to different religious presuppositions. Perhaps it is in an analysis of the particular manipulation of the pattern of order that we have a method for differentiating and relating given religious systems, as well as for apprehending their implications for the formation of social patterns of action. Burke makes an interesting comment in this connection: "Though terms, as seen [according to our method], are analysed simply as implicating one another, theological distinctions between orthodoxy and heresy can be defined by the choice of some one sequence rather than another."[62] Perhaps it is precisely in the articulation of the pattern of order that we can take hold both of the heart of Calvinism, including its view of social order, and of the relation between Calvinism and Puritanism. Perhaps here we have the key to perceiving a basic conflict between Puritanism and Anglicanism—in its theological and social dimensions—as a conflict of order.

By focusing study on an analysis of theological language in relation to the pattern of order, we attempt to systematize and refine Weber's sociology of religion, and at the same time we also shift the method and the emphasis on one important point: the matter of religious motivation. In a footnote to *The Protestant Ethic*, Weber makes it quite clear that "the point of this whole essay" is the way in which religious belief exerts independent psychological sanctions upon the economic motivation of an individual.[63]

This means, in the first place, that Weber was most interested in the effects that the "subjective adoption" of a religious position might have on " the conduct of the individual."[64] Accordingly, he never saw fit in *The Protestant Ethic* to treat the institutional context or ecclesiological pattern worked out in relation to theological affirmations.[65]

> We have quite deliberately not taken as a starting-point the objective social institutions of the older Protestant Churches, and their ethical influences, especially not the very important Church discipline . . .
> The ecclesiastical supervision of the life of the individual, which, as it was practised in the Calvinistic State Churches, almost amounted to an inquisition, might even retard that liberation of individual powers which was conditioned by the rational ascetic pursuit of salvation, and in some cases actually did so.[66]

This course strikes me as both unwise and unjustified, because to consider theological language in relation to the problem of order necessarily and very centrally involves ecclesiastical and disciplinary questions—questions, in effect, of Church order. To ignore these questions is to ignore the context in which religious ethical behavior is worked out and given meaning and direction. Certainly in the Christian tradition, and

62. *Ibid.*, 249.
63. *The Protestant Ethic*, fn. 12, 194-198.
64. *Ibid.*, 152.
65. Of course, Weber does treat the importance of ecclesiastical discipline and Church order in "The Protestant Sects and the Spirit of Capitalism," in *From Max Weber*, 302-322.
66. *The Protestant Ethic*, 152.

probably in all religions, theological language inevitably reflects upon the organization and the discipline of religious behavior. The organizational context, then, becomes one decisive expression of a given religion's pattern of order.

Furthermore, if it is true that the ecclesiastical supervision of the Calvinist and Puritan churches did at times retard the liberation of individual powers, as Weber says, then we must take such an important fact into account and be able to explain it. Weber's critics, after all, delight in pointing out the highly repressive character of much of Calvinist Puritanism, and they constantly raise the question how such a stringent idea of Church discipline could possibly have contributed to the rise of individual initiative in economics or in anything else. As the quotation above makes clear, Weber was by no means blind to the Puritan proclivity for repression, but he could not successfully answer the critics simply by lopping off consideration of ecclesiastical discipline. The critics are, in my estimation, quite justified in calling Weber to account at this point.

Neither Weber nor the critics seem to have appreciated the ambivalence and ambiguity that exist within the Calvinist Puritan position on Church order. In trying to understand the relation between repression and individual initiative, it is erroneous to identify repression with Church discipline and initiative with some sort of "subjective adoption" on the part of the believer, as Weber does. It is equally erroneous to decide too quickly that individual initiative in religious and socio-economic affairs is precluded because of the indisputable evidence of harsh repression in Reformed churches, as the critics do. We shall try to show that the Puritan Church, with all its repression, was an indispensable source of ideas for much of the individual initiative Weber found. Neither interpretation is adequate, because neither takes sufficient account of the pattern of order inherent in the theological as well as the ecclesiological presuppositions of Calvinist Puritanism. These are involved and subtle matters, requiring a good deal more theological sophistication than is evident so far.

LAW AND ORDER

Finally, as a focus for the relationship between the theological conflicts of the period and the radically changing patterns of social action, the subject of law emerges very naturally. That the dispute between the Anglicans and the Puritans was a legal one hardly requires verification. As Archbishop Whitgift put it, "[The objectives of the Puritans] all tend to one end, which is liberty of doing what men list, contrary to the lawes established, and to the practice of all well-ordered states and churches . . . "[67] The Puritans were regarded by the Anglicans as seditious and subversive not only toward Church laws, but also civil laws. They were attacked as contaminators of the social order, breeding new, foreign notions of allegiance and obedience. The exchanges between the Puritans and the Anglicans in the sixteenth century were inevitably theological and legal or, to use modern terminology, religious and secular. As one would expect, different interpretations of social institutional life grew out of this theological tension, and the question we must ask is how these different "religious" interpretations were related to "secular" legal patterns.

The question gains in importance when one observes how closely allied were the Puritans and the common lawyers in the struggle for sovereignty[68] over the province and authority of the common law in the late sixteenth and early seventeenth centuries. John Dykstra Eusden has argued in *Puritans, Lawyers and Politics*[69] that while the Puritans had little or no influence on the common law, they joined the cause of the lawyers because of a shared antipathy to the extension of royal domination. According to Eusden, the association of religion and law was little more than a temporary marriage of convenience between two groups with quite separate intellectual heritages and ultimately different purposes and values. Puritans and lawyers found a kinship based on "ideological parallelism," on certain similar characteristics.[70] There is undoubtedly something in what Eusden says. His conclusions guard against a facile identification of religious ideas with legal ideology; they point up the relative independence that the common law system had achieved in English history.

However, Eusden's account depicts the common law, at the turn of the seventeenth century, as possessing a far more stable and self-contained ideology than it actually had. He does not take into account the fact that this was a revolutionary period, in both the economic and the political spheres. England was experiencing a veritable industrial revolution, marking a phase in her life that had the deepest social and

---

67. John Strype, *Life and Acts of John Whitgift* (3 vols., Oxford, 1822), III, 127. Cf. J. W. Allen, *History of Political Thought in the 16th Century* (London, 1957), 173.

68. George L. Mosse, *Struggle for Sovereignty in England* (Lansing, Mich., 1950).

69. (New Haven, Conn., 1958).

70. *Ibid.*, viii.

legal consequences. The patterns of society were altering radically, and with them legal interpretations and regulations. Upon what were the judges to rely in making decisions to fit the times? Precedent and legal tradition? What happened when neither applied, when the heritage of the common law reflected a feudal, baronial way of life hardly relevant in a time of growing cities and new forms of trade, commerce, and industry? Were the judges to rely on "fundamental law"? Even Eusden admits that this was a highly imprecise term, meaning all things to all men.[71] The point is that during this period the common lawyers themselves were not terribly clear or consistent as to the underlying principles of legal interpretation. A study of legal activity between 1590 and 1630 must do much more justice to the ambiguities and contradictions implicit in judicial decisions and opinions than Eusden's book does.

Some scholars such as Plucknett,[72] who wish to emphasize the high degree of novelty and innovation in the legal system, go so far as to say that the most important legal figure of the time, Edward Coke, simply created out of whole cloth a conception of fundamental law, interpreting the legal traditions he inherited in the light of his own Elizabethan presuppositions. This is a contested point, but the creative role played by Coke in the determination of subsequent common law cannot be denied.

What is more, there were other legal complexities during this period: were the judges to rely upon what Coke called "judicial reason" for their authority? This term also bristles with ambiguity. Coke is altogether unclear whether it means the supremacy of the judges and courts or the supremacy of Parliament in matters of legal interpretation. Obviously, this question was not raised so long as Parliament was a "high court" in which legislative and juridical matters were indistinguishable. But now the question *was* being raised. Now the old unity of political and legal life was falling apart, and the question of authority was inevitable.

In face of the complex and dynamic character of the common law, is

---

71. *Ibid.,* 45. See also the chapter, "The Norman Yoke," in Christopher Hill's *Puritanism and Revolution* (London, 1958), 50 ff.
72. See J. W. Gough, *Fundamental Law in English Constitutional History* (Oxford, 1955) chapter 3, esp. 30-31, for a treatment of Plucknett's views. Plucknett's ideas are contained in "Bonham's Case and Judicial Review," *Harvard Law Review,* XX (1926-27), 30 ff. Many authors deal with the Elizabethan presuppositions of Coke; these will be examined in Chapter 6.

there any relation between the fundamental issues over which the Puritans and Anglicans were disputing and the inner conflicts that disturbed the very soul of the legal system? Does it make sense to say that the conflict of order which divided the two religious camps also struck at the heart of the legal thinking and activity of the time? In other words, does the common law manifest only its own independent system of meaning and interpretation, or is it related to systems of meaning that reflect wider and more ultimate questions of social order?[73]

At no point were the conflicts and tensions within the legal system revealed so dramatically as in the sphere of corporation law. The laws, royal charters, ordinances, and customs of the corporation had historically controlled and determined the character and domain of economic activity. The burning question emerging during Elizabeth's reign was who finally defines a corporation and the nature of its behavior: the crown? the common law courts? or the entrepreneur himself? In other words, was economic activity to be organized and regulated by political purposes, by legal conception, or by autonomous economic considerations? The tentative answers arrived at were by no means unambiguous or unconfused. Within the common law itself, conflicting attitudes and frames of reference are to be found. In fact, it will be one of the theses of this book that the confusions and ambiguities revealed in the legal thought of the time, and reflected particularly in the opinions of Sir Edward Coke,[74] cannot properly be understood apart from the deep-seated antagonisms between Anglicanism and Puritanism and the divergent patterns of order they represent.

On the one hand it was Coke who, in case after case, decided against

73. The questions asked here have to do with the sociology of law. It is the problem of the connection between meaning, values, and legal patterns that interests the sociology of law: "Sociology of law interprets the legal kinds of behavior and the material manifestations of the law on the basis of the inner meanings that inspire and permeate it. . . . From these it proceeds to the values and ideas of law that find expression in legal patterns, and, finally, it analyzes the contents of faith and intuition that support these values," Georges Gurvitch, *Grundzüge der Soziologie des Rechts* (Neuwied, 1960), my translation, 40-41. This book contains an extensive bibliography in the field of sociology of law.

74. Coke's role in corporation law is very important. "The conception of corporations at the foundation of the modern law of them matured in England in the fifteenth and sixteenth centuries and found its chief expounder in Sir Edward Coke," John P. Davis, in Abram Chayes (ed.), *Corporations* (New York, 1961), II, 210. The two original volumes are brought together in this edition, though the pagination remains the same.

the restriction of trade, against the long-existing political and economic controls, and at once encouraged and reflected the emergence of new values and a new conception of social order. It was he who, like so many of his fellow jurists, embodied a predisposition "to disallow any extention of restrictive practices to the new [economic] conditions which were developing on every side."[75] The impulses within legal thought toward a spirit of free and autonomous economic activity, untrammeled by the traditional legal and political restraints, manifests a "rich congruence" with some of the conclusions that emerged from the Calvinist Puritan pattern of order. The heart of Puritan thought rested in its advocacy of a new basis for obedience and a new form of authority. Out of its Calvinist heritage, it introduced a conception of social life with profoundly disruptive implications for English society, a conception that had certain affinities with the characteristics of the spirit of capitalism.

On the other hand, it was the same Coke who tried, almost obsessively, to find a basis for these decisions in the feudal traditions of English corporation law and to harmonize his revolutionary "Elizabethan ideas" with remnants and vestiges of medieval group life. Holding a point of view that understood man to be living in a legal universe in which the present and future were wedded to the past by a smooth continuity of omnicompetent law and custom, Coke vainly searched the ancient legal texts to discover a foundation for new patterns of life which called into question the very validity of his legal universe. That he did not and could not find such a foundation did not prevent him from unconsciously disguising his innovations in the clothes of the past.

In this passion for antiquity, Coke was strikingly close to Richard Hooker's theology of the old order, and to the presuppositions of Elizabethan Anglicanism. The metaphysical defense of a legal universe, with all of its rational stability, harmony, and consistency, could hardly be clearer than in Hooker's *Laws of Ecclesiastical Polity.* For Hooker, all corporate life (including economic action) is regulated and defined by an unvarying, omnicompetent "law of the realm." It is the affinities between the legal thought of the time and the Anglican theology that need exposition, so as to clarify the logic of Coke's desperate adherence to the old order in face of his unwitting encouragement of the new.

The implications of these two theological systems—Puritanism and

75. Ephraim Lipson, *Economic History of England* (3 vols., London, 1956 [vol. I, new edition] and 1948 [vols. II and III]), II, cxxxv; see Bibliographical Essay B, p. 242.

Anglicanism—sharply oppose one another, particularly in Coke's legal activity toward corporations. There, as in the more formal doctrinal disputes, the patterns of the respective positions collide head on in a "conflict of order." That conflict pits a picture of a harmonious, totally self-consistent legal universe against a dynamic conception of social change that envisions a *new* society living by a *new* law.

PART II.

THEOLOGY AND THE CONFLICT OF ORDER

3. The New Order of John Calvin

If the language and thought forms of the Puritans follow coherent patterns, the key to understanding those patterns is, to a large extent, Calvin's theology. His theology sets forth the ground rules and basic orientations of Puritan thought; it is a kind of grammar for Puritan rhetoric.

But if Puritanism and particularly Elizabethan Puritanism is not adequately apprehended except in contrast to the official Anglicanism of the day, Calvinism is little better understood apart from the Renaissance humanist context in which it was produced. In fact, the remarkable coherence between Calvinism and Puritanism is more readily apparent in the light of their common antagonism to certain presuppositions that both Renaissance and Anglican thinkers seem to share. In order, therefore, to reveal as sharply as possible the distinctiveness of the pattern of Calvinism, we begin with a brief survey of some of the characteristics of Renaissance humanism to which Calvin was so strongly opposed.

However much humanism was at bottom a method of literary investigation rather than a unitary philosophical point of view, there is no question that it embodied important philosophical biases.[1] Prominent among these, and particularly attractive to Calvin in his early career as a humanist, was the bias in favor of late classical Stoicism, particularly as

1. See P. O. Kristeller, *Renaissance Thought: The Classic, Scholastic and Humanist Strains* (New York, 1961). Cf. Kristeller's essay, "Renaissance Platonism," in W. K. Ferguson, *et al.* (eds.), *Facets of the Renaissance* (New York, 1963), 103-123.

33

found in the thought of Seneca.[2] The notion of an organic *humanitas* or *societas hominium,* regulated by one overarching, all-pervasive natural law that is manifest in man's universal reason, characterizes the writings of such humanists as Ficino[3] and Budé,[4] and, to a lesser extent, such legal thinkers as Alciat and Zasius.[5] The Stoic roots of this thought are clear. Marcus Aurelius asserts quite typically:

> If the intellectual part of us is common to all, so also is the reason which gives us our status as human beings. Grant this and the (practical) reason which bids us do or not do must also be common. Hence it may be concluded that there is but one law; and, if the law be one, we are all fellow-citizens and members of one body-politic; that is to say, the universe is a species of the state. For what other conceivable community can there be of which it may be said that the whole human race are citizens? And from this universal state must proceed those very faculties of intellect and reason, together with our concept of (natural) right.[6]

2. Calvin's first essay, "De Clementia," was a treatment of Seneca. See Lord Acton, *Lectures on Modern History* (New York, 1961), esp. his lecture on "The Renaissance," 79-80. See also Leontine Zanta, *La Renaissance du Stoicisme au XVIe siècle* (Paris, 1914).

3. Kristeller, *Renaissance Thought,* 132-133. Kristeller quotes Ficino: "For as individual men are under one Idea and in one species, they are like one man. Therefore, I believe, the sages called by the name of man himself only that one among all the virtues that loves and helps all men as brothers deriving in a long series from one father, in other words, humanity" *(Opera Omnia* [Basel, 1572], 635).

4. The classic work on Budé in which he is compared exhaustively with Calvin is Josef Bohatec's *Budé und Calvin* (Vienna, 1950).

5. C. J. Friedrich, *Philosophy of Law in Historical Perspective* (Chicago, 1963). See esp. chapter VII, "Law as a Historical Fact: The Humanists," 51-56. Friedrich argues that the Stoic influences were there in humanism, but that they were growing weaker under the impact of nationalism and historicism. He goes on to say, however: "the Humanists continued to be deeply attached to the thought that there is one law which is valid for all men. This idea, indeed, is anchored in the very foundation of Humanism" (54).

6. Meditations, IV, 4; quoted in C. N. Cochrane's study, *Christianity and Classical Culture* (New York, 1957), 166. I am indebted to this book for opening up the implicit tensions between the concept of order in classical thought and that in Christian (especially Augustinian) theology. Cochrane supplies a rich basis for the sort of analysis attempted here. This book tries to carry the theme further for Calvin. It might be argued that Cochrane emphasizes rather too heavily the role of ideas in history, in that he rather exclusively attributes the fall of Rome to the deficiencies of classical thought. However that may be, his analysis of the dimensions of order in classical thought is helpful and convincing.

In this Stoic system, God is identical with the universal order of things.[7] He is apprehended when human reason grasps the true rational coherence (the logos) of the world.[8] Consequently, the ethical demand for obedience is derived from the order of nature. Man is commanded to conform to what is. From our point of view, the command and the structural or organizational dimensions of the word "order" are completely equated, a fact of the greatest importance for the Stoic view of social action. Because man in ethical obedience can only adjust to the inexorable, eternal law of nature, there is no room for real disorder; nor, therefore, is there any kind of basis for a revolutionary reordering of things. There is, in other words, no place for genuine evil, nor for its overcoming.[9] This central teaching has not been taken seriously enough by scholars who too simply speak of parallels and similarities between Stoicism and Christianity.[10] While Stoics such as Seneca and Posei-

7. One of the most perceptive examinations of the place of natural law in Stoic thought of the "Spätantike" is to be found in Felix Flückiger's *Geschichte des Naturrechts* (Zürich, 1954). Flückiger makes the identification between God and the natural order clear. It is, of course, hard to generalize about a movement like Stoicism, which encompassed many centuries in its development. Flückiger's concern, like ours, is with the late classical period of Seneca, Marcus Aurelius, etc. I wish to emphasize, with Flückiger, the lack, in late Stoicism, of a conception of "new order" that could find institutional roots in society. My brief analysis applies especially to the thought of Seneca, Epictetus, Marcus Aurelius, Poseidonius, and with certain qualifications, of Cicero. Cicero's attempt, for example, to explain human evil as the consequence of bad custom implies a certain revolutionary zeal that must not be overlooked. On the other hand, as Flückiger points out, *De Republica* is an argument in favor of the established, or given, order of "eternal Rome."

8. Flückiger, *op. cit.*, 217.

9. E. g., Seneca, *De Providentia*, 3. See Flückiger, *op. cit.*, 199.

10. G. H. Sabine, in his widely used *History of Political Theory* (London, 1959), is clearly guilty of such a facile comparison. While there are undeniable similarities, the common overemphasis of them hopelessly misses the deep-seated differences precisely at the point of "order." The Stoics possessed no grounds for a "new order" and therefore Seneca's interpretation of the "two commonwealths" (159), unlike the Christian conception, could not receive any institutional or social expression. The profound conflict between civic and ecclesiastical duties evident in one way or another throughout the history of the Christian Church in no way bothered the Stoics. As for the conflict between the two commonwealths, Sabine himself admits that there "is no evidence that Seneca was aware of it" (164). That is certainly *not* accidental.
   However, Sabine makes a statement the importance of which he himself does not understand in much of his analysis of the relation of Christian thought to political theory: "The rise of the Christian church, as a distinct institution entitled to govern the spiritual concerns of mankind in indepen-

donius did speak of a primitive golden age which they regarded as
superior to their contemporary society, it could not—by the logic of
their system—provide them with any kind of model for reform.[11] Each
period was but another inevitable stage in the eternal predetermined
cycle of history.[12] "The condition of nature in the primitive time is,
accordingly, not a natural law norm for the present; rather it lies in the
past like Hesiod's 'golden age.' The subsequent change from that time
to the present occurred not without the will of providence and corresponds to the natural law of becoming and passing away."[13]

Out of this identification in Stoic thought of what is with what
ought to be arises something Flückiger calls a "fatalistic ethic of disposition." The individual becomes concerned with conforming to the order of reality, but this is basically a matter of inner disposition. So far
as outward action is concerned, he is a member of no social or institutional context that stands against the way things are. There is no new
command demanding a new order. The individual's obedience always
refers *back* to the old structure of things, never *forward* to something
revolutionary or transforming. In Cochrane's words, the Stoic "failed to
build a bridge between 'order' and 'process'; one main result [was] that
whatever did not fit in with the preconceptions of its ideal order was
denied or dismissed as 'unreal.' "[14]

The way in which Renaissance humanism sought in the old order of
classical antiquity the sources of true thought and action illustrates its
affinity with the Stoic pattern of order. For while the recovery of
classical thinking resulted in important intellectual innovations in the
fourteenth, fifteenth, and sixteenth centuries, very little use was made
of the revived thought for any genuine social reorientation. In general,
humanists such as Erasmus, Budé, and Ficino were much more concerned to retreat into an *arrière-boutique* to contemplate the essence of
universal humanity and to cultivate their inward rational relationship to
it than to reform the structure of things.[15] It is one of the striking

dence of the state, may not unreasonably be described as the most revolutionary event in the history of western Europe, in respect both to politics and
to political thought" (161-162). I would underscore that statement several
times.

11. See Flückiger, *op. cit.*, 200-202.
12. *Ibid.*, 199-200.
13. *Ibid.*, 217.
14. Cochrane, *op cit.*, 166.
15. This is not to argue, of course, that Renaissance figures had nothing to say
about social matters. After all, Erasmus for example did write *The Education*

features of the Renaissance, whose spirit and conclusions were usually in such direct contradiction to the scholasticism of the Roman Catholic Church, that so much intellectual activity went on with so little social effect. Ernst Troeltsch's conclusion is, in general, accurate: "The Renaissance, from a sociological point of view, was fully unproductive."[16]

How could it be otherwise when in humanism, as in Stoicism, social life was but a manifestation of the recurring, inexorable *ordo naturae* in face of which no break, no transformation is possible? As with their Stoic ancestors, the humanists' ethical activity was determined by the way things are. Any contemplation of a new heaven and a new earth was, on their understanding of life, ruled out as nonsense. Any radical pattern of behavior that called into question existing patterns was excluded for the same reason.

With John Calvin, it is quite another story. Although his thought manifests affinities with humanism and Stoicism,[17] he moves in a different direction. For him, a "new order"—a new command and a new structure—not only is possible, but already is making its mark on the world. The implications of this new order for the organization and understanding of social life are immense.

of a Christian Prince. Nevertheless, Lester K. Born, who has translated and edited this work of Erasmus (New York, 1936), puts the point quite sharply: "Erasmus was essentially a critic and an intellectual, not a militant leader. Steeped in the atmosphere and life of classical antiquity as he was, *he came to feel that his life was one of mental, not physical, activity* . . . " (20; my italics). And against those who dismiss Erasmus' social influence altogether, Born rather weakly retorts: "His [social and political] influence in the very center of the maelstrom of Europe could not have been utterly ineffectual" (fn. 107, 25).

In his essay, "Renaissance Platonism," Kristeller remarks: "In its prevailing outlook, Renaissance Platonism was individualistic rather than political . . . " (118). The main social interest that Kristeller finds has to do with the theory of love and friendship (119).

16. "Die Kulturbedentung des Calvinismus," *Gesammelte Schriften* (Tübingen, 1925), IV, 276. See Bibliographical Essay C. "The Social Implications of Humanist Thought," pp. 247-249.

17. Besides Bohatec, many scholars have treated the Stoic and humanist backgrounds of Calvin's thought. For example, Erik Wolf, "Theologie und Sozialordnung bei Calvin," *Archiv für Reformationsgeschichte,* XLII (1951), 11-31; Quirinius Breen, *John Calvin: A Study in French Humanism* (Grand Rapids, Mich., 1931); Gisbert Beyerhaus, *Staatsanschauung Calvins mit besonderer Berücksichtigung seines Souveränitätsbegriff* (Berlin, 1910); and François Wendel, *Calvin: Origins and Development of His Religious Thought* (New York, 1963), 27-37.

SOVEREIGNTY AND LAW

1. God's Command and the Moral Law

It is by the "unfathomable might of his Word" that God commands into existence the heavens and the earth and all things that exist therein.[18] God's command establishes the beautiful arrangement of the universe[19] in which "all things" testify to his authority.[20] His command goes out and "all things" obediently respond, whereupon they assume their proper places and live harmoniously by the laws and decrees of the universe. By this orderly, obedient response God is honored and praised.[21]

It is for man that the whole world is principally made.[22] He is the one who crowns the creation,[23] and upon whom rests, in one sense at least, the responsibility for preserving the beautiful arrangement. Calvin interprets the word "fulness" in Ps. 24:1 to mean "men themselves, who are the most illustrious ornament and glory of the earth. *If they should fail,* the earth would exhibit a scene of desolation and solitude, not less hideous than if God should despoil it of all its other riches" (my italics). In terms of our analysis of order, man is so central in Calvin's theology because man alone can obey or disobey God's command. No other creature possesses that possibility. The image of God in man exists when God "mirrors" himself in man, that is, when man, in due submission to the majesty of God, reflects the order ordained by God.[24] When man is obedient, he is in harmony with society and nature and within himself.[25]

18. Calvin, *Corpus Reformatorum,* eds. G. Baum, E. Cunitz, and E. Reuss (59 vols., Brunswick, W. Germany, 1863-1897), 31, 327; henceforth referred to as CR. Cf. *Institutes of the Christian Religion,* ed. John T. McNeill, trans. Ford Lewis Battles (Philadelphia, 1960), I, 14, 20; henceforth referred to simply by book, section, and paragraph.

19. *Commentary (Comm.)* on Ps. 68:34 (nearly all the references to Calvin's *Commentaries* are taken from the English edition (Grand Rapids, Mich., 1948-1950).

20. *Comm.* on Ps. 104:1-5.

21. *Comm.* on Gen. 2:16.

22. *Comm.* on Ps. 8:6; 24:1.

23. *Comm.* on Gen. 1:26.

24. T. F. Torrance, *Calvin's Doctrine of Man* (London, 1952), 51.

25. "There was an attempering in the several parts of the soul, which correspond with their various functions. In the mind perfect intelligence flourished and reigned, uprightness attended as its companion, and all the senses were pre-

But man is disobedient. The Fall occurs precisely because Adam "takes no account of the Word of God."[26] A "fearful deformity" results both within man, so that the image is "wholly defaced and wiped out,"[27] and outside man, so that he loses his proper place within creation: and "the earth was cursed on account of Adam."[28] Nature, society, and man, thus "twisted" (*déjeter*) by Adam's disobedience, are subjected to confusion and total perversity.[29]

There is, of course, a vestige of God's *ordo naturae*[30] left remaining. Even Adam's rebellion cannot fully shake the security of God's providential order. It is God, after all, who is sovereign, not man. An "external image of righteousness" still exists in man's reason and conscience by means of his perception of the natural law. But these faculties are at best tarnished tokens, for their intrinsic ambiguity demonstrates as much the deficiencies of human nature as the blessings. The "seeds of political order" that are "sown in the minds of all," the power of the conscience to discriminate "what is just and unjust," along with man's natural rational gifts in art, science, and philosophy, continue to reside in man by the mercy of God, even though human nature "is so overwhelmed—as by a deluge—from head to foot, so that no part is immune from sin."[31] "For if he had not spared us, our fall would have entailed the destruction of our whole nature."[32] Man's disobedience should, by all rights, lead to total disorder, but he cannot completely avoid the command of God. He is driven to live up to a minimal standard of civil harmony and justice[33] which is derived from certain binding legal and moral principles. These principles are made clear and sharp in the Decalogue or the "moral law," which is "nothing else than a testimony of natural law and of that conscience which God has engraved on the minds of men."[34] The apprehension of the natural -moral law by reason and conscience ought to excite man to acknow-

pared and moulded for due obedience to reason; and in the body there was a suitable correspondence with this internal order" (*Comm.* on Gen. 1:26).
26. *Comm.* on Gen. 2:9.
27. Sermon on Deut. 24:14.
28. *Comm.* on Gen. 3:17.
29. *CR* 22, 36, 7.
30. There is no question that Calvin incorporated into his thought basic humanistic, especially Stoic, ideas about an *ordo naturae* and its moral implications. But Calvin alters the conception decisively. See below.
31. II, 1, 9.
32. II, 2, 17.
33. II, 2, 13.
34. IV, 20, 16.

ledge God as the author of order and the source of the command.[35]
For despite his recalcitrance, the command ever and again drives him
back to the authority of God himself.

At the same time as the natural-moral law, at work in reason and
conscience, *prods* man to live up to the command of God it *convicts*
him of his own wilful rejection of the command and of his own inability to obey it. It is what we may call this double function of the
natural-moral law that injects an ambiguous and dynamic element.

> Both of these the Lord accomplishes in his law. First, claiming for
> himself the lawful power to command, he calls us to reverence his
> divinity, and specifies wherein such reverence lies and consists.
> Secondly, having published the rule of his righteousness, he reproves
> us both for our impotence and for our unrighteousness.[36]

The first table of the Decalogue establishes the sovereign authority of
God to command, which ought to result in humility and worshipful
obedience on the part of man. Without man's heartfelt recognition of
God's authority, the law is already disobeyed and God's order broken.
Therefore the second table, which drives in the direction of the proper
or "righteous" structure of social relations (the corresponding dimension of "order"), convicts as well as guides man. While external degrees
of harmony, or "human laws" can be maintained, "they are now
lacking in the chief point of the law ... [namely] that the 'law is
spiritual.' "[37] Thus, the command of God "accuses us when we fail in
our duty";[38] it drives home a "consciousness of guilt," a sense of
disobedience.[39] As Calvin remarks in unequivocal terms, "the purpose
of the natural law, therefore, is to render man inexcusable."[40] The
natural-moral law drives man, according to the *first use of the law,* "to
seek grace."[41]

In contrast to Stoic and humanist conceptions, Calvin subordinates
natural law to the sovereignty of God. There is no law above or outside
God: "God is above the order of nature."[42] That is to say that the

35. II, 2, 14.
36. II, 8, 1.
37. II, 8, 6.
38. II, 8, 1.
39. II, 2, 24.
40. II, 2, 22.
41. II, 7, 9. See also II, 2, 22, for an emphasis upon the inescapably compelling
    character of the law as it drives home its conviction.
42. *CR* 62, 432. Cf. also 64, 29. See Beyerhaus, *op. cit.,* 72. Cf. Richard Hauser in
    his *Autorität und Macht* (Heidelberg, 1949), 346.

command of God directs the obedience of man to something "higher" than itself, namely, to the "free will" of God as the source of order. Therefore, God is only obeyed by man's *voluntary* response, a response in which man's free will "mirrors" the freedom of God. Short of such obedience, the natural-moral law can simply compel and convict, but it provides no basis for genuine or complete coherence in itself. It can but "mirror" the servitude under which man lives so long as he lives apart from the sovereign grace of God. What Beyerhaus refers to as the "moment of voluntarism"[43] is of the greatest significance in Calvin's pattern of order, as we shall see with increasing force as we go along. Whatever superficial similarities obtain between Calvin and the Stoics on natural law are obviated by the profound difference at this point.

2. God's Command and the Positive Law

> Let us realize, then, that not without reason has God established the order of earthly justice: but because He considered the corruption that is within us. We are well warned by that as I have already said, to humble ourselves seeing that our vices require such a remedy. All the more we must extol the goodness of God because He decided to assure that harmony would prevail and that we should not despair: which would come about if there were no law in the world.[44]

"The order of earthly justice," including the political order and the institution of positive law, is decidedly occasioned by human disobedience. Calvin is clear that "if we had remained in the integrity of nature, which God had created, the order of justice, as it is called, would not be so necessary."[45] Men before the Fall responded obediently to the command of God, in the full sense, so that "*each carried the law in his own heart.*"[46] Before the Fall, the command of God was obeyed from the heart, and consequently there was an "*intégrité de*

---

43. A. P. d'Entreves, in his *Natural Law: An Introduction to Legal Philosophy* (London, 1960), mentions the relation between "nominalist" or "voluntarist" theories of law and "voluntarist ethics," for example in Calvin, 68-70. For a discussion of "voluntarist ethics" in the Reformation, see G. de Lagarde, *Recherches sur l'esprit politique de la Réforme* (Paris, 1926). I have no space or competence to discuss the relation of Calvin to the nominalist tradition. In this, as in many other matters, I find the arguments of John Hesselink's as yet unpublished manuscript, *Calvin's Concept of the Law,* very persuasive. Hesselink contends that Calvin's connection with nominalism is at best oblique.
44. *CR* 27, 409.
45. *Ibid.*
46. *Ibid.,* my italics.

nature." But as the result of disobedience the command, which in its original freedom solicits but does not coerce, becomes the order of God in a coercive and binding sense. The social structural frame of order changes from a "self-integrating" system to a system ruled by "*la police terrienne.*" The principles of righteousness must now be realized through force.[47] While political and legal institutions clearly flow, in Calvin's thought, from the will of God and are certainly part of his order, their coercive and restraining office may not be said to be "natural" or originally necessary. There is a decided change in the nature of God's order after the appearance of sin.[48]

The State in Calvin's thought, as a lawmaking and law-enforcing body, is by no means invented by men. Nor does it simply arise from some natural capacity for political order, though man is naturally a political animal.[49] It is first and foremost a theological entity, and it falls squarely under the aegis of Calvin's "passion for order."[50] It is ordained and established by God for the maintenance, at all costs, of his providential design. Consequently, political rulers are the product of God's gracious election; he bestows upon certain men (for example, the kings in the Old Testament) his holy spirit and sets them aside with "special marks" as "sons of God."[51] The rulers are the servants of God, charged with creating and maintaining order on behalf of God. They are

47. Josef Bohatec, *Calvins Lehre von Staat und Kirche* (Breslau, 1937), 23.
48. One sometimes hears that Calvin looked positively, not negatively, on the State—it is the result not so much of sin as of providence. For example, Calvin states in IV, 20, 4: "This is just as if it had been affirmed, that the authority possessed by kings and other governors over all things upon earth is not a consequence of the perverseness of men, but of the providence and holy ordinance of God . . . " The fact is—and it will be clarified as we proceed—that for Calvin political life and positive law have a double function, corresponding to the double function of the natural law. On the one hand, they propel men in the direction of harmony and integration, and away from that condition in which men "tear everything to bits" (*lanatio*). Therefore, those persons who stand in authority naturally hold positions that are "not only holy and legitimate, but far the most sacred and honorable in human life" (IV, 20, 4), just because they are specially related to God's order. On the other hand, they stand, by their inevitable use of coercion and force, as an abiding indication of the rebelliousness and disobedience of the disorder of man. This double function is fundamental to Calvin's thought. Because the pattern of order, of which it is the result, is overlooked, it is frequently neglected.
49. II, 2, 13.
50. This is Bohatec's suggestive term "*Pathos der Ordnung,*" in *Calvin und das Recht* (Vienna, 1934), 62.
51. *CR* 35, 160; 163; 579; 27, 128, 467, 511; 29, 617.

to perform their duty in the knowledge that all power stems ultimately from God, and were he to withdraw his hand, no order could exist.[52]

Because of the divine right by which the authorities rule, there is a fatherly relationship between them and their subjects corresponding to the relationship between God and man. In one sense, the political authority represents God. The subject submits to the ruler, prince, or magistrate as the result of "a divine impulsion and instinct": "it is God who has inspired in men this fear without which it is certain they would never subordinate themselves."[53] God's original order (command and social structure) has been provisionally translated into a coercive order, maintained by his chosen authorities, so that God's sovereignty will prevail over man's disobedience. Given Calvin's presuppositions, this is a necessity. Were man to have the final say on order and disorder, that is, were his No allowed to take precedence over God's order, God would no longer be God.

At the same time, it is just this necessity which injects the element of coercion into political life, and which, from our analytical point of view, means that politics and positive law can only be associated with the old order. As long as there is a necessary or compelling connection between command and structure, as there is in the civil political-legal sphere, God is not fully sovereign (in the eschatological sense), nor is man fully free. Because of man's inordinate disobedience, which at all times threatens total anarchy, the political ruler, in order to protect the sovereignty of God's order, must stay in power. He must give binding commands that will maintain and protect the society (or social structure) over which he is the ruler. The necessity for the preservation of social order provides the basis for his authority to command. His earthly control over force and coercion results directly from this "compelling" character of his office. It is this condition, incidentally, that introduces what can be called a conservative bias into Calvin's political thought. It explains his hesitancy to recommend to Christians any sort of revolutionary action.[54]

Nevertheless, God's order, as well as man's obedience, is not ultimately identified with any existing political structure. God's command is not bound by or restricted to the preservation of any historically given society. On the contrary, it drives beyond and stands in tension with the coercive character of all existing political-legal structures. God

---

52. Bohatec, *Calvin und das Recht,* 30.
53. *CR* 29, 660.
54. See fns. 63, 66 below.

in his sovereignty is essentially free of (though never unrelated to) the binding imperatives of historical social existence. In a word, his will is not defined by what is. Correspondingly, man is not really man so long as he is ordered by such necessities, so long as he is obedient only because of political constraint.

But if man is not fully man until he mirrors the freedom of God in his own voluntary obedience, he is not man at all when he rejects the rulers. Such an act plunges him into animal-like anarchy. Government was instituted by God, "so that men might not live like dogs and cats."[55]

Accordingly, the function and character of the governing authorities are spelled out in relation to the creation and enforcement of positive law. The purpose, norms, and limits of positive law are laid down in the natural law:

> For it is an axiom of positive law that the law is valid in so far as it is determined and carried out by the ruler; however, it is an axiom of natural law that the validity of positive law is not guaranteed through the naked authority of the ruler, rather its form and contents are just in so far as they correspond to the godly law and to the natural law.[56]

Ultimately, God's order as expressed in natural law and in positive law and political authority do not contradict each other. Each comes from the same source. But there is no possibility of *deriving* positive law from natural law in any direct way. Were it derived immediately from natural law, the accuracy or inaccuracy of the derivation would be the final court of appeal for the validity of a particular positive-legal decision. This would call in question the final earthly authority of the rulers, for if positive laws could be generally debated or appealed, then the ruler would no longer possess the last temporal word on order. He would be "under" rather than "over" the law.

Following Cicero's maxim, "The law is a dumb ruler, while a ruler is a living law," Calvin definitely states in certain places that the sovereign is released from the law. He *is* the law, the *lex animata*.[57] The abso-

55. *CR* 55, 559.
56. Bohatec, *Calvin und das Recht,* 126. Translation is mine.
57. Beyerhaus (*op. cit.,* 76-78) shows the influence of Roman notions on Calvin's political and legal thought. In the same vein, Bohatec demonstrates the influence of the humanists on Calvin: "Der Vergleich der Lehre des Zasius mit derjenigen Calvins ergibt eine so auffallende; *Übereinstimmung, dass man füglich von einer direkten Abhängigkeit Calvins von dem deutschen Humanistensprechen darf." (Staat und Kirche,* 50; my italics.)

lutistic implications of this side of Calvin's positive-legal formulation, which clearly bears a strong relation to Roman legal theory, are strikingly expressed in his theory of rebellion. Calvin holds resolutely that even the tyrannical ruler ought to be obeyed.[58] His commands (laws) bind the subjects not because they are necessarily just (and therefore in accord with natural law or a higher "court of appeal," such as the wishes of the people), but because they are commanded by him who is the *lex animata*, the one who *even in his tyranny has his government from God.*[59] Even a corrupt administration is better than anarchy.[60] The intensity of Calvin's passion for order at any price is very strong.

There is, however, another side to Calvin's position on the matter of *princeps legibus solutus* which, although it is sometimes thought to be inconsistent or contradictory, is quite consistent when viewed within the framework of his pattern of order. Calvin occasionally makes the point that "godlessness" equals "lawlessness."[61] In his later writings, especially in the Sermons on Samuel, the idea is emphasized that willful and immoral acts on the part of rulers flow from an overemphasis upon their freedom from the law.[62] They are under God, and responsible to him; they must not use their power arbitrarily, but in God's service.[63] God always reserves the right to make the ultimate command:

> If they [the godless rulers] *command* anything against Him [God],
> it ought not to have the least attention; nor, in this case, ought we to
> pay any regard to all that dignity attached to magistrates; to which
> no injury is done when it is subjected to the unrivalled and supreme
> power of God.[64]

58. *Comm.* on Rom. 13:1 ff; *Comm.* on I Peter 2:14-15.

59. IV, 20, 25.

60. Bohatec says (*Staat und Kirche*, 60): "die verunstaltete und verderbte Regierungsform ist besser und nützlicher als die Anarchie." Cf. Beyerhaus, *op. cit.*, 99-100.

61. *Comm.* on Ps. 10:4: "The ungodly . . . permit themselves to do anything . . . because their own lust is their law; yea, rather, as if superior to all laws, they fancy that it is lawful for them to do whatever they please."

62. *CR* 43, 253.

63. *CR* 29, 555. See Bohatec, *Staat und Kirche*, 63; M.-E. Chenevière, *La pensée politique de Calvin* (Geneva, 1937), 171; cf. *CR* 5, 18, 14. In this connection, Beyerhaus makes an interesting point: he argues that Calvin's unswerving emphasis upon the sovereignty of God has a "thoroughly levelling" effect when translated into political terms. Consequently, Calvin is suspicious of monarchy and favors aristocratic government because it does not lend itself so readily to usurpation of the power of God (IV, 20, 8).

64. IV, 20, 32.

This exception in Calvin's view of rebellion is, of course, predictable. Calvin remarks frequently that when the ruler attempts to set himself above God, the situation has no longer anything to do with positive law, but falls under the overreigning law of God.[65]

This is precisely the point that if a ruler commands anything against God, it is by definition *no* command, and, therefore, "ought not to have the least attention." Likewise, the ruler who makes such a command is *no* ruler because, as we have seen, all rulers derive their power from God himself. Such a "ruler" may rightfully be overthrown by lesser magistrates who, as political authorities, still legitimately represent God's order.[66] He may not be overthrown by the people, for they have already forfeited their ability to decide aright with respect to order.[67] The ruler remains above the positive law only to the extent that he conducts himself according to the "all encompassing sovereignty of God,"[68] and according to "the obligations that are imposed on him by God."[69]

There exists, then, a demand for inward obedience, on the part of the ruler, to the true order of God. He is called to compel and to regulate his citizens according to the purposes, norms, and limits of the natural-moral law, so that they may be properly prodded in the direc-

65. *CR* 24, 603; 51, 228, 685, 785; cf. Bohatec, *Staat und Kirche*, 80.
66. It is true that Calvin is extremely hesitant to take the full consequences of his own recommendations in special cases, such as his advice to the beleaguered French Protestants. Clearly, the French crown was requiring Reformed Protestants to reject their faith, and yet Calvin wrote Charles IX in January 1561 that the Reformed Churches had properly been exhorted "to remain in peaceable subjection to their prince" (*Letters of John Calvin*, ed. Jules Bonnet [4 vols., Edinburgh and Philadelphia, 1855-58], IV, 169). Nevertheless, in keeping with the tension in his own thought, Calvin is considerably less passive in other advice to French Protestants. In April 1561, he wrote Admiral Coligny, a potential insurrectionist, "if the princes . . . demanded to be maintained in their rights for the common good, and if the Parliament joined them in their quarrel . . . it would be lawful for all good subjects to lend them armed assistance" (*ibid.*, 176). In September 1562, he even goes so far as to urge all Reformed Churches to support financially the soldiers employed for the purpose of defending Reformed Protestants after the massacre of Vassey. "God has reduced us to such an extremity that if [the troops are not supported], we can expect nothing, according to human probability, but a pitiful and horrible desolation . . . " (*ibid.*, 279). Good order is sorely threatened, thereby making a violent response permissible.
67. Chenevière, *op. cit.*, 165; IV, 20, 31.
68. Bohatec, *Staat und Kirche*, 80.
69. Chenevière, *op. cit.*, 172.

tion of obedience to God himself. Consequently, the same double function at work in Calvin's idea of natural and positive law is equally clear in his attitude toward political rulers, with a variation. Political authority is by definition, a manifestation of order—it drives toward harmony and regulation. On the other hand, its very reliance upon coercion points to the disobedience and disorder of man, or to the inadequacy of his relation to God. Furthermore, since the rulers are themselves human beings (with the exclusively human characteristic of ethical choice) and not "forces" such as natural and positive law, they are themselves responsible to God. The legitimacy of their kingdom is ultimately judged according to their own obedience to the true order of God.

We have surveyed, roughly, Calvin's understanding of the second use of the law[70] which "constrains" sinners, even though "their *hearts* are not disposed to fear and obey God." The incompleteness implicit in the first and second uses of the law establishes the necessity for the third use, which falls under the heading of the redeeming activity of Christ.

3. Jesus Christ and God's Sovereign Command

The third and principal use, which pertains more closely to the proper purpose of the law, finds its place among believers in whose hearts the Spirit of God already lives and reigns. For even though they have the law written and engraved upon their hearts by the finger of God, that is, have been so moved and quickened through the directing of the Spirit that *they long to obey God,* they still profit by the law in two ways. Here is the best instrument for them to learn more thoroughly each day the nature of the Lord's will to which they aspire, and to confirm them in the understanding of it.[71]

70. II, 7, 10.
71. II, 7, 12; my italics. In order to understand the systematic implications of the law for social life in general, it is instructive to place this passage alongside II, 8, 51-57 and IV, 20, 15-16. For Calvin, the final twofold purpose of the law is to inspire heartfelt reverence for God and love of man (II, 8, 53). What we wish to emphasize is that in IV, 20, 15-16, these two ultimate purposes become the end of the natural-moral law as well. As I have tried to show throughout this analysis, the first two uses of the law press toward and entail the third use in Calvin's scheme: "For it is his eternal and unchangeable will that he himself indeed be worshiped by us all, and that we love one another." "Surely every nation is left free to make such laws as it foresees to be profitable for itself. Yet these must be in conformity to that perpetual rule of love, so that they indeed vary in form but have *the same purpose*" (my italics). Accordingly, those who embody in their hearts and lives the "third and principal use"—namely, members of the new order—become the model of social life. It is they who obey law as it was intended to be obeyed.

For Calvin the creation of order and the redemption of order inhere in the "living Word of God," namely, in Jesus Christ.[72] He is the incarnated command of God, as well as the "Head" of the true social structure. The purpose of redemption is the same as that of creation: the bringing into proper order of all things. It is Christ who confronts and overcomes the source of social confusion and disorder, namely, the heart (or will) of man. It is only by gaining obedience from the heart, in a completely voluntary sense, that man iș restored to the image of God. Only then can man take his proper place in relation to God and the rest of creation.[73]

Christ is the obedient one. He does what man cannot do by himself, he obeys with his whole heart. His life, as a consequence, is a perfect pattern of order: " . . . in Christ the feelings were adjusted (*compositi*) and regulated (*moderati*) in obedience to God and were altogether free from sin."[74] Christ is the manifestation of perfect harmony between the "will of God and the will of man, so that they differed from each other without any conflict or opposition."[75] Thus, Christ is the "living image of God his Father."[76]

Because of Christ's total obedience even to death, "sin has been abolished, salvation has been given back to men, and in short the whole world has been renewed and all things restored to order."[77] Or, as Calvin comments in interpreting John 12:31,

> "Judgment" is interpreted variously as "reformation" and "condemnation." I agree rather with the former view, with those who say that the world shall be restored to right order. For the Hebrew, *Mishpat*, which is rendered "judgment," means a state of good order. Now, we know that apart from Christ there is nothing but confusion in this world. Although Christ has already begun to set up the Kingdom of God, his death was the real beginning of a right order and the full restoration of the world![78]

In terms of our analysis, obedience to God's command entails the fulfillment of God's social-structural design. Christ is entailed in the Calvinist pattern of order, for if God is to be God (the authority of

72. *Comm.* on Col. 1:15, John 1:13.
73. *Comm.* on Luke 17:20.
74. *Comm.* on John 11:33.
75. *Comm.* on Matt. 26:39.
76. *CR* 33, 59.
77. *Comm.* on John 13:31.
78. *Calvin: Commentaries*, ed. and trans. by Joseph Haroutunian and L. P. Smith (Philadelphia, 1958), 339.

order), and obedience fulfills the harmonious arrangement of all things, then his order must be completely obeyed. God would cease to be God not only if his provisional agents of coercion did not prevail against the No of man, but also if he were not somehow able to overcome even the heart of man, and thereby inaugurate the Kingdom. In short, if "God" equals "perfect order," his order (command) must order perfectly (structure all things perfectly harmoniously and coherently).

Therefore, those who participate in the new order in Christ's Body, those "who voluntarily devote and submit themselves to be governed by him,"[79] owe their decision to the decision of God in Christ on their behalf. They respond to God's command from the heart because in "le grand secret conseil de Dieu," they were so elected.[80] Calvin's doctrine of predestination[81] betokens the freedom of the sovereign will of God over the creation of order. Man is not the final authority; God is. That some men truly obey and some do not can be ascribed to no other cause than the "free grace" of God, which is "confirmed" and "sealed" in Christ. It is just the point of the doctrine that "in Christ" men eagerly acknowledge (or confirm) that it is *God* who is sovereign.

79. *Comm.* on Matt. 6:10.
80. *CR* 8, 114; 22, 47.
81. See III, 21-25, for Calvin's discussion of predestination. It may be pointed out, in passing, that the relation between God's electing will and man's elected (or predestined) will differentiates Calvin's doctrine of predestination from "fatalism," insofar as that term means passive acceptance of what is. He who is elected now *actively* wills God's order—he "mirrors" God's active free will. Thus, the creation of a new order that stands in tension with the way things are is basic to Calvin's theory of predestination. A man manifests his election by electing in new ways, in ways that an "old man" under the bondage of sin is prevented from choosing. Calvin himself deals with the allegation that Christian predestination entails quietism and passivism in an extremely important passage—III, 23, 12: "To overthrow predestination our opponents also raise the point that, if it stands, all carefulness and zeal for well-doing go to ruin. For who can hear, they say, that either life or death has been appointed for him by God's eternal and unchangeable decree without thinking immediately that it makes no difference how he conducts himself, since God's predestination can neither be hindered nor advanced by his effort?" However, Calvin replies: "Paul teaches that we have been chosen to this end: that we may lead a holy and blameless life. If election has as its goal holiness of life, *it ought rather to arouse and goad us eagerly to set our mind upon it* than to serve as a pretext for doing nothing. What a great difference there is between these two things: to cease well-doing because election is sufficient for salvation, and *to devote ourselves to the pursuit of good as the appointed goal of election!* Away, then, with such sacrileges, for they wickedly invert the whole order of election" (my italics); cf. III, 22, 2-3.

The command of God (the law) is fulfilled in Christ by his voluntary loving obedience, and therefore can become fulfilled by the members of the Body. Christ himself is not only the correct interpreter of the law, by means of his life, death, and teachings, but he *is* the law, insofar as he embodies the end toward which the law points—the free and reverent submission to the sovereignty of God. By constraining themselves increasingly under the "yoke of Christ," by accepting Christ's "pattern" of obedience, Christians come to grasp the real purpose and function of the law. They come progressively to attain "the perfection of righteousness."[82] In other words, they come to affirm the law not as an unavoidable necessity that coerces and restrains them, but as the command of God that sets them free for loving, voluntary response. "When men willingly honor God's glory and acknowledge the world to be ruled by him and themselves to be under his authority, then they give true evidence of religion."[83]

In this framework, Calvin's theory of conscience in relation to Christian liberty is extremely important.[84] The conscience is the

82. II, 8, 51. There is unquestionably in Calvin's thought the basis for a "developmental" or "progressive" ethic. "The Kingdom means ... the spiritual life, which begins in this life by faith, and in which *we grow daily as we progress in a constant faith*," *Calvin: Commentaries*, 138. See also III, 19, 4. The most striking elaboration of this point is found at III, 7, 5: "Let each one of us, then, proceed according to the measure of his puny capacity and set out upon the journey we have begun. No one shall set out so inauspiciously as not daily to make some headway, though it be slight. Therefore, let us not cease so to act that we may make some unceasing progress in the way of the Lord. And let us not despair at the slightness of our success: for even though attainment may not correspond to desire, when today outstrips yesterday the effort is not lost. Only let us look toward our mark with sincere simplicity and aspire to our goal; not fondly flattering ourselves, nor excusing our own evil deeds, but with continuous effort striving toward this end that we may surpass ourselves in goodness until we attain to goodness itself." These sentiments inspire the kind of future-oriented, achieving, aspiring ethic that Weber found to be so characteristic of the Protestant ethic. We shall encounter these same notions in the Puritans.

83. *Calvin: Commentaries*, 146.

84. See "On Christian Liberty," III, 19. It is certainly true, as Edward A. Dowey, Jr., puts it in *The Knowledge of God in Calvin's Theology* (New York, 1952), that conscience for Calvin "is an element of the subjective revelation of God the Creator, given in the created order itself, not in Scripture. It is a universal endowment, part of man as man, an element of the *imago Dei*" (56). Conscience is the "knowledge of what is right and just" (*Comm.* on Rom. 2:14), and as such it is firmly grounded in the law of creation or the natural law (see Dowey, 57-59). Thus, conscience plays a noetic function for Calvin;

medium between God and man, in which are gathered up all the complexities and dynamics of Calvin's pattern of order. It is both the locus
of man's deepest relationship to God and the center of unrelenting
torment to him. To begin with, the conscience reveals the basis of
man's disobedience; "it brings him to conviction" because he turns the
order of God (in both dimensions) into disorder.[85] He does not revere
God as the ultimate authority, rather he reveres the command of God,
the law, above God himself. That which was given in order to lead man
to the heartfelt dependence on God in which true liberty consists is
transformed into a "yoke," and man is bound to his own disobedience.
When the conscience shackles the freedom of God to his created order,
its own distinctive freedom becomes shackled also. The fatal flaw is
that God's order is regarded as over, closed or "old," something that
can be identified with God himself and relied upon as one would rely
upon God. So regarded, the law becomes coercive and binding. It drives
man against his will (in the various forms of natural and positive law
and political authority) in the direction of the sovereign God. At the
same time, it convicts man *just because he must be driven toward God*,
because he does not freely heed the Word in "voluntary obedience,"[86]
with "alacrity and promptitude."[87] The command which was meant to

it constitutes a kind of moral reason which, like natural law, abides despite
the Fall. This is an important point to emphasize lest it be thought—as, for
example, August Lang mistakenly thinks in "The Reformation and Natural
Law," in Emile Doumergue, *et al.* (eds.), *Calvin and the Reformation* (New
York, 1909) that a capacity for moral reasoning no longer exists in man after
the Fall.

It ought not to be inferred, however, that Calvin is interested in developing
a theory of natural law and conscience into a self-contained moral philosophy
independent of Christian revelation. On the contrary, when Calvin defines
conscience, as when he defines natural law (see below), he invariably implies
the direct relevance of the Christian revelation of sin and redemption to these
terms. "It first behooves us to comprehend what conscience is; we must seek
the definition from the derivation of the word. For just as when through the
mind and understanding men grasp a knowledge of things, and from this are
said 'to know,' this is the source of the word 'knowledge,' so also *when they
have a sense of divine judgment, from being accursed before the Judge's
tribunal, this sense is called 'conscience.'* For it is a certain mean between God
and man, *because it does not allow man to suppress within himself what he
knows, but pursues him to the point of convicting him*" (III, 19, 15, my
italics; cf. IV, 10, 3).

85. III, 19, 15.
86. III, 19, 4.
87. *Ibid;* I prefer Allen's translation of these phrases to McNeill's. See *Institutes*,
    trans. John Allen (Philadelphia, 1936), II, 79.

set the conscience free, now binds it in such a way that its passion for harmony with God cannot possibly be satisfied, but can only be at once intensified and frustrated through its bondage to the old order. So the conscience is dynamic, craving "confidence," "tranquillity," and "appeasement" from the "terror" and "disquietude" produced by the haunting conviction of the law. It drives and disturbs man, and will not let him rest in less than God himself. Here, in sum, is the double function of the command noted throughout this section.

Analytically, we again face the separation of the command and the structural dimensions of order. The law (command) does not automatically create social coherence (it is not identical with it). To hold that real and true harmony will exist if only man fulfills the law is, according to Calvin, the very seat of perversity. By the same token, the way things are structured does not itself issue in a reliable ethical or legal command. The world is, after all, fallen. As we have seen, command and structure find their unity only in a dynamic, indeterminable fashion, that is to say, in the sovereignty of God. It is Christ who is the consummation of God's sovereign combination of command and structure. It is he, for reasons mentioned above, who removes the conscience from coercion and necessity and bequeathes to it a liberty fully in the image of God's liberty. "In Christ" man may now participate in that dynamic, indeterminable interweaving of command and structure that is in God. Such participation defines his obedience insofar as man recognizes "with alacrity and promptitude" that God's command is fulfilled only in a new, harmonious structure of relationships and, at the same time, that this structure is fulfilled only when it includes the free response of a totally voluntary will.[88]

It is, therefore, clear why Calvin writes:

> Now, since believers' consciences, having received the privilege of their freedom, which we previously described, have, by Christ's gift, attained to this, that they should not be entangled with any snares of observances in those matters in which the Lord has willed them to be free, we conclude that *they are released from the power of all men.*[89]

The conscience now stands directly before God and, in obedience to

88. It must be re-emphasized that law is not completely eliminated, but its status is radically revised: the law "still continues to instruct and exhort, and stimulate to duty, although *it has no place in their consciences before the tribunal of God*" (III, 19, 2; my italics).

89. III, 19, 14; my italics.

him, nothing else can be relied upon. In Christ there is a new break-through of God's authority that demands a total reorientation of allegiance. However, in keeping with Calvin's understanding of political authority, liberty of conscience is "spiritual" and may not be "mis-applied to political regulations."

> There is a twofold government in man: one aspect is spiritual, where-by the conscience is instructed in piety and in reverencing God; the second is political, whereby man is educated for the duties of humanity and citizenship that must be maintained among men. These are usually called the "spiritual" and the "temporal" jurisdic-tion . . . by which is meant that the former sort of government per-tains to the life of the soul, while the latter has to do with the concerns of the present life—not only with food and clothing but with laying down laws whereby a man may live his life among other men holily, honorably, and temperately. For the former resides in the inner mind, while the latter regulates only outward behavior. The one we may call the spiritual kingdom, the other, the political kingdom. Now these two, as we have divided them, must always be examined separately; and while one is being considered, we must call away and turn aside the mind from thinking about the other. There are in man, so to speak, two worlds, over which different kings and different laws have authority.[90]

As long as man exists in his present state, as one for whom the com-plete Kingdom of God has not yet come, God's political order of coercion must still prevail. The old order does not lose its provisional control, at least over the external conduct of man. But it is obvious from our study of Calvin that the realm of the free conscience—as a key to the whole question of order—is ultimate, and provides the guidelines for understanding God's plan and his work in the world. In terms of Calvin's pattern of order, nothing is surer than that the Kingdom of God, toward which all things move, includes overcoming the engines of coercion in favor of voluntary obedience to the will of God. Of course, the Christian lives in constant tension between two orders, but the tension will finally be set aside. There is absolutely no basis in Calvin's system for conceiving of the two orders as eternally coexistent, as part of some natural hierarchy of order.[91] The pronounced developmental or progressive character of the Kingdom of God signals the entire move-ment of history as a movement from political-legal regulation and

90. III, 19, 15.
91. This is one of the crucial distinctions between Calvinism and Thomism.

coercion toward the self-determining, self-integrating freedom of the conscience.[92]

In this matter we confront the central ambiguity and uncertainty in Calvin's pattern of order. It is the ambiguity which underlines what I shall call the dilemma of earthly power in the Calvinist system. Calvin's thought pulls in essentially two directions (directions that in one way or another attend the entire development of the Christian Church): one is "other-worldly" or "world-denying," to use Weber's terminology. There is an emphasis upon the "otherness" as well as the "inwardness" of the Christian life, a strain that comes out particularly strongly in III, 6-10. For example, "whatever kind of tribulation presses upon us, we must ever look to this end: to accustom ourselves to contempt for the present life and to be aroused thereby to meditate upon the future life."[93] This tendency, if heavily emphasized, individualizes and spirit-ualizes the new order; in effect, it makes the new order irrelevant to society. If the passage about the two kingdoms were allowed to stand alone, its implications would be clearly world-denying. Luther and, in a different way, Hooker move very far in this direction. However, the second, or "inner-worldly," direction is extremely strong in Calvin— much stronger than in either Luther or Hooker. In terms of this direction, the new order is strongly relevant to the reshaping of all things. Accordingly, the Gospel is socialized and externalized. It is because of this second direction, which we have been mainly exploring, that Calvin and his followers could never divorce completely one order from the other. Indeed, the whole point of this analysis has been to show how systematically *interrelated* the new is with the old.

On the logic of the system, it is therefore quite impossible to do what Calvin admonishes, to abstract the mind from all consideration of one realm while the other is being discussed. Neither Calvin nor his followers were ever able, practically or theoretically, to make such a complete disjunction. As Calvin himself says, "Jesus Christ is thus the beginning of the second and the new creation; for the first creation was destroyed by the first man."[94] In the "new creation," *all* forms of order point toward and will eventually be transformed in Christ; if they do not accept that fact, they may no longer be considered as order.[95]

92. K. Fröhlich in *Gottesreich: Welt und Kirche bei Calvin* (Munich, 1930) rightly remarks that the entire basis for the Christian's life in Calvin is "das Wissen um das Fortschreiten des Regnum Christi" (42).
93. III, 9, 1.
94. *Comm.* on Col. 1:18.
95. See the Dedication to the *Institutes.*

The relation, as well as the distinction, between the old order of political-legal coercion and the new order of the liberated Christian conscience is particularly apparent in Calvin's view of the State and Church, as we shall see more fully in the next section. While the State as the locus of coercive power is certainly distinguished from the Church in Calvin's pattern, it has no other function than to serve the Church. *In the nature of the State's differentiation from the Church lies the basis for its subordination to the Church.* Coercion must give way to freedom; the old order must give way to the new. Accordingly, the Christian religion is envisaged as the foundation for social order, an assumption that is underlined by Calvin's stipulation regarding the "religion offices" of the State: "Civil government has as its appointed end, so long as we live among men, to cherish and protect the outward worship of God, and to defend sound doctrine of piety and the position of the church."[96] The framework for proper order is provided by the consistent maintenance of the Reformed Christian faith. There is no true order without the honor of God.[97]

However, if the differentiation of Church and State means subordination, it also still means differentiation.[98] The common assumption that Calvin sought simply to reinstate a theocracy after the fashion of the Old Testament is mistaken. He always resisted suggestions, by such people as Karlstadt, that the Mosaic law ought to be legislated into practice.[99] He rejected the notion that Genevans should establish a new Davidic Kingdom. The relevance of such forms was, for him, clearly over.[100] Therefore, Calvin was inclined to accept the established forms

96. IV, 20, 2, 9.

97. *CR* 53, 140: "Voilà pourquoi (Dieu) a établi les rois et magistrats, et la police humaine. C'est en premier lieu: que nous vivions, dit Saint Paul, en toute pieté." (Cf. *CR* 52, 267; 52, 130, 134, 137, 139.)

98. For a discussion of the differentiation of Church and State, see Wendel, *op. cit.*, 74, and André Biéler, *La pensée économique et sociale de Calvin* (Geneva, 1961), 129-130.

99. Ernst Pfisterer, *Calvins Wirken in Genf* (Essen, 1957). Pfisterer confirms what we have already seen: that the Mosaic law and especially the Decalogue is for Calvin the basis for the "fundamental moral framework" of the positive law, but not for its contents (52-56). There is a great deal of room for discretion on the part of the authorities in the light of their own legal traditions and historical circumstances. Cf. IV, 20, 15-16.

100. A most important statement by Calvin, in this connection, demands comment: "Whereas kings, in times now over, were virtually the spirit of social life, now Christ is that spirit, and he reigns *per se* in the church, 'vivifying' its life. *'Today'* we by no means have earthly kingdoms that are in the image of

of government and law in Geneva without trying to recast them in a biblical image.[101] We have already seen that for him given rulers are, generally speaking, ordained of God *as they stand.*

This is a decisive point in Calvin's pattern of order not only because it reveals the often mentioned conservative bias in the reformer's political thought. Much more important in this context, it indicates Calvin's fundamental antipathy toward confusing the true Christian order with the political-legal order. That is to say, the irreducible coercive element endemic to political order cannot finally be accommodated to the voluntaristic, free-willing characteristics of the Christian life. It is for this reason that though Calvin consistently attempts to adjust the law of God to the law of the world, he will never allow them to be collapsed into one another. A basic differentiation between new and old order obtains throughout. "So, then, the Kingdom of Christ extends, no doubt, to all men; but it brings salvation to none but the elect, who with *voluntary obedience* follow the voice of the Shepherd; for the others are *compelled by violence* to obey him, till at length he utterly bruise them with his iron sceptre."[102]

This is not, of course, to say that there are no tensions and confusions between the differentiation of the Church from the world on the one hand, and the subordination of the world to the Church on the other. Quite the opposite, this is the very dilemma of earthly power which, as we shall see, consistently haunts the Calvinist experience. But these tensions and confusions ought not blind us to the clear direction of Calvin's pattern of order. It is only when the pattern is borne in mind that the complexities in Calvin's political and social theory are fully understandable.

> *Christ.* Since the coming of Christ, and the differentiation of the church from the state, the rulers have decidedly taken a subordinate place. The locus *per se* of Christ's Lordship is the church" (*CR* 66, 635; my italics). Beyerhaus cites convincing evidence to refute Choisy, the classical representative of the idea that Calvin wished to found a new Israelitic Kingdom. See esp. Beyerhaus, *op. cit.,* 142-145. For Calvin, Christ had come and the Old Testament form of social life had ended. In face of so many misunderstandings along these lines, these aspects must be re-emphasized.

101. Chenevière, *op. cit.,* 197-221, has an instructive discussion of Calvin's legal and political role in Geneva. There is reason to believe that he was true to his idea that secular political order is to be accepted "as is" from God, though he also, of course, introduced some political innovations, particularly with respect to the relations of Church and State.

102. *Comm.* on John 17:2; my italics.

SOVEREIGNTY AND SOCIETY

1. Society and God's Sovereign Order

Just as God's Word commanded or "ordered" creation into existence, and just as his Word commands man to participate in fully integrated obedience, so also, God's Word "orders" or structures all things perfectly. The world before the Fall was one grand harmony. All of nature and all men performed their functions cooperatively in an organic testimony to God. In other words, creation in the Eden period did what was ordered.[103]

Just as man alone is the one who possesses the choice between obedience and disobedience, so he is responsible for the maintenance or destruction of the full integration of creation. Just as man's role in relation to God's command is unique because he faces a decisive alternative, so man's role in relation to the socio-natural order is unique because he is potentially the principal benefactor as well as despoiler of order. It is for this reason that man stands at the top of creation: "But as we know . . . the world was made chiefly, for the sake of mankind."[104] It is in this sense that creation "is subjected" to man. Its coherence depends (to a certain extent) upon man's obedience.

God's socio-natural design dictates optimum economic abundance and the highest degree of its just distribution. Perfect enjoyment of the "good things" of creation is the object of God's order:

> The Prophet makes it known that God not only provides for the needs of men and gives to them as much as is sufficient for the ordinary needs of this life, but by His mercy He treats them still more generously when He gladdens their hearts with wine and oil.[105]

But this enjoyment must be seen in the context of harmonious social relationships. In the discussion of Matt. 25:20, Calvin asserts that the economic processes of labor, trading, and gain, as part of the gifts God has committed to men, ought to be performed for "the profit or advancement of the whole company of believers in common." The "use or object" of the gifts of God, Calvin goes on, "is to promote mutual intercourse among men. . . . Now the *gain* which Christ mentions is general usefulness, which illustrates the glory of God."

103. *Comm.* on Ps. 104:1-27, 19:1.
104. I, 16, 6.
105. *Comm.* on Ps. 104:15.

It must be emphasized that in God's original order this ideal of general usefulness entails the vigorous initiative and involvement of every individual member. Each member is, of his own accord, to be assiduously useful for the good of the whole. This emphasis upon "utility," or instrumentality or functionality, is extremely important in Calvin's understanding, particularly so since it is placed in an economic context:[106]

> It is not the will of the Lord that we should be like blocks of wood, or that we should keep our arms folded without doing anything; but that we should apply to use all the talents and advantages which he has conferred upon us. It is indeed true that the greatest part of our labours proceeds from the curse of God; and yet although men had still retained the integrity of their primitive state, God would have had us to be employed, even as we see how Adam was placed in the garden of Eden to dress it. Solomon, therefore, does not condemn watchfulness, a thing which God approves; nor yet *man's labour, by which when they undertake it willingly, according to the commandment of God, they offer to him the acceptable sacrifice* . . . [107]

> *Let each of us remember, that he has been created by God for the purpose of laboring, and of being vigorously employed in his work;* and that not only for a limited time, but till death itself, and what is more, that he shall not only live, but die, to God.[108]

Man is, then, created by God for voluntary labor that is offered in a spirit of eager, uncompelled devotion to the service of God and the community. Indeed, not only does God curse "laziness and loafing"[109]

---

106. There is, in other words, a good deal of evidence in the Calvinist system for what Parsons has called "instrumental activism." Weber called attention to the "utilitarian" aspect of Calvinist thought in fn. 33, 265-266, of *The Protestant Ethic.* For an interesting examination of this, see E. Harris Harbison, "The Idea of Utility in John Calvin," *Christianity and History* (Princeton, N. J., 1964), 249-270.

107. *Comm.* on Ps. 127:1 (my italics).

108. *Comm.* on Luke 17:7 (my italics).

109. Quoted in Biéler, *Social Humanism of Calvin* (Richmond, Va., 1964), 45. Biéler continues: "By associating man with his own labor, God assigns an earthly goal to his creature. Man is created to work. Here on earth, man accomplished his destiny by working. Consequently, idleness is against nature. Idleness is therefore an offense to God. . . . . Hence Calvin denounces the fault of those men who draw their resources from the work of others without bringing a real service to the community. He decries these 'idlers and good-for-nothing individuals who live by the sweat of others and yet bring

in Calvin, but indolent people are to be regarded as pre-eminently the source of disobedience and disorder:

> [Paul] applies the appellation of *disorderly persons*, not to those that are of a dissolute life, or to those whose characters are stained by flagrant crimes, but *to indolent and worthless persons, who employ themselves in no honorable and useful occupation*. For this truly ἀταξία (disorder)—nor considering for what purpose we were made, and regulating our life with a view to that end, while it is only when we live according to the rule prescribed to us by God that this life is duly regulated. Let this order be set aside, and there is nothing but confusion in human life. . . . *For God has distinguished in such a manner the life of men, in order that every one may lay himself out for the advantage of others*. He, therefore, who lives to himself alone, so as to be profitable in no way to the human race, nay more, is a burden to others, giving help to no one, is on good grounds reckoned to be ἀταξία (disorderly).[110]

The interweaving of economic abundance, voluntary labor, and social integration is crucial for our study. According to Calvin, "man was rich before he was born,"[111] but abundance is unthinkable apart from "general usefulness" or "mutual intercourse." And, of course, social integration is unthinkable apart from "the glory of God." In other words, the very object of mankind is to enjoy the fruits of God's creation, but this can be done only within a framework of order, a fact

no common means to help mankind.' " " 'Though we receive our food from the hand of God,' Calvin writes, 'he has ordained that we work. Is now work taken away? Behold, the life of man is thrown under' " (45).

110. *Comm.* on II Thess. 3:5 (my italics). In the light of such passages as this, one is puzzled by Georgia Harkness's comments in *John Calvin: The Man and His Ethics* (New York, 1958): "But when one searches Calvin's own words, one finds comparatively little about the duty to labor. Denunciations of the blasphemer, the adulterer, the drunkard, and the spendthrift, appear on almost every page. Also, of the avaricious person who covets his neighbor's goods and amasses riches dishonestly. But one must seek diligently to find references to the sin of idleness, or praises for the virtue of toil" (168). Miss Harkness has simply not been diligent enough! My list of relevant passages is already quite long and is still growing: see, for example, Calvin's commentary on Gen. 2:15; 3:17, 19; John 9:4 Matt. 25:20 (to be dealt with below); II Thess. 3:10, 11. And, as the passage quoted above makes clear, idleness is not of incidental consequence in the problem of order: disorderly persons are not those "of a dissolute life" or those who "are stained by flagrant crimes," but *indolent persons*.

111. *Comm.* on Gen. 1:26.

that implies two things: (1) Unless man accepts the fruits of creation as the fruits of God's creation, he will not enjoy them; he will pervert them. Man must concede from his heart that God is the giver, the sustainer. The material enrichment of man is subsumed under God's command, under his system of order. (2) Only as there is true obedience to God's order will there be true economic order at the social level, and true economic order alone can produce a satisfactory appropriation and distribution of abundance.[112]

Calvin has what we might call a functional view of economic life as distinct from a preferential or hierarchical view, which organizes the economy in favor of special groups. The economic order is to be evaluated in terms of general usefulness—that is, of maximum production and just and equal distribution among the community of mankind. Furthermore, roles or vocations in this scheme are assigned fundamentally with reference to functional utility or "eminent usefulness." "It is certain that a calling would never be approved by God that is not socially useful, and that does not redound to the profit of all."[113] In Biéler's apt summary:

> "God has created man," Calvin says, "so that man may be a creature of fellowship." . . . Companionship is completed in work and in the interplay of economic exchanges. Human fellowship is realized in relationships which flow from the division of labor wherein each person has been called by God to a particular and partial work which complements the work of others. The mutual exchange of goods and services is the concrete sign of the profound solidarity which unites humanity.[114]

The primitive or original society which stands directly under God's sovereign order, then, is consistently and strikingly portrayed by Calvin in economic categories.

2. Disobedience and the Disordered Society

As the Fall was the result of man's disobedient response to God's command, so it signified the breakdown of the harmonious, well-ordered primitive community. As mentioned in section 1 above, "the earth was cursed on account of Adam."[115] It was precisely man's

112. Biéler, *La pensée économique et sociale*, 321.
113. *CR* 51, 639.
114. Biéler, *Social Humanism*, 17-18.
115. *Comm.* on Gen. 3:17.

breaking of God's command which spelled the breaking of God's pattern of social structure. Since there is just social relationship only when the design of God is maintained, the breaking of that design leads to social dysfunction. Preferential relationships now characterize the "perverse society." Men no longer deal with each other as brothers under the lordship of God, and therefore they do not contribute to society (for the sake of "general usefulness") their particular abilities and offices. On the contrary, "in their pride and haughtiness they despise their neighbors, and they also make war on heaven."[116]

The prerogative of ordering or arranging men in social hierarchies according to the highest degree of functional effectiveness is usurped from God by man in the Fall. Man attempts to dominate the socionatural order *in his own name and by his own right*, rather than in the name and by the right of God. Consequently, as his relation with God is inundated with pride and haughtiness, issuing in a "war on heaven," so man's relation with his brother is controlled by concern for his own honor and dignity. The attempt to attain prestige by himself and for himself results in social division and strife. In his disobedience man tries to replace God as the source of ultimate order and this, of course, provokes the "fearful deformity" of all things. Calvin indicates that man's system of order is directly contrary to God's:

> Let us take careful note, then, that each time men who have been raised to high estate are beaten down, and conversely, each time those who were scorned are honoured, this does not happen without reason.[117]

This is the "total perversity" of which we spoke earlier. It infects sexual[118] as well as familial relationships.[119]

Total social perversity also affects the economic order. Both optimum production and just distribution were impeded by the Fall. God is no longer taken as the one who provides the gifts of creation and properly organizes men that they may benefit from the gifts to the utmost. Man now seizes these for himself. What was God's design becomes man's design. As a result, men "are burning in such covetousness that always entices them . . . and they are never content."[120]

Envy, vanity, pride, avarice—all of which lie at the heart of the fallen

116. *CR* 46, 136.
117. *CR* 46, 136.
118. *Comm.* on Rom. 1:24-26.
119. *CR* 28, 454.
120. *CR* 28, 200.

economic system of man—beget social alienation. The abundance that economic activity yields becomes the God, and the attainment of abundance—in itself—the driving command of human life. The system of order is formulated in terms of Mammon. Like the political order, which set itself up in place of God, such a system is no order at all; it is *bouleversée*—"overturned" (Biéler).

However, just as in the politico-legal order man's No to God's command was not allowed to produce *complete* disorder (which would mean God was no longer God), so in the socio-economic realm man's divisive disobedience does not triumph totally over God's order. According to Calvin, material goods continue to have a "pedagogical use" even after the Fall.[121] The nourishment and satisfaction which these material goods continue to bring men, if only in a fragmentary way, serve as an adumbration of the coming Kingdom of God.[122] The gifts of creation continue to serve the purpose of God even in spite of man's rejection of him. God continues to be Lord over creation and its fruits even though man does not acknowledge it. He continues to give gifts and to organize men in such a way that these gifts can be produced and to a limited extent enjoyed. It is another aspect of God's providential order which prevails and directs things according to his design, even if that design has for the time being become a coercive order.

3. God's New Order: The Kingdom and the Church

If God is to remain God it is necessary[123] that both dimensions of order be fulfilled completely. As Jesus Christ was the fulfillment of the command of God in creation and redemption, so he is the expression and fulfillment of God's social-structural design.[124]

Man's wholehearted decision against God plunges him into the consequences of disobedience and disorder. Man is trapped in a situation that (from the point of view of his own capabilities) affords no exit. His dilemma is compounded exactly by his attempts to make himself obedient and to order his own existence. Since God alone is the author of order, it is he alone who can provide perfect order. Only when man

---

121. *CR* 25, 623.
122. *Comm.* on Ps. 128:2.
123. Biéler, *La pensée économique et sociale,* 246: "La dessein de Dieu reste immuable; son plan de restitution de l'univers est déjà conçu et arrêté au moment où il donne la vie à l'homme."
124. See p. 48, fn. 78, above.

concedes this from the heart, as we have seen, may he participate in true order. But such a concession is made, not through reliance on man's own will (that would be simply another manifestation of destructive self-reliance), but through God's gracious act in Christ. It is in the Body of Christ that all the bitter fruits of disobedience and disorder are done away with. There men become perfectly obedient and perfectly ordered. In a striking passage, Calvin indicates these two dimensions of Christ's lordship: his perfect obedience and his accomplishment of order:

> He humbled Himself to exalt us, He enslaved Himself to free us, He impoverished Himself to enrich us, He was sold to redeem us, a captive to deliver us, condemned to pardon us, He was made a curse for our blessing, an oblation of sin so we should receive justice, He was disfigured to reconstitute us, He died so we could live. To such an extent that through Him harshness is softened, anger appeased, shadows brightened, injustice made just, weakness made virtuous, misery consoled, sin prevented, scorn scorned, fear reassured, debts paid, labours lightened, sadness gladdened, misfortune made fortunate, difficulties made easy, disorder ordered, division unified, ignominy ennobled, rebellion subjected, threats threatened, snares ensnared, assaults assailed, effort strengthened, combats combatted, war subdued, vengeance avenged, torment tormented, damnation damned, destruction destroyed, Hell put in chains, death abolished, mortality immortalized.[125]

The Kingdom of Christ, in Calvin's view, is a new order of decidedly cosmic proportions:

> All that is created is subject to mortality but the Kingdom of Christ is an eternal kingdom. Hence all creation must be fashioned anew and transfigured.[126]

> The fundamental materials of the world will pass away in order that, as it were, a new structure may arise; but their inner kernel remains. . . . harmony with the Lordship of Christ.[127]

> In completing the redemption of man God will restore order to the present confusion of earth. . . . We are content with the simple doctrine that such measure and order will prevail in the world as will exclude all distortion and destruction.[128]

125. *CR* 9, 813-815.
126. *Comm.* on Heb. 12:27.
127. *Comm.* on II Pet. 3:10.
128. *Comm.* on Rom. 5:21.

For the result of the sad disorder ensuing upon the fall of Adam
would have been at any moment to break up the machinery of the
world, to bring its wheels to a standstill, if a mighty power of
another order in accordance with its secret purpose had not inter-
vened to hold it together . . . . [129]

The Kingdom is the order or structure toward which all things in-
cline and in which all things are properly fulfilled. But, as we would
expect, it is not something that emerges naturally or without interrup-
tion from things as they are: not from the world of nature, not from
established societies, not even from man as he is. The "inner kernel" of
all these things remains, but they must be "fashioned anew and transfigured" by an independent decision or action on the part of God. Such
is the crucial sovereign or voluntary character of God that he—in a
manner recognizably distinct from the created cosmos—initiates the
perfection of order. Thus, as God is not equal to or identical with the
existing socio-natural order, so his order (his Kingdom) is not equal to
or identical with what is. Both God's command and his structure are
characteristically differentiated from the commands and the structure
of the world.[130]

In describing the central characteristics of the new order, Calvin
employs economic language and imagery to an impressive degree:

> *Those who employ usefully whatever God has committed to them
> are said to be engaged in trading. The life of the godly, is justly
> compared to trading,* for they ought naturally to exchange and
> barter with each other, in order to maintain intercourse; and the
> industry with which every man discharges the office assigned him,
> the calling itself, the power of acting properly, and other gifts, are
> reckoned to be so many kinds of merchandise; because the use or
> object which they have in view is, to promote mutual intercourse
> among men.
>
> Now the *gain* which Christ mentions is general usefulness, which
> illustrates the glory of God. For, though God is not enriched, and
> makes no gain, by our labors, yet when every one is highly profitable
> to his brethren, and applies advantageously, for their salvation, the
> gifts which he has received from God, he is said to yield profit, or
> gain, to God himself. So highly does our heavenly Father value the
> salvation of men, that whatever contributes to it he chooses to place
> to his own account. That we may not become weary in doing well,

129. *Ibid.*, 5:20
130. See Fröhlich, *op. cit.*, 75-93.

Christ declares that the labour of those who are faithfully employed in their calling will not be useless.[131]

If we are rightly to understand what Calvin means by true order, we shall not be able to leave economic categories out of account. Biéler has put Calvin's view well: "The religous life and the material life of the believer are both subjected to the same order of God."[132]

As the primitive community was bound together by economic interdependence and mutuality, so is the "restored society." Accordingly, "Christ re-established among Christians, the members of his church, a just redistribution of goods that was destined [ultimately] for all. This transformation prefigured the restoration of the economic order in the whole of society."[133] This means that the disruptive aspects of the perverse society, such as monopoly, hoarding, and gross economic inequities, are done away in the Body of Christ.[134] The Church is called to manifest a harmonious "diversity of grace" in which "whatever benefits God confers on [the members], they should mutually communicate to each other."[135]

Two things about the "diversity of grace" implicit in the new order should be emphasized: (1) As the preceding passage makes clear, this sort of communication must be engaged in willingly or voluntarily. As Christ, who is Head of this Body, voluntarily participated in the reconciliation of mankind, so must those participate who benefit from his action:

> We ought to give to our brothers much more bountifully and generously than men are usually in the habit of doing. For men are somewhat grudging in what concerns their neighbors. Few do their

131. *Comm.* on Matt. 25:20; my italics.
132. Biéler, *La pensée économique et sociale,* 154.
133. *Ibid.,* 256.
134. Biéler summarizes the evidence on this point very nicely in *Social Humanism:* "Evangelization by calling forth the birth of man to new life makes him apt to commercial service. From external submission to the law, which man defrauds as soon as possible, the Christian passes to willing obedience, to the ethics of liberty. . . . Speculation, cornering and monopolizing are the principal forms of a vitiated economic order. . . . Monopolists are nothing less than murderers because they block the circulation of goods necessary for life. 'Today when everything has such a high price,' Calvin says, 'we see men who keep their granaries closed; this is as if they cut the throat of the poor people, when they thus reduce them to extreme hunger,' " 52-53. See also *La pensée économique et sociale,* 306 ff.
135. IV, 1, 3.

duty eagerly and promptly, or give their labor and kindness without
calculation. To correct this fault, *God praises above all alacrity*.[136]

(2) Christian obedience is to be conducted without preferential regard
for persons:

> [James] denies that our neighbours are loved, when a part only of
> them is through ambition chosen, and the rest neglected. This he
> proves, because it is no obedience to God, when it is not rendered
> equally according to his command. Then as the rule of God is plain
> and complete or perfect, so we ought to regard completeness; so that
> none of us should presumptuously separate what [God] has joined
> together. Let there be, therefore, a uniformity, if we desire rightly to
> obey God. As, for instance, were a judge to punish ten thefts, and
> leave one man unpunished, he would betray the obliquity of his
> mind, for he would thus show himself indignant against men rather
> than against crimes; because what he condemns in one he absolves in
> another.[137]

Though social distinctions are by no means dissolved in Calvin's new
order, the function and behavior of every member is finally judged by
one overriding *uniform* law:[138] the eager edification of the Body of
Christ.

This sort of pattern, then, with all its economic overtones, is *specially related to and bound up with* the eschatological purposes of God.
What man was created to be—a freely obedient being who responds
gratefully to the gifts of God, ardently sharing them with all his
brothers and turning them to corporate use—is put by Calvin again and
again in the language of economic action.

Of course, such totally harmonious economic life is part of the
ultimate purpose of God; it is, as such, ideal and never altogether real-

---

136. *Calvin: Commentaries,* 336; my italics.

137. *Comm.* on Jas. 2:10

138. "No one was exempt from this discipline, both princes and common people
submitted to it. And rightly! For it was established by Christ, to whom it is
fitting that all royal scepters and crowns submit" (IV, 12, 7; cf. II, 8, 53).
"Christ declares himself the light of the whole world. By this universal
statement, he takes away the distinction not only between the Jew and the
Greek, but also between the learned and the ignorant, the distinguished and
the common people," *Calvin: Commentaries,* 139-140. Cf. Biéler, *La pensée
économique et sociale,* 253-256. In fn. 2, 255, Biéler speaks of Calvin's emphasis upon "universalism" over against the "particularism" of some
Genevans who wished to make their Church exclusively Genevan. See also
104 ff.

ized in the "present state." But it is expressive of that toward which all things move, of that which characterizes the Kingdom of God; expressive, therefore, of what exists proleptically in the Body of Christ and stands in tension with the old order. For the time being, the economic life of the world must continue, like all secular life, to be partly organized by coercion; it must be subjected to political power and authority. But such a situation is only provisional. It is now in process, and it finally must give way to the complete kingship of Christ, under whom all the members of society shall become fully self-integrating.[139]

The discussion of the central characteristics of the new order in economic terms sets the stage for understanding Calvin's general conception of the Church. For there are the profoundest parallels in Calvin's thought between action and organization expressed in economic terms, and action and organization expressed in ecclesiological terms:

> "The Communion of Saints" ... very well expresses what the church is. It is as if one said that the saints are gathered into the society of Christ on the principle that whatever benefits God confers upon them, they should in turn share with one another. This does not, however, rule out diversity of graces, inasmuch as we know the gifts of the Spirit are variously distributed. ... If truly convinced that God is the common Father of all and Christ the common Head, being united in brotherly love, they cannot but share their benefits with one another.[140]

In the "diversity of grace," or the spiritual division of labor,[141] there is a greater and richer unity: *"sed in distinctione esse unitatem."*[142] "When a man possesses some particular excellence it is not for himself alone, but it has as its end the common benefit of all."[143] According to Bohatec's suggestive phrase, members of the Church are not so much individuals as "individualities";[144] they are distinguished from one another according to their various specific capabilities in order to serve

---

139. See Biéler, *La pensée économique et sociale,* 155-168, 391-476, for a discussion of Calvin's economic activity in Geneva. Cf. Nelson, *op. cit.,* 68, on the significance of Calvin's radical reinterpretation of usury for economic life. See Bibliographical Essay D, p. 250.

140. IV, 1, 3.

141. To use a phrase that underlines the close similarity between ecclesiological and economic language.

142. *CR* 49, 497.

143. *CR* 41, 373.

144. *Staat und Kirche,* 282. Cf. *CR* 34. 663.

or to complement one another. It is in his differentiated function rendered for the good of the whole Church that the member takes on his
individuality. [145] Put theologically, he who is elected in Christ finds
his personhood by taking his place in the harmonious structure of the
holy community. A Christian is *elected or called to order*. Analytically
considered, this is quite in keeping with Calvin's general conception: a
person is not truly obedient until he takes his proper place in God's
order; he does not take his proper place until he apprehends the order
(command) of God in his heart or conscience and responds to it
"freely"; he does not apprehend until he acknowledges eagerly that his
own freedom has been granted by God's grace (or God's sovereign
freedom, which is governed by no further necessity). His heart is truly
integrated, and he becomes himself, when he is integrated in the new
order. The reverse is also true: he is integrated in the new order when
his heart is integrated in Christ.

Accordingly, Calvin's doctrines of Spirit and Word must be seen in
connection with this view of the Church:

> When the Spirit of God governs us it reshapes our emotions in such a
> way that our souls are tied together . . . that we are united together,
> one to another, each one according to his calling.[146]

Christ is no longer with his Church in the flesh, but he reigns over it
"through the inestimable power of his Spirit."[147] The Holy Spirit is that
which organizes and binds together all the members into a harmonious
structure of unity and integration. It is, by definiton, a social power
that dynamically liberates wills for active reconciliation in the membership of the Christian Church. It distributes gifts primarily *"in solidum,"*
that is, it gives particular talents to the Body *by means of* the various
individuals who are entrusted with them. There is nothing preferential
about the Spirit's distribution, rather differences are purely functional.
They give no member greater claim than any other before God. The
basic work of the Spirit, then, is the edification or building up of the
Body of Christ.

Closely linked to the activity of the Spirit is the function of the
Word in preaching and teaching.[148]

145. The point Émile Durkheim made so classically in *Division of Labor in
     Society*—that "individualism" is a social or institutional phenomenon—could
     have been found in the theological terminology of Calvin.
146. *CR* 51, 523.
147. *CR* 46, 82.
148. We can obviously provide merely a sketch here of these dimensions of

We must hold to what we have quoted from Paul—that the church is built up solely by outward preaching, and that the saints are held together by one bond only: that with common accord, through learning and advancement, they keep the church order established by God.

As he was of old not content with the law alone, but added priests as interpreters from whose lips the people might ask its true meaning, so today he not only desires us to be attentive to its reading, but also appoints instructors to help us by their effort. This is doubly useful. On the one hand, he proves our obedience by a very good test when we hear his ministers speaking just as if he himself spoke. On the other, he also provides for our weakness in that he prefers to address us in human fashion through interpreters in order to draw us to himself, rather than to thunder at us and drive us away. Indeed, from the dread with which God's majesty justly overwhelms them, all the pious truly feel how much its familiar sort of teaching is needed.[149]

Nothing fosters mutual love more fittingly than for men to be bound together with this bond: one is appointed pastor to teach the rest, and those bidden to be pupils receive the common teaching from one mouth. For if anyone were sufficient to himself and needed no one else's help (such is the pride of human nature), each man would despise the rest and be despised by them. The Lord has therefore bound his church together with a knot that he foresaw would be the strongest means of keeping unity, while he entrusted to men the teaching of salvation and everlasting life in order that through their hands it might be communicated to the rest.[150]

Calvin's thought; much of great importance must be neglected. His understanding of the Word involves the complex question of the place of the Bible and the sacraments, which we cannot go into. But it is clear that Calvin guards against a wooden biblicism precisely by his doctrine of Word and Spirit (in theory if not in practice). The Bible does not become the Word unless quickened by the Spirit, which means that it must drive toward and be fulfilled in the edification of the Body. Calvin's emphasis upon preaching (see below) illustrates that the Bible has inextricable social significance. Similarly, the sacraments are directed toward the confirmation of the covenant granted by the Lord, which allows new social relationships: "Car comme le pain, qui est là sanctifié pour l'usage commun de nous tous, est fait de plusieurs grains tellement mêlés ensemble, qu'on ne saurait discerner l'un de l'autre, ainsi devons-nous être unis entre nous d'une amitié indissoluble. Et qui plus est, nous reçevons là tout un même corps de Christ, afin d'en être faits membres." (CR 5, 443; cf. IV, 15, 6, 13, 15).

149. IV, 1, 5.
150. IV, 3, 1.

The Word of God comes as an ever new command driving toward an ever new order. The command to the Church and the structure of the Church become effectively combined in the joining of Word and Spirit.[151] In this union, the Word of God and its obedient apprehension in the members fulfills itself in the formation and deepening of the holy community, and the community anchors itself in the obedient apprehension of the Word. Consequently, for Calvin the Word must be "preached," "taught," and "spoken," for it is by its very nature only relevant in the living social context of the Church. Only when it binds people together anew and "matures" relationships, reforming, re-expressing, and renewing them, is it really the Word of God. By the same token, relationships are only renewed and made right when individual members heed the preached Word "as if [God] himself spoke." For this reason, the "human ministry which God uses to govern the church is the chief sinew by which believers are held together in one body."[152] The preached Word of God comes as a special command direct from God himself, a fact that accounts exclusively for its authority.[153] On the other hand, it fulfills itself only in community: it realizes its authority in its integrative effects. These two dimensions of the Word (the command and the structure) account for a deep tension in Calvin's thought regarding the actual polity of the Church.

In discussing ecclesiastical government, Calvin uses a phrase the significance of which cannot be missed in the light of our discussion: he speaks of an *administratio spiritus*.[154] It means, of course, that offices of authority in the Church have no independent status or superiority— Christ is the only real authority in the Church.[155] Such offices are established and evaluated with respect to their special service in the edification of the Body. Though ministers be "of inferior rank," they are to be honored because they speak the Word of God.[156] A bishop in the early Church "was not so much higher in honor and dignity to have lordship over his colleagues." He simply had certain "functions" that had been decreed "by the general voice."[157] There is in Calvin's thought a radical functionalization of administrative roles, which

151. III, 1, 2.
152. IV, 3, 2.
153. IV, 3, 1.
154. *CR* 2, 779.
155. *CR* 41, 84; 55, 240.
156. IV, 3, 1.
157. IV, 4, 2.

corresponds exactly to the same emphasis made in economic and general ecclesiological terms.

Precisely because all churchly offices find their significance in relation to the activity of the Spirit, namely, in building up the community, they must be referred finally to "the general voice" of the community in order "not to diminish any part of the common right and freedom of the church."[158] Calvin is clear about this. He quotes Cyprian favorably: "A priest should be elected publicly in the presence of all the people, and . . . he should be approved as a worthy and fit person by the public judgment and testimony."[159] The reasons for the election of Church officers are extremely important from our point of view: the Church member with the truly obedient heart (the liberated conscience) will naturally "elect" as he has been "elected,"[160] that is, in relation to God's proper order. (As we have seen this is what election means.) Therefore, choice or election in matters of Church organization (or structure) is part of the "common right and freedom of the Church." The Church is that one organization truly at liberty to choose its own correct relationships.[161]

On the other hand, Calvin certainly did not unqualifiedly assert a democratic principle. While it is true that officers should be elected by the Church, "pastors ought to preside over the election in order that the multitude may not go wrong either through fickleness, through evil intentions, or through disorder."[162] Calvin's reason is, of course, that

---

158. IV, 3, 15.
159. IV, 3. 15.
160. The political and theological use of the same word is hardly accidental.
161. It is important to remember the "covenantal" or consensual context in which the Reformation of Geneva took place. First, there was a conscious break with Geneva's Roman Catholic past and, second, there was an opportunity for the entire city to pledge its loyalty to the new Confession of Faith drawn up by Calvin and Farel in 1536. H. D. Foster, who so admirably treats this matter in his essay, "Calvin's Programme for a Puritan State," *Collected Papers* (New York, 1929), calls this "the first Protestant creed to be adopted by a representative body and sworn to and permanently observed by the inhabitants of a republic . . . " (53). He continues: "The Confession reaffirms the profoundly ethical emphasis . . . in the *Institutes* and Articles. It was more than a creed; it was a religious and social compact. Professedly following the examples of the covenants of the Old Testament, it was the forerunner of the Scottish National Covenant of 1638, the Solemn League and Covenant signed by the English Parliament in 1643, and the covenants entered into by the early New England town churches" (54).
162. IV, 3, 15.

so long as the world exists, the visible Church can never be identified
with the invisible; the elect and unelect remain mixed.[163] Furthermore
even the elect, many of whom are, perhaps, more obedient and respon-
sive to the Word of God than the unelect, "have a great part of their
heart and soul still occupied with fleshly desires by which they are
drawn back and prevented from hastening toward God."[164] For the
time being, therefore, Calvin places more confidence in the direct Word
of God and its proclaimers as an agency of order, than in the still
equivocal hearts of the people. He provides the basis for a certain
aristocracy of the ministers, but it is obviously a temporary, pro-
visionsal arrangement. It is a refinement of the logic at work in Calvin's
understanding of civil politics and law: disobedience makes necessary
special forms of regulation and control. The tension, however, is there,
for the Word presses dynamically toward fulfilling itself in a voluntary,
harmonious community in which election rests with the elect. The very
tension observed throughout this investigation of Calvin—between the
old order (the order of coercion and necessity with its provisional forms
of control) and the new order (the harmonious order of free, voluntary
obedience)—is also present in the Church, albeit in a modified way.
Because Christ reigns in Word, sacrament, and Spirit in the Church, the
old order is decisively broken there and the new is beginning. Therefore, the hallmark of the old order, coercion, is by definition excluded
from it. But there remain these special and temporary forms of control
within the church, because the community of wills cannot yet be
trusted: it still has a long way to go. Because the wills are partially
redeemed, the Word of God controls the Church through the ministers
and elders with *partial* force (that is, short of actual coercion). These
officers are certainly more than members like everyone else; they are in
a preferential position, analogous to the preferential position of political rulers for precisely the same reason. Their status is made necessary
because of the actual or potential disobedience within the Church. (One
is tempted to say that the subsequent heavy emphasis upon the prestige
of the ministry in Calvinism—with its requisite of a "special call" different from and perhaps better than the layman's "call," has been a
formalization of this principle.)

It is interesting to note here the similarities as well as the differences
in Calvin's attitude toward polity in the Church and in the State.

163. IV, 1, 2-3.
164. III, 19, 4.

Ideally, Calvin favored a consensual polity in both. The emphasis on collective agreement in Church order already encountered finds its way into discusssions of civil government as well: "This is the most desirable kind of liberty, that we should not be compelled to obey every person who may be tyrannically put over our heads; but which allows of election, so that no one should rule except he be approved of by us."[165]

However, because both Church and State are liable, under temporal conditions of disorder, to the arbitrariness and disobedience of their members, it is preferable, in both places, to create a polity which checks sedition, on the one hand, but guarantees "maximum feasible participation" on the other. Such an arrangement, applicable to both Church and State, is a combination of democracy and aristocracy.[166] This form of government presupposed, primitively to be sure, a system of checks and balances whose importance was not lost on later Calvinist political thinkers.[167]

To propose the ideal of consensual polity in both Church and State, even to the extent Calvin did, obviously could have revolutionary or at least reformist consequences. Calvin was willing to take these consequences with respect to Church reform. For example, his discussion of Roman Catholicism has rather direct and explicit revolutionary implications:

> If anyone should duly weigh and examine this outward form of church government which exists today under the papacy, he will not find a robbers' den in which thieves riot more brazenly without law and restraint. Surely everything there is so unlike, indeed, so alien to Christ's institution, and has so degenerated from the ancient ordinances and customs of the church, and so conflicts with nature and reason, that *no greater injury can be done to Christ than when they put forward his name to defend such a disordered government . . . [such a] formless chaos, full of desolation.*[168]

Men could not wait to transform Church order, at least in face of such obvious "desolation." Their lives depended on reform.

Because of his intense fear of anarchy in the civil sphere, Calvin was, as we have seen, deeply suspicious of political agitation. However, the

165. *Comm.* on Deut. 1:16.
166. IV, 20, 8.
167. See IV, 20, 31, and esp. fn. 54, 1518-1519.
168. IV, 5, 13; my italics.

language he was using toward the end of his life about resisting the lawlessness of tyrants and even "spitting on their heads" proves that the political revolutionary zeal of some of his descendants was not without foundation in the master's own words. Nevertheless, the new order, as embodied in the Church, was always the primary focus of Calvin's considerable energies for organizational reform.

Calvin's conception of a new order, in part institutionalized here and now in the Church, bears an extremely important implication for understanding social relationships. As we have seen, social roles within the Church are radically functionalized according to the economic, social, and spiritual needs of the community. The Body of Christ, energized by the Holy Spirit, is (and becomes) a community in which members willingly and eagerly harmonize their own specific gifts with the gifts of others, for the good of all. This kind of self-integrating, uncoerced system is the meaning of God's order. By their willing participation, members witness to the real purpose and end of social life. They are the wave of the future, the new elite. Thus those who manifest their obedience in the Body of Christ become a special group. Those who voluntarily take their functional place in the holy community, subjecting their wills to the Word of God, are, by definition, the community. The final distinction is, of course, known only to God, but a partial distinction must be made by man. "Thus in each parish there was actually a double roll of membership: on the one side there were the true, genuine, faithful, and active Christians, and on the other those who were merely nominal or worldly. . . . The effect of Calvinism was the separation of the pure body of communicants from the impure. . ."[169] As Calvin himself states: "It is the godly man's duty to abstain from all familiarity with the wicked, and not to enmesh himself with them in any voluntary relationship."[170] We have here the basis for a "new aristocracy" or new elite, whose credentials are not birth, wealth, or position, but voluntary obedience and functional responsibility. Because "pure Christians" are related to true order, to God's order, they assume a privileged place. Directed by the Holy Spirit, they become a new model for society. They set its sights and guide its action. However, their object is not typically aristocratic. They seek urgently to extend the new community to all society. Their whole aim

169. Ernst Troeltsch, *Social Teaching of the Christian Churches* (2 vols., New York, 1960), II, 596-597.
170. IV, 1, 15. The use of the word "voluntary" is significant in this context.

is to participate in the transforming Kingdom of Christ, which will one day be "all in all."

Throughout this treatment of Calvin, I have indicated that the most intense, as well as the most perplexing, problem is relating the new order to the old. Calvin's discussion of the central characteristics of the new order is carried on in terms of functional, voluntary, self-regulating behavior. However, his discussion of civil political-legal action refers to life outside the Church, life that is regulated by force and convention. At several points, he makes this distinction crystal clear:

> The church does not have the power to coerce, and ought not to seek it (I am speaking of civil coercion). . .[171]

> For the church does not have the right of the sword to punish or compel, not the authority to force; not imprisonment, nor the other punishments which the magistrate commonly inflicts. Then, *it is not a question of punishing the sinner against his will, but of the sinner professing his repentance in a voluntary chastisement.* The two conceptions are very different. The church does not assume what is proper to the magistrate; nor can the magistrate execute what is carried out by the church.[172]

It is, as we have seen throughout, the question of coercion that is central. When there is no *free, voluntary* response to God, there is no true order. This means, according to the logic of Calvin's system, that the new order in both its economic and strictly ecclesiological dimensions is, finally, above the political-legal sphere.

To be sure, Calvin believed the law and the political ruler must drive men toward spontaneous, co-operative economic action. Similarly, the state must drive man in the direction of true religion. But in neither case can it compel or control the essential voluntary ingredient that distinguishes true economic action and entails a separate context of action over which the agents of earthly power have no authority.

We confront once again, then, what we have referred to as the dilemma of earthly power in Calvin's thought: of power which is fundamentally differentiated from the new order because of its coercive characteristics and which is, at the same time, subordinated and harnessed to the achievement of the new order. This is, in the last analysis, the underlying dilemma that Calvin sought practically to

171. IV, 12, 16.
172. IV, 11, 3; my italics.

resolve throughout his years in Geneva, and that the English Puritans so agonized over during the late sixteenth and early seventeenth centuries.

In surveying briefly the institutionalization of Calvin's pattern of order in Geneva, I wish to suggest in a general way that the dilemma of earthly power for the Calvinist must be resolved one way or the other, either in favor of differentiation (emphasis upon the independence of the Church, voluntarism, and so on) or in favor of subordination (emphasis upon theocratic control, establishment, and so on).[173] Furthermore, I suggest that, together with the matter of theological inclination, the particular historical circumstances will play a large role in determining which emphasis is made.[174] It is important to remember, of course, that while Calvin's thought invariably "slips" one way or the other, both directions are always present, and each acts as a qualification and condition upon the other.

There can be little question that in instituting the new order in Geneva, Calvin's solution was weighted toward subordination, toward harnessing political power in the service of the Church. However, unless we understand the full proportions of this dilemma, as well as the pattern of thought that underlies it, we cannot possibly comprehend the "Genevan experiment."

On the one side, whether the word "theocracy," "christocracy," "bibliocracy," "ecclesiocracy," or "pneumatocracy" is used to describe the state of affairs in Calvin's Geneva (all, in my judgment, more or less equally inexact and inaccurate terms), each points to a fundamental fact: during the years of Calvin's ascendancy, Genevan life was con-

173. This sort of interpretation is in general accord with the thinking of Troeltsch in his *Social Teaching of the Christian Churches.* Troeltsch sees Calvinism as the somewhat unstable combination of "sect-type" and "church-type" tendencies. The former involve separatism, voluntarism, equalitarianism, as well as a strong eschatological flavor. The latter involve uniformity, inclusiveness, and hierarchical chains of authority. (See *Social Teaching*, II, 590-602.) It is to be noted that the tension is not à la Tawney between "individualism" and "collectivism," but between two contrasting, though interrelated, conceptions of social order. Certainly in Calvinism, both tendencies are heavily communal in nature.

174. By putting the matter in this way, I am attempting to take account both of the significance of a religious framework and of historical contingencies in the molding of institutional patterns. Thus, against many of Weber's critics, I am contending that Calvin's Geneva was not simply a product of its times. On the other hand, Calvinism came to emphasize one or the other of its tendencies, depending on the historical and sociological environment in which it found itself.

sistently and specifically ordered by a theological conception of human behavior. Political, legal, familial, economic, and social institutions were all interwoven with and oriented toward the characteristics of Reformed life and belief as Calvin and his followers developed them. No one who reads the record of the elaborate welcome Calvin received upon his return to Geneva in 1541, or of the extensive power he was permitted to accumulate in Genevan affairs thereafter, can doubt that providence had provided him with a co-operative city in which to advance the cause of the Gospel.

Given the fundamental emphasis in Calvin's system of thought upon government and law as prods in the direction of the new order, it is quite logical that he and his supporters should similarly view Genevan politics. For example, the Consistory—a combination of ministers and politically appointed elders—acquired tremendous power in regulating and supervising the moral life of all Genevans.[175] The controls imposed by the Consistory rigorously restricted social amusements by means of severe civil punishment against offending parties. What is more, the Church's moral interpretations became in many instances part of the civil law. Pfisterer in his well-documented study cites numerous cases in which "Calvin's point of view jumbled together the spiritual and the worldly powers."[176] In a word, "everything had to contribute to making a saintly city of Geneva."

Calvin was very pessimistic about the extent to which the new order could be realized this side of the Kingdom. Men—even redeemed men— were so susceptible to disobedience, so inclined to disrupt God's harmonious design, that the use of earthly power to stimulate righteousness was, wherever feasible, a simple necessity. Nevertheless, close practical co-operation between the old order and the new is obviously subject to circumstance. Had Calvin not encountered a tractable political situation in Geneva, had the authorities fundamentally opposed his program as they did elsewhere, the sort of emphasis that was made in Geneva would have been quite different. Under such

175. Regulations extended to matters of belief and action considered to be blasphemous, denunciatory, or otherwise subversive. In order to enforce these regulations, various means of control were contrived, consisting of observations by "city servants" (a kind of semi-police) and periodic "house-visitations" by local clergy, "from which no one could exclude himself" (Pfisterer, *Calvins Wirken in Genf*, 98). More systematic and extensive thought control could hardly have been devised.

176. *Ibid.*, 24.

circumstances, the distinctiveness, the differentiation of the new order from the old, would naturally have been stressed.

For even in the ideal conditions of Geneva, Calvin never allowed the Church to become organizationally co-terminous or identical with the magistracy. To a degree unknown in Zwingli's Zürich, Luther's Germany, or Hooker's England, Calvin maintained the independence of the Church over against the civil society, however much he blurred and jumbled the lines of demarcation. The critical problem that Calvin faced throughout his career in Geneva was a problem common to the entire age of the Reformation: the inclination of temporal governments to gain extensive control over the life of the Christian Church and, in effect, to subjugate it. This is clearly what the magistrates of Geneva had in mind, and heated conflict precisely over how independent the Church would be in supervising its own affairs led to Calvin's ouster in 1538. When he returned in 1541, he attempted to formulate a clear distinction between Church and government in his famous *Ecclesiastical Ordinance of the Church of Geneva*. The impact of this document, after some modification, is correctly summarized by Wendel:

> Although, in the final reckoning, the Ordinances had given the State more than Calvin wanted to concede, one could no more speak of an annexation of the Church by the Magistracy than of a preponderance of the Church over the civil power. The distinction between the two powers was the foundation of the entire edifice.[177]

That Jesus Christ is sole authority over his Body is made abundantly clear in the preamble to the *Ordinances:*

> It has seemed good to us that the spiritual government, such as our Lord demonstrates and institutes it by his word, should be set down in good form, to take place and be observed among us. And thus have we ordered and established, to obey and to maintain in our

177. Wendel, *op. cit.,* 79. In confirmation of this point, Thomas G. Sanders in *Protestant Concepts of Church and State* (New York, 1964) states: "The practical consequence of Calvin's theocratic views was to maintain the authority and independence of the church against the Erastianism into which Germany and England fell. Wherever Calvinism spread, it found means for combating the political absolutism that was enveloping Europe . . . Calvin did not seek rapport between the church and the state through a control of the state by the church. He held rather that the church should determine freely, without interference from the political order, the dimensions of life directly concerned with religion" (254-255). Further, cf. Foster, *op. cit.,* esp. 38-51.

town and territory the Ecclesiastical policy, which follows, as we see it is taken, from the Gospel of Jesus Christ.[178]

There are, as we have seen, firm grounds in Calvin's system of thought both for stressing the subordination of earthly power to the purposes of the new order and for differentiating the one from the other. Though as the result of favorable circumstances political power was pervasively turned to the advancement and defense of the Kingdom during the height of Calvin's domination, the crucial practical distinction Calvin drew between the Church and the government must not be ignored. Lord Acton is certainly right: "The secret of Calvin's later influence is that he claimed for the Church more independence than he obtained." By instituting a context of action that transcended the confines of political-legal coercion, Calvin "checked the reigning idea that nothing limits the power of the State."[179]

John Calvin—not to mention the movement he inspired—has been described in many conflicting ways. He has been called medieval and modern, authoritarian and liberal, tyrannical and democratic, a visionary and a creature of his times. Often it is said that he combined all or many of these tendencies within himself in a thoroughly contradictory way. However, it is hoped that by means of the investigation undertaken here, many of the contradictory elements will fall into place and be seen in the wider context of Calvin's thought. The whole point is that the dynamic, living, vital elements in Calvinism spring, not from the conflict of irreconcilable ideas nor simply from the conflict between ideas and historical circumstances. They spring from, or are reflected in, the inner dynamics of Calvin's pattern of order.

This is not to say that Calvinism is nothing more than the extension of Calvin's system of ideas.[180] Calvinism spread far and wide. It confronted new and varied historical situations, and underwent new and varied pressures. It had to adjust to new demands and withstand new

178. *Calvin's Theological Treatises,* ed. J. K. S. Reid (Philadelphia, 1954), fn. 1, 58.
179. Lord Acton, *Lectures on Modern History,* 134, 136.
180. Nor is it to say that Genevan Calvinism came only from John Calvin's head. Circumstances were extremely important. My only point is that Calvinism can be understood as a system of coherent meaning with its own independence. I am not convinced by those who argue, for example, that the Geneva theocracy was a concession to circumstance and that it did not really represent Calvin's central thinking. I believe we have shown that an "aristocracy of the Word" is quite as logical as the more democratic tendencies, that totalitarian dimensions fit with the impulse toward freedom.

challenges. Of course, it was influenced, and of course it changed. But with all its new emphases, an essential coherence can be traced. As Weber saw, in no place was the Calvinist pattern of order more significant than in England. At the end of the sixteenth century, the new order, heralded earlier by John Calvin against his humanist and Roman Catholic contemporaries, was proclaimed with renewed vigor by such men as Thomas Cartwright and William Perkins against their English opponents.

4. The Elite of the New Order: The Puritans

The term "Puritan" has been the source of much scholarly consternation. Although many different definitions have been offered, it is often said that Puritans were those English Protestants fundamentally interested in radical ecclesiastical reform. Otherwise, in matters of theology and doctrine, runs this opinion, they differed rather little from their Anglican compatriots. It is difficult, say the Georges, to discover "what all the fuss was about."[1] And Rowse informs us that the attention paid the Puritans is all out of proportion to their actual importance.[2]

However, serious scholarship has long since made clear that there specific reasons why there was so much fuss, and why the fuss was considered important in the sixteenth and seventeenth centuries.

[Puritanism] was ... more than an affair of church government, more than the logomachy of churchmen and schismatics. It was a new way of life, overrunning all the divisions which from time to time seamed its surface and threatening in each of its manifestations to disrupt the existing society. Eventually it was to subdue English civilization to an attitude of mind, a code of conduct, a psychology, a manner of expression, the vitality of which far outran the particu-

---

1. C. H. and K. George, *The Protestant Mind of the English Reformation* (Princeton, N.J., 1955), 341. In his article, "A Social Interpretation of English Puritanism," *Journal of Modern History* (December, 1953), 332, C. H. George defines the Puritans exclusively as "those people in the Church of England who wanted to institute further reforms in the national church worship."
2. A. L. Rowse, *England of Elizabeth* (New York, 1961), 464. See Bibliographical Essay D, pp. 252-253.

lar forms of religious life which sprang up from time to time in the course of its irresistible advance.[3]

Haller's definition is particularly helpful because it designates Puritanism specifically as a new way of life, whose central characteristics are clearly delimitable, even though they manifest themselves in various forms. He continues: "The disagreements that rendered Puritans into presbyterians, independents, separatists and baptists were in the long run not so significant as the qualities of character, of mind and of imagination, which kept them all alike Puritan."[4] Puritanism was, indeed, a distinct system of meaning and values with an indomitable logic that shook the very foundations of Elizabethan and Stuart society. If certain modern scholars have trouble recognizing it as such, contemporaries were hardly so undiscerning. One would not have found Elizabeth, James, or Charles, Whitgift, Bancroft, or Laud questioning the distinctiveness and singular vitality of Puritanism. They all felt its threat and knew its power.

It is the characteristic pattern of order of the Puritan system that needs analysis if we are to discover where the real issue between Puritanism and Anglicanism lay. When that is the focus, some of the confusions and unclarities fall away, and it becomes easier to determine who can and who cannot properly be called Puritan. Of course, the great bulk of Elizabethan Puritans were concerned with ecclesiastical reform. But to limit the term to them is to overlook significant Protestant thinkers who, upon close scrutiny, deserve the title every bit as much as Thomas Cartwright, Walter Travers, or John Field. The point is that agitation for Church reform points to something far more basic than simply ecclesiastical adjustments; it points to a method of thought and action that, as Whitgift and Hooker plainly saw, involved conclusions totally incompatible with the old order of English society. In the last analysis, whether the pattern was expressed in parliamentary admonitions and bills, subversive tracts of Church reorganization, sermons, "prophesyings," or university lectures and learned pamphlets did not much matter. It was the pattern itself that counted.

The personal relationship of John Calvin and Theodore Beza to Tudor Puritanism should have provided the clue that Puritanism amounted to more than "genevating"[5] the Church of England. When

3. William Haller, *Rise of Puritanism* (New York, 1957), 18.

4. *Ibid.*, 17. See Bibliographical Essay D, pp. 253-254, for a discussion of Puritanism as a general movement.

5. The term is Archbishop Bancroft's. McNeill mentions that Bancroft speaks of

for example in 1551 John Hooper, the Bishop of Gloucester, was imprisoned because he refused to wear vestments and even denounced them from the pulpit, Calvin agreed with Hooper that vestments ought to be abolished but expressed regret at Hooper's unstrategic intransigence.[6] During the Edwardian period, Calvin maintained a consistently conciliatory attitude toward Cranmer and the Anglicans.[7] Then, when the Marian exiles arrived in Europe (1553-58), he, like other reformers in Switzerland, opened Geneva to the émigrés, and sponsored the formation of an exile Church there. In other words, he helped to sow the seeds for the kind of ecclesiastical agitation that was to develop upon the return of the émigrés, while at the same time he tended to discourage open conflict over Church orders.

Calvin died in 1564 before the issues were really drawn, but his successor, Beza, showed a comparable ambiguity toward the Puritan movement. In 1566 he wrote Archbishop Grindal, himself rather soft on Puritanism, in clear support of the movement.[8] He also supported the Admonition to Parliament of 1572. However, in 1591 he confided to Whitgift that he "never had the intention of opposing the ecclesiastical polity of your Anglican Church."[9] It is, no doubt, this ambiguous attitude which accounts for the fact that some of the returning exiles continued within the Anglican fold, while others joined the Puritans. Such equivocation on the part of the master himself and of his successor only underlines the fact that Calvinist influence can neither be divorced from nor reduced to agitation for Church reform.

"Scots genevating" and "English scottizing," John T. McNeill *The History and Character of Calvinism* (New York, 1954), 320. See Bibliographical Essay D, pp. 250 ff., for a discussion of the relation of Calvin to Puritanism.

6. McNeill, *op. cit.,* 309-310. See also M. M. Knappen, *Tudor Puritanism: A Chapter in the History of Idealism* (Chicago, 1939), 85-90, for a discussion of the same event.

7. However, Calvin by no means took an agreeable view of the Henrician formulation. For example, in his *Comm.* on Amos, 7:13, he writes: "They who at first extolled Henry, King of England, were certainly inconsiderate men; they gave him the supreme power in all things: and this always vexed me grievously; for they were guilty of blasphemy when they called him the chief Head of the Church under Christ."

8. G. Yule, "Theological Developments in Elizabethan Puritanism," *Journal of Religious History* I, (June 1960), 16-25.

9. McNeill, *op. cit.,* 315. McNeill mentions, on the other hand, Beza's controversy with Adrian Saravia, a friend of Hooker's, in which he "created the impression of hostility to an episcopal polity." This simply further emphasized the equivocation on this matter.

Calvin's influence upon English religious developments, then, exceeded questions of Church reform and touched the heart of the broader theological issues that were of such importance in this period. But here again, we totally misunderstand the relation between Calvinism and Elizabethan Protestantism if we merely identify the former as a collection of assorted doctrines (such as predestination, supremacy of Scripture, and the like), and undertake to trace their respective fortunes individually. As we demonstrated in the previous chapter, Calvinism must be seen in its entirety, with its central emphasis and impetus. Its connection with England must be similarly gauged. In such a light, the deep coherence between Calvinism and Elizabethan Puritanism—in sharp contrast to the Anglicans—cannot be missed.

THOMAS CARTWRIGHT (1535-1603)

In 1564, the year of Calvin's death, Cartwright inaugurated his career as an Elizabethan disputant in a formal debate that was, in a way, a dramatic preview of things to come. He was at the time a fellow at Cambridge University and, apparently because of the respect he enjoyed, was chosen to refute the case for monarchy before none other than Queen Elizabeth herself. He argued that neither God nor nature ordains monarchy, for "mere men," he said, "require a fellowship of labour and counsel."[10] The queen was evidently impressed by the whole debate, although for fairly obvious reasons she was particularly pleased with Cartwright's opponent. She could not foresee that the Cambridge fellow who had harmlessly challenged the foundations of her throne was, in but six short years, to bring to a sharp focus a vigorous movement that would provide the severest internal threat of her entire reign.

While Cartwright was studying theology and law in Cambridge and London, the sporadic rumblings of Puritan opposition could already be heard. The twin tenets of Elizabethan religious policy, supremacy and uniformity, provoked the various phases of the "vestiarian controversy" during the 1560's. It was not only that extremist and moderate sentiment came into conflict regarding "things indifferent." A much more fundamental question was raised by the queen's enforcing the use of vestments: did the secular ruler have the last word in

10. Quoted in A. F. S. Pearson, *Thomas Cartwright and Elizabethan Puritanism* (Cambridge, 1945), 14.

ecclesiastical affairs or not?[11] Could the émigrés, recently returned from their continental schooling in the ways of the Reformed Church, abide the terms of the Supremacy Act of 1559, which described the queen as the "only supreme governor in this realm . . . as well in all spiritual and ecclesiastical things or causes as temporal"?[12] Many thought not, although Elizabeth and Archbishop Parker were bound to see that they should. "God save us," said Parker, "from such a visitation as Knox has attempted in Scotland; the people to be the orderers of things." Convinced that the queen knew best and that the wages of divided authority is social chaos, Parker staunchly upheld the supremacy of the crown in religious affairs. His stand resulted in the expulsion of certain students from Cambridge—the center of the agitation—but the general turmoil was simply a prelude of what was to come.

There is no evidence that Cartwright took part in the controversy, nor that he ever thought it particularly crucial. It is probably because of his detached attitude that he was appointed preacher at the university in 1567, and then, in 1569, Lady Margaret Professor of Divinity. Cartwright's interests lay at a deeper and still more explosive level; on the basis of his study of scriptures, he became preoccupied with questions of Church government. His opening series of lectures was delivered on the first two chapters of the book of Acts, in which he contrasted what appeared to him to be the simple, consensual polity of the early Church with the hierarchical and authoritarian form of the Anglican Church. He urged, among other things, that archbishops and archdeacons be abolished, that each church be governed by its own minister and presbytery, that pluralism and nonresidence be abolished, that each minister be attached to one specific congregation, and that ministers be called by the consent of the whole congregation, rather than by the hierarchy. The far-reaching revolutionary implications were plain enough to students and university authorities alike. The lectures naturally caused an immense uproar, and after a brief tenure, Cartwright was deprived of his professorship and expelled from the university in 1570. According to the leading authority on Cartwright, "the chief result of his conduct was the resuscitation and reformation of English Puritanism. He made the question of polity the distinctive and

11. Knappen, *op. cit.,* 187-195.
12. J. E. Neale, *Elizabeth I and Her Parliaments* (2 vols., New York, 1958), I, 83, remarks that "it is not surprising that the first phase of the Elizabethan Puritan movement was a struggle over vestments; it was the aftermath of the 1559 Parliament."

foremost note of the movement."[13] This action secured his position as "head" of Elizabethan Puritanism.

However, the concern Cartwright had with Church polity in these inaugural lectures, as well as in his subsequent debates with Whitgift and in his other writings, points, as we hinted, to something deeper in Puritan mentality. It points to a radically new conception of social life and authority; it points in effect to a new order. Without question the essential distinction between Cartwright and his Anglican antagonists concerned the relationship of State and Church[14] or, in the language of our previous chapter, the relationship of coercion and freedom:

> Where for as muche as our Saviour Christes kingdome was not of this world / and that against horrible disorders in his church / punishable by the sworde / he did not (one extraordinary whipping excepted) draw yt: and considering that this lawfull ordinance of God / is not onely in the churche / but withowt: yt is manifest that our Saviour Christ in respect off his mediatourship towardes us / exerciseth not the civill sword. For in that he said his kingdome was not off this worlde / he made an opposition not unto the wicked off the worlde / as other some times: but unto Cesars authoritie / which was the ordinance of God / whereto he was falsly charged to have made claime. . . . And in that the autoritie off the sword in heathen princes (although not a like used) is the same ordinance of God that (is) in Christian (magistrates): the one proceeding off God immediately / and not from our Saviour Christ as mediatour / the other doth likewise.[15]

> For that which may be conveniently wonne with a worde / shoulde not be gotten by the sworde: and that which may be gotten to bee donne with conscience / should not be essaied by compulsion.[16]

It is Cartwright's underlying differentiation between old and new order, as well as his method of elaboration, that thrusts him squarely into the Calvinist tradition. If he never succeeded in becoming the "English Calvin" he aspired to be because, with his one-track mind, he lacked

13. Pearson, *op. cit.*, 44.
14. See, for example, A. F. S. Pearson, *Church and State: Political Aspects of 16th-Century Puritanism* (Cambridge, 1928). Pearson contrasts the conception of the Anglicans with the "Two-Kingdom Theory" of the Puritans (8). Chapter II (9-40) is a helpful analysis of this essential theory in Puritanism.
15. *The Second Reply against M. Doctor Whitgift's Second Answer touching the Church Discipline* (Zürich?, 1575), 417; referred to henceforth as *SR*.
16. *SR*, 234.

Calvin's brilliant comprehensiveness and perception, he did succeed in enunciating the central conclusions of the Calvinist pattern of order.

Basic to Cartwright's system of thinking is the idea that God is bound neither by his commands nor by the structure of order he has created.[17] God is free or sovereign over order; he is not identified with it. The direct Word of God, which betokens his inbreaking sovereign freedom, exacts from man a corresponding voluntary or consenting obedience within the conscience. Nothing short of free, conscience-felt submission to the sovereign God himself will do. "No man can glorify God in anything but by obedience; and there is no obedience but in respect of the commandment and word of God: therefore it followeth that the word of God directeth a man in all his actions."[18] "If there be anything wherein we do not according to that which is commanded (by magistrates), it is because we cannot be persuaded in our consciences that we may so do (whereof we are ready to render a reason out of the word of God) . . . "[19]

Accordingly, the command of God fulfills itself in that structure of relationships in which the free-willing individual conscience converges with the harmonious integration of all, in which voluntary obedience to God's command issues in proper social order. For Cartwright that structure is the Church, or the Body of Christ. "Wherefore whosoever in feeling to profite the church according to his calling / doth anything to the preservation off this body: he doth yt as an eye / an arme / an eare / or as some other member . . . "[20] The church is "the depository of the conscience," to use a phrase translated by Cartwright from Walter Travers's Latin edition of *A Full and Plaine Declaration of Ecclesiasticall Discipline* (1617). It is the context of obedience.

The Church may be properly designated a new order, because it is the result of the revolutionary "obedience of the Sonne," by which "all redemption is purchased unto us . . . which obedience was most special-

17. D. J. McGinn, *Admonition Controversy* (New Brunswick, N.J., 1949), 247. This book (referred to henceforth as McGinn, *AC*) contains a valuable collation of primary resource materials from the writings of both Cartwright and Whitgift. The references used here are usually direct quotations from their works.
18. *Works of Whitgift* (3 vols., London, 1851-53), I, 190; referred to henceforth as *WW*. These volumes contain most of the primary material constituting the debates between Whitgift and Cartwright.
19. *WW*, I, 79.
20. *SR*, 415.

ly and most signally declared in the shedding of his blood."[21] It is
decisively "in Christ"[22] that the conscience is set free from the bonds
of sin and recalcitrance against God's Word, and, therefore, from the
bonds of disorder. Christ alone *willingly* followed the command of God
(his law)[23] and, as a result, willingness becomes the hallmark of his
Church. "This libertie as hathe been shewed / is a peece off the libertie
which Christ hath purchased unto his churches / by the shedding of his
precious bloud."[24]

The only tolerable authority in the Church is the Word of God made
manifest in Jesus Christ. That voluntary, conscience-felt obedience
which is in Christ must characterize the system of authority within the
Church. Since Christ is the direct and exclusive head of the Church,[25]
his elected members embody (or institutionalize) that voluntariness
which characterizes his headship. Precisely their ability to consent freely to right order is what distinguishes them as the Body of Christ; it is
their full inheritance as sons of God. Against this background, Cartwright lashes out at Whitgift:

> It is no smale owtrage yowe doe the churche of God / to account of
> yt / as of an ignorante multitude. For onlesse yowe meane the
> churche / when yowe saye / then a thousand other whiche be ignor-
> ant: yowe speake beside the matter / seeing wee do not permitte
> either examination / or election off the ministers to every multitude
> / and blinde assemblie: *but unto those onely / which make an open /
> and cleare profession off the trewthe.*[26]

Cartwright's preoccupation with consensual Church polity is hardly to
be explained as the result of an eccentric or arbitrary compulsion simply to reform the Church. As with Calvin; the pattern of order in these
matters is quite consistent: the capacity to elect rests with the elect. His
whole analysis of Church life and organization makes the dimensions of
this pattern clear.

21. *A Commentary upon the Epistle written to the Colossians* (London, 1612),
    47.
22. On the basis of my research in Cartwright and Perkins (certainly, in their
    different ways, two leading expounders of the Puritan pattern of order), I can-
    not agree with Knappen's judgment that there is virtually no Christology in
    Tudor Puritanism, *op. cit.*, 376.
23. *SR*, 96.
24. *SR*, 226.
25. *SR*, 410-411: "If Christ be onely head: then that I set downe / that the civill
    magistrate is head of the commonwealthe / and not of the church / standeth."
26. *SR*, 130; my italics.

For Cartwright the congregation must be so ordered that Christ might rule and reign in his church by the scepter of his word only."[27] At bottom, the Word of God is that which calls forth a new community with distinctive patterns of organization and action. Indeed, the Word would be incomprehensible to Cartwright and many of his fellow Puritans apart from such activity. The Word of God, after all, demands *new* obedience issuing in a *new* order, "as though matters of discipline and kind of government were not matters necessary to salvation, and of faith."[28] It is, therefore, first to scripture, as the written record of the Word of God, that one must go to determine the character and structure of the Body of Christ.[29] There God "has set before our eyes a

27. McGinn, *AC*, 374.
28. *WW*, I, 180-181.
29. It is often argued that the Puritans, and Cartwright in particular, were first and foremost biblical literalists, grounding their entire position on proof texts. There is a real question, however, whether such a person as Cartwright was quite so literalistic as has been implied. In a letter *To a Godly and a Zealous Lady*, he states that if a biblical text contradicts the "general tenor of the Bible's teaching," the spirit ought to be preferred to the letter. That is hardly an expression of literalism; A. Peel and L. Carlson (eds.), *Cartwrightiana* (London, 1951). (See also Davies, *The English Free Churches* (London, 1952), 27, for the same view.) Along the same line, Pearson in *Church and State* 124-125, remarks: "The real reason why the Puritans held many of their distinctive tenets was not necessarily because Scripture enjoined them; they sought Scriptural support because they already believed in or were inclined to such tenets."

Furthermore, the Puritan position is hardly exhausted by calling it literalist or biblicist, unless it be assumed that there is in fact one clear "biblical position" which can be readily extracted from the Bible. The question is why the Puritans emphasized the brand of biblical interpretation they did, and what the particular coherence of their position was. Was there not something more at work than a wooden use of the Bible? Our analysis of the pattern of order in certain Puritans attempts to suggest that there was, and it suggests at the same time that there were quite consistent reasons why the Bible itself was regarded as an expression of the Word of God, calling for new obedience and new order.

Finally, Cartwright's generally Puritan emphasis upon the centrality of the preached Word within particular congregations—that is, of an interpreted or "living" Word—militates against an oversimple understanding of the Puritan view of Scripture. Cartwright argued heatedly that simply reading the scriptures aloud has no saving effect. Hooker took strong issue with that point. See Hooker's *Of the Laws of Ecclesiastical Polity*, ed. Christopher Morris (2 vols., London, 1960), II, 76-79; and also the note on Calvin's view of Scripture; fn. 148, pp. 68-69 above.

perfect form of his church."[30] The central characteristic of that "perfect form" is the preaching of the Word to a specific community by an elected pastor. According to Scripture, says Cartwright, preaching is and must remain public or social. It does not serve the pastor alone, or isolated individuals; on the contrary, the Word is regularly proclaimed for the "common profit" of a given congregation: "forasmuch as it pertaineth to the commoditie off the whole body / that the part which he [the preacher] hath the nourishment off / be well preserved."[31] The purpose of the Word is the dynamic edification of the Church.

Consequently, Cartwright was dead set against the homilies, or stereotyped readings, that passed for sermons in Anglican communions. A genuine sermon must apply the Word of God to "present circumstances" and to the "change of times."[32] Very significantly Cartwright remarks, only the minister as preacher of the Word "is the mouth of the Lord from him to the people."[33] "The guiding and ordering [of] the whole body is to follow the voice [of the mininster]."[34] That is to say, nothing prescribes or predetermines the dynamic upbuilding of the new order of Christ, save the living Word of God spoken in ever new contexts to the Church. The particular sermon must be determined by the minister in relation to the present situation and status of a given community; what will be said cannot be decided out of context by some central Church authority that distributes the same message to many different congregations. To make the Word of God merely conventional, to rob it of its specific communal significance is, according to Cartwright, to kill it.

By the same token, Word and sacrament may not be separated, as they were in the Anglican Church, nor may there be any private sacraments. A sacrament simply signifies the social emphasis of the preached

30. *WW*, I, 176-177.
31. *SR*, 346.
32. *SR*, 363 ff. Cf. Walter Travers, *A Full and Plaine Declaration of Ecclesiasticall Discipline* (Leyden, 1617), 80: "Here the Pastour had need of great and profound knowledge to the change of times, the diversitie of things, the variety of persons, and to deale thus or otherwise, according to that variety and difference." In this connection, I want to emphasize the implicit relation in Puritan mentality between the Word of God and what is "new." The importance of this idea of preaching in contrast to the Anglicans (for whom the Word of God was always related to the "old") cannot be exaggerated.
33. McGinn, *AC*, 157.
34. *Directory of Church Government* (London, 1644), n.p.

Word of God;[35] they are two inseparable aspects of the same thing;[36] The Lord's Supper is "a seal and confirmation of the promises of God unto us [and] a profession of our conjunction as well with Christ our Saviour and with God as also . . . a declaration and profession that we are / at one / with our brethren . . ."[37] Private sacraments, like stereotyped homilies, tear the heart out of God's new creation.

Because the minister, as preacher and administrator of the sacraments, fulfills his calling only in relation to a specific congregation, that congregation fulfills itself only when it "calls" or elects him. Cartwright was strongly opposed to the Anglican custom of pluralism and nonresidence whereby a clergyman could have several different parishes, or be rector of a parish, and not be present very often. As we have seen, the pastor's role made no sense to Cartwright apart from his constant direct contact with one congregation.

The preached Word of God does not order aright unless it converges with conscience-felt, voluntary obedience or consent. The minister, above all, may not impose himself, for that would override the decisive consensual character of the new order; nor may he be imposed by some hierarchical authority,[38] for that would introduce coercion where, at all costs, liberty of Christian conscience must prevail. Cartwright even goes so far as to say that if the minister is not called, "there is no obedience."[39] The obedience of the preacher is manifested only in the context of the *free decision* of the congregation, just as the congregation's obedience is manifested only in response to the unstereotyped Word of God. Election of the minister, on the basis of proper examination, takes place "so that the consent of the churche in the election of the ministrie / being profitable unto the godlie / and those which are trewe sheepe / that their love maie abounde towardes their minister / and in respect off the Hypocrites / and goates / that they maie be more inex-

---

35. This fact is illustrated by the conflict between Cartwright and Whitgift on whether "take ye" ("you" plural and collective) or "take thou" (singular) should be used in the communion service. Cartwright, of course, favors the collective or social interpretation; see Hooker's *Laws*, II, 333, fn. 3.

36. McGinn, *AC*, 200-205.

37. *Ibid.*, 239. Cf. *WW*, II, 61.

38. Cartwright claims that there is no love of the minister where coercion or external control is brought to bear. The essence of the relationship between preacher and congregation is "freedom" or love. The minister must not be "thrust upon [the people] against their wills," *WW*, I, 375.

39. *SR*, 337.

cusable before God / and lesse hurtefull to men."[40]

"Election[s] made by the people where everyman giveth his voyce," according to Cartwright's translation of Travers, "are compared by some to a banket, where everyman bringeth his dish: which is so much the daintier the more there be that come unto it."[41] Or, as Cartwright himself says to Whitgift:

> I would ask if the church be not in as great danger when all is done
> at the pleasure and lust of one man, and when one carrieth all into
> error, as when one pulleth one piece with him, another another
> piece, and a third his part also with him. And it is harder to draw
> many into an error than one, or that many should be carried away
> by their affections than one. . . . (Even though ecclesiastical monar-
> chy might be said at times to keep the peace) yet the peace which is
> without truth is more execrable than a thousand contentions. For as
> by striking of two flints together there cometh out fire, so it may be
> that sometimes by contention the truth which is hidden in a dark
> place may come to light, which by a peace in naughtiness and
> wickedness, being as it were buried under the ground, doth not
> appear.[42]

It is not simply any kind of order and peace that is desired within the Church, but the specific peace and order of God that demands heartfelt human participation and response. The criterion of such participation is, as we have seen, "an open and clear profession of the trewthe." Nothing else is required. The Word of God is a radical equalizer: it places all on the same footing before God. None of the social distinc-tions of the old order obtain within the new community,[43] for every member of the Body of Christ has a voice on the basis of his assumed election by God.[44] It is even true that God often chooses the poor and simple before the rich and noble, although "I plainely affirme that manie of the Nobilitie and gentrie are Zealous and Religiouse. . . . The common and most usual calling of God / resteth in more off the poorer then off the richer sorte: that the riche and noble that have received that benefite of this holie callinge / maie learn therby the better to es-teeme the treasure they have / and the faste to hould yt."[45] In other

40. *SR*, 230-231.
41. *Full and Plaine Declaration*, 30.
42. *WW*, II, 238.
43. *WW*, II, 356.
44. See Bibliographical Essay D, for a discussion of the place of predestination in
    Cartwright's thought, p. 255.
45. *SR*, 10-12.

words, every member of the Body stands by his own personal obedience, and not by the traditional rank and status of the world. The
only social distinction that makes any difference to Cartwright and his
fellow Puritans is the one that exists between the new and the old
order, between the Church and the world. God is not bound by the way
things are or have always been; he elects whom he will, and on the basis
of his free, sovereign election alone is the member's status and function
sealed.

Accordingly, "simple men which carry no great countenance or shew
will undoubtedly do more good unto the church . . . . "[46] "They are
the church of God, although they be called sheep in respect of their
simplicity and harmlessness, yet are they also for their circumspection
wise as serpents in the wisdom especially which is to salvation; and how
vile account soever you will make of them, they are the people of
God . . . . "[47] Each member was to have a part in determining the order
of the Body of Christ: "none," said the First Admonition to Parliament
in describing the early Church, "came to be over the people but by
their voices and consents."[48]

At the same time, these Puritan leaders could not abide any purely
democratic polity within the Church. It was impossible for "mere men"
to make any final judgments between the sheep and the goats, and since
the view of Cartwright and Travers favored an established, uniform
Church, a number of goats were likely to participate in the vote. For
this reason, the elders and other ministers in a given locale "must goe
before the people in the election."[49] They must supervise the examination of and voting for a prospective minister, although if all members
"were so taught of God" there would be no need for such supervision;
it is a concession to necessity. If there were no corruption in the congregation, *there would be no fear of choosing unworthy people.* Total
obedience would coincide with total order.

The similarity of this formulation with the position of Calvin should
be stressed. Earlier we described the element of corruption still present
within the Church and pointed out that for Calvin this condition modified or limited the amount of freedom each believer could enjoy in the
existing Church. All coercive measures and special power were by no
means excluded from the Church; yet this situation was provisional, not

46. McGinn, *AC,* 472-473.
47. *Ibid.,* 449-450.
48. *WW,* I, 411. Cf. *SR,* 140.
49. *Full and Plaine Declaration,* 29.

ideal. Coercion was in no way a part of the ultimate new order already breaking in. So long as the world existed, the Calvinist would have to adjust in some tolerable way the claims of free obedience with the necessity of "holding owte" willful disobedience. But while he made "concessions to necessity," as we say, the final aim of his position was of the greatest importance in introducing a conception of social order that devalued and subordinated political forms of coercion.

As it is, the ministers and elders, once elected, compose a provisional center of special authority. They, after all, are the designated guardians and proclaimers of the Word. Cartwright sketches the relationship among the various authorities in the Church as follows: "For, in respect of Christ the head, it is a monarchy; and, in respect of the ancients and pastors that govern and with like authority among themselves, it is an aristocraty, or the rule of the best men; and, in respect that the people are not secluded, but have their interest in church matters, it is a democracy, or a popular estate."[50] The "best men" should be classified according to the four apostolic and scriptural offices, bishop, minister, elder, and deacon. The offices of archbishop and archdeacon should be abolished (a recommendation that, naturally, threatened the whole hierarchical structure of the Church of England). Above all, these offices should be radically functionalized, and therefore generally leveled in terms of power and status: the authorities must not be called "simply governor or moderator *but governor or moderator of that action and for that time and subject to the orders that others be and to be censured by the company of the brethren as well as others if he be judged any way faulty."*[51] Cartwright argues that even St. Peter retained his office on this basis; he was "chosen of the apostles unto the presidentship in those actions"![52]

Cartwright makes a great deal of the principles of consensuality and equality among the bishops and ministers. "Whereas it is said, for the preservation of unity one must be over all, St. Cyprian sheweth that the unity of the church is conserved not by having one bishop over all, but by the agreement of the bishops with one another. For so he writeth, that 'the church is knit and coupled together as it were with the glue of the bishops consenting one with another.' "[53] Quoting Cyprian further, he says: "We do not use any compulsion or violence over any, nor

50. *WW*, II, 390.
51. McGinn, *A C*, 326, my italics.
52. *Ibid.*, 328.
53. *WW*, II, 211.

appoint no law to any; seeing that every one that is set over the church hath in the government the free disposition of his own will, whereof he shall give an account unto the Lord."[54] From the point of view of the pattern of order involved, it is easy to understand Cartwright's dismissal of Whitgift's assertion that there must be an archbishop to settle contentions and disputes among the bishops and thereby restore order. It is fundamental to the Calvinist scheme that the mutual decision of obedient authorities dedicated to the Word of God and properly "elected" by the consent of the Church will equal true order. Indeed, *only in voluntary consent can true order be achieved. Consent is the glue of the Body.*

While it is true that Cartwright generally expresses his preoccupation with consensual or voluntary action in ecclesiological terms, he makes some remarks about liberty and economic action that are most important for our purposes. The remarks are found in a short but vigorous exchange with Whitgift over the question of observance of holy days.[55] Cartwright strongly resists the idea of having many different arbitrary holy days that prevent the individual from performing a good day's work. He supports the text of the First Admonition, which lays down as God's command, "Six days shalt thou labor." He even resists celebrating Easter on a special day, for "it tieth and (as it were) fettereth a meditation of the Easter to a few days, which should reach to all our age and time of our life ..."[56] But if holy days are to be kept at all, they ought to be kept by custom, and not by the command of the Church or the magistrate: "which thing if it had remained in that freedom, that it was done by custome, and not by commandment, *at the will of every one, and not by constraint,* it had been much better than it is now ... "[57] He continues: " ... it tendeth to no policy nor wealth of the people, or preservation of good order, that there should be so many days wherein men should cease from work, being a thing which breedeth idleness and consequently poverty, besides other disorders and vices, which always accompany idleness." ... "Seeing that therefore that *the Lord hath left it to all men at liberty that they might labour, if they think good,* six days; I say, the church, nor no man, can take away this liberty from them, and drive them to a neces-

54. *WW*, II, 208.
55. The exchange is found in *WW*, II, 569-592. For further reference to economic liberty and holy days, see Cartwright's *Directory of Church Government.*
56. *WW*, II, 577.
57. *Ibid.*, 582; my italics.

sary rest of the body."[58]

For Cartwright, upholding the Calvinist system of thought, liberty in the Church corresponds to liberty of economic behavior. Voluntary obedience to the calling of God inevitably expresses itself in economic terms because, just as with Calvin, the realms of economic and ecclesiological action are so profoundly interrelated. Against Whitgift's separation of worldly and "spiritual" callings, Cartwright adopts a view that must have appeared very secular to Whitgift: "All lawful callings came from God, and return to him again, that is, he is both author of them, and they ought to be referred to his glory."[59]

These essential components that go into making up the Church's life form the present embodiment of the ultimate order of God. The Church is, as Cartwright says, "the foundation of the world." Therefore, "it is meet that the commonwealth which is builded upon that foundation should be framed according to the church . . ."[60]

> It is true that we ought to be obedient unto the civil magistrate which governeth the church of God in that office which is committed unto him, and according to that calling. But it must be remembered that civil magistrates must govern according to the rules of God prescribed in his word, and that as they are nurses so they be servants unto the church, and as they rule in the church so they must remember to subject themselves unto the church, to lick the dust of the feet of the church. Wherein I mean not that the church doth either wring the sceptres out of the princes' hands, or taketh their crowns from their heads, or that it requireth princes to lick the dust of her feet (as the pope under this pretence hath done), but I mean, as the prophet meaneth, that, whatsoever magnificance, or excellency, or pomp, is either in them, in their estates and commonwealths, which doth not agree with the simplicity and (in the judgment of the world) poor and contemptible estate of the church, that they will be content to lay down.
>
> And here cometh to my mind that wherewith the world is now deceived, and wherewith M. Doctor [Whitgift] goeth about both to deceive himself and others too, in that he thinketh that the church must be framed according to the commonwealth, and the church-government according to the civil government, which is as much as to say, as if a man should fashion his house according to his hangings, when indeed it is clean contrary, that, as the hangings made fit

58. *Ibid.*, 587 and 569; my italics.
59. *WW*, III, 437.
60. *WW*, III, 189.

for the house, so the commonwealth must be made to agree with the church, and the government thereof with her government. For, as the house is before the hangings, and therefore the hangings which come after must be framed to the house which was before, so the church being before there was any commonwealth, and the commonwealth coming after must be fashioned and made suitable unto the church.[61]

If the Church is the manifestation of the new consensual or voluntary order, the State is the manifestation of the old coercive order. As such, it is distinctly subservient to and, indeed, fulfilled in the Church. The state must become fashioned according to the Body of Christ until ultimately (or eschatologically) it ceases to be needed as a constraining agent. It is, thus, decidedly subordinate to the Church. "Every nation and kingdom which shall not serve the church shall be destroyed."[62]

Of course, the State has its own special mandate from God. It plays an extremely important role in "holding owte sinne," and it is owed great obedience and honor from the Christian. It maintains order to the "glory of God."[63] In fact, argues Cartwright, his doctrine is a "friend unto princes and magistrates." He desires, simply, that the commonwealth truly fulfill its mandate by submitting itself to the purposes of the genuine order of God, for "the full and whole placing of our Saviour Christ in his throne is the perpetual stay and stayed perpetuity of all princes in their seats."[64]

Although Cartwright and other Presbyterians, along with Calvin, said they desired no disturbance to the State but only its security, Whitgift rightly identifies what we might call Puritan double-talk on this matter. On the one hand, like Calvin before him, Cartwright would leave the State untouched and simply reform the Church. Yet, on the other hand, Cartwright proclaims in good Calvinist fashion a totally new order in which the State's whole position is changed—"the commonwealth must be made to agree with the church, and the government thereof with her government," as he said. They could not, as Puritans

61. *WW*, III, 189.
62. *WW*, I, 25.
63. *WW*, I, 20; cf. *WW*, III, 295: Cartwright claims (like other Presbyterians) to be a loyal subject of the queen's—"her authority be the greatest in the earth ... " But he continues in a vein that is strikingly like the words of Archbishop Grindal to the queen, "it is not infinite, but it is limited by the word of God ... " See Bibliographical Essay D for mention of the relation of Grindal to Queen Elizabeth.
64. *WW*, I, 19-20 and 25; cf. *WW*, III, 295.

were soon to learn, have it both ways.

Still, that which subordinates the State to the Church—namely, the use of the sword—is also what differentiates the two.[65] At all costs the functions of Church and State must be kept distinct from each other. The Church must not use any form of coercion or corporeal punishment, nor must it in any way assume the form of the State.

> And whereas in the policy of M. Doctor it seemeth a furtherance to the gospel to join these together, which was also the policy of the idolaters . . . in the wisdom of God it hath seemed far otherwise; which I doubt not did therefore separate the ministry from this pomp, which is commendable in the civil magistrate, lest the efficacy and power of the simplicity of the word of God, and of the ministry, should be obscured, whilst men would attribute the conversion of souls unto the gospel (due unto the word and to the Spirit of God) to these glorious shews; and lest, whilst the minister have the word in one hand and the sword in the other, men should not be able to judge so well in their consciences of the mighty operation of the word of God in them. For they might doubt with themselves whether the fear and outward shew of the minister carried some stroke with them in believing the word.[66]

Ministers must not "meddle in civil affairs," nor hold civil office, as was the custom in the Anglican communion. In so doing, they not only take the sword into their hands, but they also lend the legitimacy of the Word of God to the provisional structure (including degrees of rank and status) of the old order.[67] Furthermore, there ought not to be Church courts under any circumstances. To demand for the Church legal, coercive jurisdiction over such things as marriage, divorce, wills, and testaments, and to claim for the Church special courts with peculiar means of legal administration, such as *ex officio mero*,[68] is again to

65. McGinn, *AC*, 346.
66. *WW*, III, 436.
67. McGinn, *AC*, 349.
68. The process called "*ex officio mero*" (the capacity of the judge on his own responsibility to move cause against a defendant) was, as is well known, one of the main weapons used by the Chancery Courts to root out Puritans. The defendant was required to swear to charges before they were cited, and he could obtain legal advice only after he so swore. Consequently, he might often have to swear and under further interrogation to testify against himself. If the charges were contested, then witnesses were produced and almost any kind of information accepted. The prosecution enjoyed, obviously, a distinct advantage. The whole process was strongly resisted by the Puritans, for understand-

confuse the old order with the new. It is to claim for the Church what rightfully belongs to the magistrate and the civil courts.[69]

Cartwright is very clear on the way in which the State must employ its coercive power in the service of the Church. Atheists and disobedient people, he says, are

> . . . of and in the commonwealth, which neither *may nor can be in or of the church;* therefore the church having nothing to do with such, the magistrate ought to see that they join to hear the sermons in the place where they are made, whether it be in those parishes where there is a church, and so preaching, or where else he shall think best, and cause them to be examined how they profit, and if they profit not, to punish them; and, as their contempt groweth, so to increase the punishment, until such times as they declare manifest tokens of unrepentantness; and then, as rotten members that do not only no good nor service in the body, but also corrupt and infect others, cut them off: and, if they do profit in hearing, then to be joined unto that church which is the next place of their dwelling.[70]

Since those who are obedient members of the Church are the *true citizens* of the new order, they constitute the new elite in relation to whom the whole society must be organized. They it is who set the tone and direction for social life. In fact, a citizen's very usefulness to society is to be judged, finally, on the basis of his obedience to the Church. It is quite clear, on Cartwright's position, that no member can take his proper place in society without first taking his proper place in the new community. Accordingly, the State must be marshaled in the service of driving citizens toward true obedience, that is, toward the Church. Those citizens who incorrigibly refuse to be so driven must be lopped off by the State "as rotten members" that do "no good nor service in the body." Quite literally, they can be of no earthly use.

able reasons. See H. C. Porter, *Reformation and Reaction,* (Cambridge, 1958) 158-160.

    However, the common lawyers also resisted this practice, which rested on civil and canon law procedure. R. A. Marchant in *Puritans and the Church Courts in the Diocese of York, 1560-1642* (London, 1960), 5, remarks: "One of the distinct advantages of canon and civil law procedure was that only very rarely did a judge give any reason for his sentence. The tradition of precedents built up in the common law courts, by the publication of reasoned judgments, was one of their greatest strengths, and gave them much influence. A similar practice, had it existed before the eighteenth century in civil law procedure, would undoubtedly have done much to enhance the prestige of those courts."

69. *WW,* III, 265, 438.
70. *WW,* I, 386; my italics.

They are as injurious to the commonwealth as they are to the Church, for their disobedience can produce nothing but disorder.

Here we see again the basis for the inseparable unity between ecclesiological and economic action in this system of thought. Only in direct, voluntary response to God's command does one fulfill his function or service (calling) in God's true order, and only when one fulfills his function in God's order, is he obedient to God's command. Obedience and fulfillment of function take place in the Church insofar as they are the proleptic embodiment of the new society that is breaking in. Therefore, membership in the Church must contribute to true social order, while willfulness against the Church can only mean drastic social disintegration. In that sense, the genuine member of the Body of Christ is the measure of true citizenship for the commonwealth.

On the pattern of the system, it would be as impossible for a person to fulfill his "lawful calling" in economic life without heartfelt obedience as it would for him to have heartfelt obedience without fulfilling his "lawful calling." True obedience equals true order in the total sense. Cartwright did not spend much time working at the economic implications of the system although, as we have seen, he did not altogether neglect them. These dimensions were much more spelled out by Perkins (see below). But the fact that Cartwright was preoccupied with ecclesiological aspects does not mean that the economic implications are not there.

In its separate and subordinate position to the new order of God, the State may be said to operate by "reason of church." Insofar as it defends and extends the Church and the Word of God, as Cartwright understands it, the State most adequately performs its own task. "The only way," he writes, "of purging the Commonwealth of these pestilences (murders, thefts, etc.) is to bend the force of sharp and severe punishments, *especially* against idolaters, blasphemers, contemners of true religion and of the service of God."[71] Cartwright rather frequently calls for the death penalty against such people, and at times his words reach a pitch of vindictive brutality.[72] So much so that McGinn—not without justification—labels Cartwright's writings as an "outline for an Elizabethan concentration camp."[73] He finds in the leading Puritan's words the rankest expression of totalitarianism.

71. *SR*, 118; my italics.
72. *SR*, 69-70.
73. McGinn, *AC*, 132-133.

Pearson[74] attempts a defense of Cartwright, arguing that his position must be understood in the setting of the times, times in which intolerance was not uncommon. While this is partly true (the argument is a familiar one used by nearly all apologists on behalf of favorite figures who indulged in intolerance), it is not the last word, and when it is so taken it confuses rather than clarifies the dynamics of thought at work. Hence, McGinn's reluctance to accept Pearson's rather half-hearted justification is, I think, quite in order. There are important reasons in the Calvinist Puritan system for the unrelenting intensity with which it sought to sponsor the transformation of the widest possible number of consciences. Therein lay the hope of order. And while Elizabethan tolerance is often exaggerated, there is a vast difference between the defensive intolerance of Whitgift, Bancroft, and Laud and the decidedly offensive intentions of the Elizabethan Puritans.

But if totalitarian regimentation was advocated in the name of the new elite, the fundamental differentiation between State and Church, the old order and the new, was maintained. The all too common view that English Puritans "wished to do in England what they later did in New England, that is, destroy the ancient law, decisions in equity, and the ancient monarchical constitution" and that they "wished to set up the Mosaic law as the only legal code for the land" is mistaken.[75] Such a suggestion simply misunderstands the dimensions of thought at work here. Cartwright explicitly denies Whitgift's assertion that he and the Puritans are seeking to abrogate all the existing laws of the land by substituting Mosaic laws for them:

> As for the casting away / of the studie / and large volumes of the lawe / which he imagineth to followe of this assertion: he decieveth hym selfe. . . . If he aske our lawiers / upon what groundes the great-

74. *Church and State,* 110.
75. John S. Marshall, "Richard Hooker and the Origins of American Constitutionalism," *Origins of the Natural Law Tradition* (Dallas, Tex., 1954), 48. This widespread view—with respect to New England at least—has been demolished once and for all by G. L. Haskin's most interesting book, *Law and Authority in Early Massachusetts* (New York, 1960). Haskins shows the impact of common law tradition on Massachusetts Bay, even though certain adjustments were made; see esp. chapter X "After English Ways," 163 ff.: "The Bible in Massachusetts was an indispensable touchstone, but not the cornerstone, of Puritan legal thinking" (162). The same regard for the common law tradition most certainly existed among the English Puritans.

est part of their houghe volumes (as he calleth them) stand, they will
answer him / they partly stand uppon the plaine wordes off the lawe
off Moses / and partly of reason uncorrupt / which is the equitie off
the lawe urge'd off us. And therfore althoughe our lawes / be some
time in forme diverse / from the lawes off Moses: yet they will never
graunt him ... that our healthsome lawes, be contrarie to Moses
lawes. For both being Good / one of them can not be contrarie to
the other.[76]

Not only is there no insinuation that the whole body of English law
should be thrown out to make room for Mosaic law; there is, in fact, an
assertion that in general English law already exists in harmony with
Mosaic law, even though it is articulated differently. Nor will Cartwright accept Whitgift's accusation regarding the replacement of lawyers with clergymen:

Where he saith that we of the clergy, should be the best judges by
this means, it is to open injurie / to charge us with that / which we
openly renounce / and condem in him: which is / that in medling in
civil affaires / they put their sickle in an other mans harvest.[77]

"It is not," he continues, "as the Answer [from Whitgift] surmiseth
untruly that the magistrate is simply bound unto the judicial lawes off
Moses: but that he is bound to the equitie / which I also called the
substance / and marrowe off them."[78] Cartwright makes ample room for

76. *SR*, 103-104; cf. *WW*, I 273.
77. The passage continues not altogether clearly: "Notwithstanding if in establish-
ing of lawes / for the Godly / and peaceable governement of the common
welth / there may be no assistance of the ministerie / whereby the lawes
should be the better compassed / to the equitie prescribed in the word of God
/ and to take heede that nothing be doon against it: there is no just cawse / to
uphold the Bishops presence in the Parlament howse" (*SR*, 104).
78. *SR*, 95. For Cartwright the term "equitie" is equated with the "morall lawe."
Although the Old Testament ceremonial laws and many of the judicial laws
were abrogated with the coming of Christ, the moral law was not (*SR*, 96). It
is the moral law that is related to "our reconciliation with the Lord" and "our
good agreement with men," or to the ultimate end of God's order fulfilled in
Christ. It is that toward which all good law and order is now directed, which is
why the law of the land ought to be framed with reference to it. This notion,
a replica of Calvin's doctrine of natural law, means two basic things in our
analysis: (1) God's command is related to and bound up with the driving
forces of the law of the land. Secular law is brought under the service of God.
(2) God's command can never be reduced to nor fulfilled by the administration of the law of the land. It remains, by definition, an indefinite, indeterminable "equitie," "substance," or "marrowe" that resides in the indeter-

the discretion of the political and legal authorities in the application and interpretation of the law of God: "yt followeth / that even in making politike lawes / for the common wealth / Christian Magistrates owght to propound unto themselves those lawes (of Moses) / and in the light of their equitie / by a just proportion off circumstances, off person / place / etc. frame them."[79] Of course, the "core" of English law must agree with the law of God,[80] but the meaning of "core" remains quite vague and subject to the determination of the God-ordained secular authorities. On the face of it, Cartwright's formulation is not much different from what many non-Puritan jurists were saying.[81]

The real point at issue was Cartwright's urgent request that the force of law be intensified in order to give the inward consciences and heartfelt commitments of men no respite until they rest in voluntary obedience to God's new order.[82] The "substance and marrowe" of the law of God was precisely that God is the sovereign who must be obeyed directly and before whom there may be absolutely no other authorities. That is why, for Cartwright, crimes against the first table of the Decalogue must be enforced most severely.[83] Secular law serves the purposes of God, it "agrees" with the command of God, when it drives

minable sovereignty of God's will. In complete agreement with the Calvinist themes running throughout this study, here is the foundation for the two superficially contradictory impulses in Calvinist Puritanism: (1) the intensification of the law by which men are thrust toward active, heartfelt allegiance to God, and (2) the devaluation of the law as the means of true obedience because of its reliance upon coercion. Both these aspects indicate the reasons why there was no specific suggestion for essential or structural reform of English law. On the one hand, English law was already related to the moral law; and on the other, no legal system could in itself reproduce true order. Only God can do that.

79. *SR*, 97.
80. *SR*, 104.
81. Eusden, *op. cit.*, 124: For example, Sir Edward Coke, hardly a Puritan, favorably quoted a fifteenth-century chief justice: "To those lawes which the holy church hath out of scripture, we ought to yield credit; for that . . . is the common law, upon which all lawes are founded" (from II *Institutes*, 625). Eusden continues: "The Bible supported, in the mind of the lawyers, the authority of ancient common law rules and parliamentary enactments and thus helped to effect the ultimate authority of fundamental law." Cf. Haskins, *op. cit.*, 144.
82. Heresy laws and laws against adultery had long since been part of the common law. Cartwright and the Puritans would simply intensify and expand their enforcement; Haskins, *op. cit.*, 144 ff.
83. See Pearson, *Church and State*, 108-110.

man toward that community whose mark of membership is the consent of the free conscience.

The profound threat that Cartwright and the Puritans represented for late sixteenth century English society was not that they wished to substitute the law of Moses lock, stock, and barrel for the common law. To be sure, they would sharpen specific aspects of the law; but their fundamental objective called into question the very *nature* of the State and the law as agencies capable of determining and producing ultimate order. As Whitgift perceptively remarked: "this doctrine of yours . . . tendeth to the overthrowing of states of commonwealths . . . "[84] They attempted so to harness the power of the old order to the service of the new, that when it had finally accomplished its task—namely, of pressing men to stand voluntarily before God and alongside one another—it would, at the same time, have lost its reason for being. The Church, after all, is the foundation of the world, and its character, by definition, rules out coercion. As with Calvin, on Cartwright's pattern of order, coercion is its own undoing.

Implied here is a withering away of the State and, consequently, a devaluation of the State (and of the law) as the source or expression of ultimate earthly order. The State cannot of itself set the fundamental tone for social life, even though it retains its own distinctive mandate from God. Nor is there, in this pattern, a static subordinationism in which State and Church are relegated to an eternal, "natural" hierarchical relationship; nor is there a notion of the omnicompetence of given political-legal structures in all worldly affairs, as was the case with official sixteenth-century Anglicanism.

So long as the world exists, rebellion and disobedience naturally need restraint in the terms of the old order. But the days of the State and the law as agents of force are clearly numbered. The whole emphasis of what we call the Calvinist pattern of order, consistently extended by Thomas Cartwright, was a radically new structure of relationships in which the free individual conscience coincides with harmonious social integration. A decisive sector of social life becomes emancipated from political-legal control—it develops its own autonomy, its own inner order.

Cartwright elaborated this system of thought almost exclusively in ecclesiological terms. The wider social implications remained to be articulated by the Cambridge divine, William Perkins.

84. *WW*. I, 278.

WILLIAM PERKINS (1558-1602)

If Cartwright was the explicit leader of Elizabethan Puritanism, who provided theological and biblical ammunition for the front-line ecclesiological concerns of the movement, William Perkins was the dominant systematic theologian, who expounded and elaborated the Puritan system from well behind the lines. At one time, these two central figures were associated in an underground classis in Cambridge, and early in his career Perkins defended certain Puritan liturgical ideas. But in 1587 he recanted his opposition to kneeling and in 1590, when the Puritan persecutions were heightened, he more or less dissociated himself from those particulars of Church reform so passionately emphasized by Cartwright. Wright accurately calls him a moderate Puritan with rather uncontroversial nature.[85] In several places, Perkins prudently defends the Church of England, arguing that it is still within the pale of the true Church.[86]

Perkins's generally moderate view in these matters has led various writers to argue that he was, at heart, a good Anglican and possibly the leading defender of Anglicanism against the Roman Catholics. The Georges even produce the idea that Perkins and Laud were in "complete agreement" on affairs of Church and State![87] Such conclusions not only fly in the face of what Perkins himself says about Church and State, they in no way reflect an awareness of the components and complexities either of Puritanism or official Anglicanism. As we saw above, Calvin and Beza themselves held ambivalent views toward the Church of England, and we have argued that both soft and hard views could find support in their vacillating attitudes. In any case, there is no value in lighting on a few random passages in a man's thought and using them as a basis for comparison. Perkins was a professional theologian whose ideas manifest a sophisticated and coherent point of view profoundly at odds with the official position of the Church of England, whether he cared to indicate that fact openly or not.

85. L. B. Wright, *Middle-Class Culture in Elizabethan England* (Chapel Hill, N. C., 1935), 281.
86. See I, 307, II, 161, III, 240-241, in Perkins's *Works* (3 vols., I, Cambridge, 1612; II, London, 1617; III, London, 1631). The pages in III are renumbered after 265. Those subsequent pages are marked in these footnotes with an asterisk. Perkins's *Works* are henceforth referred to by volume and page number.
87. Georges, *op. cit.*, 188.

Perkins is especially concerned with ethical action and social affairs, so that he focuses the Calvinist tradition in ways that reflect and speak to the spirit of the times. Yet he is by no means simply a tractarian, and his social analyses and ethical pronouncements cannot be understood apart from his theology. Perkins forcefully and consistently applies the central theological components of the Calvinist system to social activity. The inbreaking new order of God has for him the greatest practical relevance.

He lived only forty-four years, but managed, during that time, to achieve immense influence and popularity as a lecturer at Cambridge and as a preacher at St. Andrews University. "In a word," says Fuller,[88] "the Scholar could heare no learneder, the Townsmen plainer Sermons." He numbered many leading Puritans among his students and followers: Preston, Sibbes, Ames, Cotton, Gouge, Thomas Goodwin, and he was very widely read among the New England colonists. "No books, it is fair to say, were more often to be found upon the shelves of succeeding generations of preachers, and the name of no preacher recurs more often in later Puritan literature."[89]

For Perkins, as for Calvin and Cartwright, God's will is "his essence of Godhead indeed."[90] "God must first will a thing before it can be just. The will of God doth not depend upon the quality and nature of a thing, but the qualities of things in order of causes follow the will of God. For everything is as God wills it."[91] Without God's active determination, there are no right relations among men, no harmony; in short, there is no genuine order. The "just" order of the world depends upon God's preceding Word, which is his order or command. "The world was ordained by the Word of God."[92]

> God framed the Ages, that is, all creatures, visible and invisible, in a most excellent, perfect, and absolute order. As in campe every man keeps his ranke and order, and no man goeth out of his standing appointed him: So every creature hath his due place, and his proper use assigned him of God: so that the workmanship of the world in

88. Thomas Fuller, *The Holy and the Profane State* (Boston, 1864), Book II, chapter 10.

89. Haller, *op. cit.,* 65.

90. I, 722.

91. I, 288. At III, 23*, Perkins underlines God's total sovereignty: "God is not tied to the order of Nature." This emphasis should be firmly borne in mind when we come to compare the thought of Richard Hooker.

92. III, 10*.

every creature, and in every respect was absolute: and thus ordained is as much as perfectly made. And the whole world was as the perfect body of a man, where every member, bone, joynt, veine, and sinew, is in his proper place, and no thing out of square.

Also, as with Calvin and Cartwright, the essential ingredient in God's true order is the voluntary, conscience-felt obedience of man. Adam, in the state of innocence, possessed the possibility of such obedience, and therefore embodied, temporarily at least, "the integritie of man's nature"; in him was wisdom and justice "which is a conformitie of the will, affections, and powers of the body to doe the will of God."[93] Man's inner integrity, as well as his outer or social integrity, is deeply bound up with the freedom in which he wills to be obedient to God's Word. Just as God freely creates order by an assertion of his sovereign will, so man participates in the creation of true order and fulfills it through the uncoerced agreement of his will with God's: " . . . in every good act, God's grace, and mans will, concurre: Gods grace as the principall cause; mans will renewed, as the instrument of God. And therefore in all good things, industrie and labour, [and] invocation on our parts is required."[94] "When a creature is in that estate, that it willingly serves God, and cannot but serve God, then is our perfect libertie."[95]

But Adam rejected God; he sinned. Consequently, he was overcome by the "corruption, or rather the deprivation of the first integritie." He fell into a state of disorder, characterized by "the confusion or disturbance of all the powers and actions of the creature."[96] Disobedience infects the whole life of man so that even " . . . the best inclinations and motions of the mind of a naturall man, are not onely enemies, but even enmities to God." "And though he which is captive to sinne can do nothing but sin, yet may hee in sinning use his liberty: and in divers kinds of evils intended, shew the freedome of his will."[97] Man freely rejects God and becomes trapped in his own willful recalcitrance. The bitter fruit of human dereliction is radical social disintegration. There is disorder, dissension, and strife in the world, says Perkins, because

> . . . the state of all creatures is changed, for that wherein they were created, by the fall of our first parents. God made no disorder . . .

93. I, 17.
94. I, 738.
95. I, 722.
96. I, 18.
97. I, 730.

therefore it was in a most perfect order: For orderly comlinesse is a part of the goodnesse of a thing: but disorder is the effect of sin: it entered with sinne, and it is both a companion and a reward of sinne. Had we continued in our innocence all creatures had continued in their excellent order: but when we had broken the perfect order, that God had appointed us: immediately all creatures broke that order wherein they were afore both towards us, and amongst another. Whil'st we obeyed God, all creatures obeyed us: but when we shooke off the yoke of obedience unto God, and rebelled against him, then they became disobedient unto us. . . .

. . . So God created man rich in all blessings, put him into the palace of the world: garnished this house of the world with exceeding beauty: his meat, his apparell, his recreation, his house were all excellent and glorious; he made all other creatures, amongst which there was nothing but concord, love, agreement, uniformity, comeliness, and good order: now man by sin fell, and by his fall, not onely spent all his riches (that is, defaced the glorie of his owne estate:) but also set this house (that is the world) on fire: that is, defaced the beauty of heaven and earth: brought confusion, corruption, vanitie, deformity, imperfection, and monstrous disorder on all creatures; set all the world together by the eares, and one creature at variance and deadly hate with another: so that one creature doth fight, teare, wound, destroy, and eat up another. O cursed and damnable sinne of man, that hath so shamefully disordered that heavenly order, wherein God created all things in the beginning![98]

There remain, to be sure, vestiges of God's image "in certain notions concerning good and evill . . . " which abide in man's conscience. But they serve simply "to bereave man of all excuse before Gods judgement seate" by continually disturbing and condemning man on account of his disobedience.[99]

Man thus "dead in sin" can be restored to order only through an overreigning act by God himself. That act, according to Perkins, is Jesus Christ. The creation and perfection of true order is the work of God, and his "call" or law points man to a heartfelt, voluntary acknowledgment of that fact. In such acknowledgment is obedience, and in such obedience is the fulfillment of order. It is Christ alone who meets these requirements. He " . . . stands in our place, roome, and stead; and before God represents the person of all the elect: and in this respect is he

98. III, 10-13*. One could hardly find a more striking example of the interrelation between "order" and "obedience."
99. I, 20.

subject to the law, *not by nature, but by voluntarie abasement and condition of will.*"[100] All the sins of the elect are imputed to him, so that his "obedience is a fulfilling of the law for us, and his whole righteousness is ours to make us stand righteous before God."[101] In Christ those men who were elected or predestined by God to obedience are "chosen,"[102] and the possibility of realizing their election begins: theologically put, Christ's justification makes sanctification possible.[103]

The election of God, made manifest in Christ, is "an effectual calling, whereby a sinner beeing severed from the world, is entertained into God's family."[104] He who is chosen becomes a member of the new order, which is Christ's Body: ". . . the whole person of every faithfull man, is verily conjoyned with the whole person of our Saviour Christ . . ."[105] "Christ, because he is the head of the faithful, is to bee considered as a publike man sustaining the person of all the elect."[106] It is, in other words, in the Church that the new order of God is inaugurated; there men participate in Christ's free-willing conformity to God's law.

> As a king by his lawes brings his people in order, and keeps them in subjection, so Christ by his word, and the preaching of it, as it were by a mightie arme, drawes his elect into his kingdome, and fashions them to all holy obedience. . . . In this kingdome all men live not, but only those that are subject to Christ, obedient to the lawes of his kingdome, and ruled by his authority and are continually taught in his word by his spirit. But those that refuse to live according to the lawes of this kingdom, and choose to live at their owne libertie, are in the kingdome of darknesse, that is, sinne and Satan.[107]

The elect are restored to true order. Final obedience to the "law of Christ," that is, to the command manifested in Christ's life, death, and Resurrection, is that structure of human relationships integrated and

100. II, 273; my italics.
101. I, 309.
102. I, 24.
103. I, 81-85.
104. I, 76.
105. I, 78.
106. *Ibid.* In another connection, Perkins describes Christ as a "publike person" who represents the elect as does a burgess in Parliament (II, 214-215). This political metaphor is particularly interesting in the light of the strong parliamentary activity of the Puritans during the reign of Elizabeth.
107. I, 336.

harmonized according to the needs of the community: "for the common good is to bee preferred before any one man's private good."[108]

> ... Those that are strong must support the infirmities of the weake,
> that so the whole building beeing compact and knit together, may
> grow up to a holy temple in the Lord. ... For each member has
> need of the others and must adjust and yield to the infirmities and
> weaknesses of the others ... [109]

> As a candle spendeth it selfe to give light to others: so must Gods
> people spend those gifts which God hath given them for the benefit
> of their brethren. A Christian man howsoever he be the freest man
> upon earth, yet he is servant to all men, especially to the church of
> God, to do service unto the members of it by love for good of all.
> And this good is procured, when we convey the graces of God be-
> stowed on us to our brethren.[110]

It is in Christ and in him alone that this ultimate social structure can
be realized, for it alone stands directly under the command of the
author of order. As Christ directly opposes Satan (power of disorder),
so his Body—the Church—stands over against Satan's old order of sin
and bondage, representing God's providential design. To be elected by
God is to find and actively to fulfill one's place in the new order. For
Perkins, as for Calvin and Cartwright, predestination is inseparable from
the Church: "the Church is a peculiar company of men predestined to
life everlasting, and made one in Christ."[111] Analytically considered,
God's sovereign election determines true order; therefore, those elected
by God are elected *in relation to* each other. As we have seen throughout our analysis so far, predestination in the Calvinist Puritan pattern of
order is in no sense atomistic or "solitary" (to use Tawney's description), but decidedly organic.[112] The Church as the body of believers is

108. II, 359.
109. II, 360.
110. I, 309.
111. I, 277.
112. At the risk of beating a dead horse, we emphasize something already emerging from our study: that "individualism" and social order are by no means
  necessarily antithetical terms as, for example, the Georges (along with
  Tawney and others) argue. In their discussion of Perkins, *op. cit.,* 129, they
  claim there is no individualism in Perkins because, as they see it, he stresses
  concern for the community. H. M. Robertson says the same thing of Calvinism in general. The point of Perkins's thought is, of course, that when one
  individually obeys God's order (command), he voluntarily takes his proper
  place in God's order (community). His election is fulfilled when *he himself*

as crucial to God's scheme as his act of predestination itself. One without the other is quite illogical, as Perkins makes clear in a significant rejection of Arminianism.

> ... It puls downe the pale of the Church, and laies it waste as every common field: it breeds carelessness in the use of means of grace, the word and Sacraments; when as men shall be perswaded, that grace shall be offered to every one effectually, whether hee be of the Church or not, at one time or other; whersoever or howsoever he live: as in the like case, if men should be tolde that whether they live in the market towne or no, there shall be sufficient provision brought them, if they will but receive it and accept of it, who would then come to the market?[113]

The heart of the pattern of order before us is that God's decision demands a human decision for social action, a decision between the old order and the new, between the world and the Church. In good Calvinistic tradition, Perkins argues that there is no salvation outside the Church militant, "and such as remaine forever out of the same perish eternally. . . . And the reason hereof is plaine: for without Christ there is no salvation: but out of the militant Church there is no Christ, nor faith in Christ: and therefore no salvation."[114] In other words, salvation is defined in terms of membership in the new community. It is for this reason that "everyman must be admonished evermore to joyne himself to some particular Church, being a sound member of the Catholike Church." In short, God's Church on earth is "the most excellent of all societies."[115]

> The companies and societies of men in families, townes, and kingdomes, and in other common affaires of this life, be the ordinance of God, and good in their kinde; but yet the society of the Saints in the Church of God, doth farre surmount them all, and that in these respects; First, because in Gods Church salvation may bee obtained,

elects to act harmoniously toward the "greatest" and the "meanest." This kind of autonomous action is made possible precisely by differentiating the Church from the State, or from coercive control. The Church in this scheme "institutionalizes individualism"—to borrow a term from Parsons—it provides a context for behavior that takes place by virtue of individual decision, and not by means of the sword. To put it another way, the Church becomes a sphere of autonomous order.

113. I, 295.
114. I, 301.
115. III, 245*.

but not in other societies as they are societies, though sundrie benefits arise from them, unlesse they bee either particular Churches, or
members thereof. Secondly, the Church of God is the end of all
other societies: and they are all ordained to preserve and cherish the
Church, which is the society of the Saints. Thirdly, the Church
beautifies all other societies: the principall dignitie of any towne,
houshold, or kingdome is this, that they are either Churchs of God,
onely is Lord over all . . . .[126]

The Church, as the institutionalization of the perfect blend of command and structure present in Christ, stands naturally under his direct
authority: " . . . he neither hath nor can have any creature in heaven or
on earth to bee fellow herein."[117] "Nay," Perkins continues, "Christ
needes no vicar or deputy; for he is all-sufficient in himself and alwaies
present with his Church . . . " Even kings and princes who, as we shall
see, have great political authority in the Church "with all others owe
homage unto Christ: there he hath the Canonicall Scriptures to be his
lawes, whereto every one must subject himselfe."[118]

On the basis of these and other passages, one can only surmise that
certain scholars, as well as the Anglican authorities of the time, did not
read Perkins very carefully or bother to think through the implications
of what he was saying for the Anglican Church. The whole foundation
of Anglicanism, as we shall see more fully, rested on the postulate that
the queen was the "only supreme governor in this realm . . . as well in
all spiritual and ecclesiastical things or causes as temporal." Perkins's
position, fully consistent as it is with Calvin's and Cartwright's, strikes
at the heart of that postulate. The Church lives by a new authority and
a new law. Further, Perkins sounds exactly like Cartwright on the possibility of deriving Church government from Scripture: "And deare
Father of all mercie plant that word, that the Saints may worshippe
thee in those meanes, in order and comeliness, which thou hast appointed . . . "[119] For profound reasons, such words were fully heretical to
official Anglicanism. On the basis of these arguments alone it is pre-
posterous to conclude, as some do, that Perkins was a great defender of
Anglicanism.

116. III, 245-246*.
117. I, 301; my italics.
118. III, 209*. Christ alone must determine scriptures, says Perkins, for neither
     the ministry nor the Church has any authority of its own *(op. cit.)*. Our
     comments on Cartwright's view of Scripture would also apply, in general, to
     Perkins. See fn. 29, p. 89, above.
119. I, 381.

Christ's authority over the Church is implemented by means of the ministers, who are first and foremost preachers. The Church is "gathered by the word preached."[120] Even ministers, however, are not deputies but "onely instruments"[121] of what Christ himself is doing in the Church. They articulate the Word of God which calls for *direct* and wholehearted response from the believer. By the logic of Perkins's system, man can rely upon the sovereign Word of God shown forth in Christ for his authority; and only the ministers, whose very office of preaching refers to and embodies that sovereign Word, can be taken as authoritative. It is, undoubtedly, because of the fact that God's Word is sovereign and free and therefore irreducible to set patterns or generalizations that Perkins, like Cartwright, sharply rejects the Anglican practice of reading stereotyped homilies.[122]

At the same time, the authority of the preacher is inseparable from the electing consent of the Church. Like Christ, the Christian is called first and foremost to a voluntary decision about the order of God. In fact, the order is complete only when such a decision occurs. Therefore, the authority of the preacher concurs with the authority of the elect, who possess the decisive capacity to elect. Perkins states quite plainly that ministers must submit to examination and election before entering their office. What he calls "allowance from men" for the "outward calling" is indispensable in determining the validity of God's calling. "And here it is to be remembered, that triall of gifts and free election, without partiality, should be in the designment of all, specially of publike callings." For so it was in the primitive Church![123]

The capacity to elect or choose in matters of Church government naturally entails an egalitarian principle within the new order. "The members thereof are all alike in heart and affection."[124] "Wee must come naked before him [God], and hee will have no respect to our birth, our riches, our learning. Therefore it is good for us to put on Christ, that in him we may be accepted."[125] Within the "regiment of the Gospell," says Perkins,

> . . . there is neither father nor mother, neither master, mistres, maid nor servant, nor husband nor wife, nor Lord, nor Subject, nor

120. I, 304.
121. I, 609.
122. I, 348.
123. I, 760.
124. I, 309.
125. II, 194.

inferiour, but Christ is all, and each to other, is Christ himselfe, there is none better than other, but all alike good, al brethren, and Christ onely is Lord over all . . .[126]

This does not mean that all such divisions are eliminated here and now. The vision of the Kingdom of God in which Christ shall "put downe all power, rule, and authoritie," thereby completely wiping away rank and status (including, significantly, the temporary distinction between pastor and people),[127] remains, in general, an eschatological vision. But this new order is already breaking in,[128] overcoming the old order, giving new direction to the trend of history, while at the same time radically if incompletely embodying the outlines of God's ultimate order. It is in the Church that men reap the first fruits of the inner and social integrity of their humanity. For with Perkins, as with Calvin and Cartwright, to be a man is fully and freely to decide for God as the sovereign of all things. That is the basis for all proper relationships. That is the basis for the only kind of status and division that really matters: the distinction between the old man and the new.

Accordingly, the Church is the context or locus of man's genuinely voluntary, heartfelt action. It is, to use Travers's phrase, "the depository of the conscience . . . "

Now Christ being a King, must needs have a Kingdome, which is not of this world, standing in the might and policy of a man, as earthly kingdomes doe; but it is spirituall, directly concerning the hearts and consciences of men, where he ruleth by his lawes. And this is his privilege, which cannot be given any creature, man or Angell, to rule and raigne spiritually in the heart and conscience. This spirituall Kingdome of Christ is exercised, not by dint of sword, or force of armes, but by his holy word, through the work of the spirit.[129]

Like Calvin, Perkins claims that the conscience stands "in the middest between [God] and man, as an arbitratour to give sentence, and to

126. I, 394.
127. I, 667.
128. Hill in "William Perkins and the Poor," in *Puritanism and Revolution,* 236-237, indicates the revolutionary agitation already at work within the Elizabethan Puritan congregations. "A Puritan petition of the fifteen-eighties asked that noblemen should be compelled to join with the nearest congregations, their houses 'being commonly not convenient . . . to have such Officers as ought to be in everie Church, and the want of mynisters yet being so great.' " Such a radical proposal for integration horrified Hooker. The Puritan outlook was clear, continues Hill, "in the common depreciation of mere aristocracy of birth as contrasted with the aristocracy of the spirit."
129. III, 219*.

pronounce either with man or against man unto God."[130] It is the center of man's existence insofar as it is the point of direct relationship between God and man, and insofar as it is the center for the reception and execution of God's order. "The proper end of conscience is, to determine of things done, [that is] a mans own actions . . . " Conscience is thus closely connected with the will in Perkins's thought.

Just as God's sovereign will is decisive for achieving "right order," so, too, is man's conscience and will. And as God's will is not *his* unless it is free, or uncompelled by any higher authority, so there is no genuinely human will or conscience unless it freely acknowledges and acts upon the sovereign authority of God—"considering [a] will constrained is no will."[131] "We must be a lawe to ourselves: we must be voluntaries, without constraint, freely yielding subjection to the will of God . . . "[132]

> . . . Seeing Gods preventing and working grace turnes our wils, and makes them, of unwilling, most willing wils, all our obedience must be voluntarie, and come from such freenesse of will, as if there were no bond in the law of God, to force and compell us thereto. The people of God, that are turned and guided by the free spirit of God, must be a voluntarie people, and with all alacritie and cheerefulnesse, doe the duties that pertaine to them of a readie minde, even as if there were neither heaven nor hell, Judge or judgement after this life.[133]

Perkins described the Kingdom of God, toward which all things are moving, as a place "wherein Gods lawes are the onely lawes, and they shall be written in mens hearts: where each one is a sufficient governour of himselfe, and yet all subject to God; and their God unto them all in all."[134]

It is this heavy emphasis upon the consenting will and conscience as the crucial ingredient in true order that has led to some misunderstanding over Perkins's viewpoint. For example, Mosse concludes that only the intention of the conscience, and not the ethical action itself, is of consequence in Perkins's thought.[135] It is Mosse's understanding of Perkins that if one's intention concurs with God's will, whether or not

130. I, 517.
131. I, 559; cf. I, 721.
132. II, 276; cf. II, 252.
133. I, 739.
134. III, 79*.
135. George L. Mosse, *Holy Pretence. A Study in Christianity and Reason of State from William Perkins to John Winthrop* (Oxford, 1957).

one actually performs a good deed is unimportant. This leads Mosse to argue that Perkins had an ethical and political theory that promoted (à la Machiavelli) "reason of state" as a justification for political "policy." So long as intentions were right, any action can be justified. He further argues that Perkins's ruler is a *legibus solutus*—virtually uncontrolled and acting by "divine right." Mosse's case is intriguing, and may have a certain limited validity, but it will not bear the weight of the conclusions he draws from it. In the first place, Mosse's separation of intention and action in Perkins is too strong. In the second place, it is simply untenable to equate Machiavelli, who held that the state is . . . the supreme and all-inclusive good, with the Calvinist Puritan position. It could certainly be argued that this was in general Elizabeth's viewpoint, as well as that of James I and Charles I. But the way in which Calvinist Puritanism restricts (and thereby depreciates) political life by summarily excluding its authority and control from a sector of social life can hardly be called Machiavellian, especially when the excluded sector is the embodiment of ultimate social value. Religious and, inchoately at least, economic actions are decisively withdrawn from the direct regulation of the State. That is not the basis for a thoroughgoing policy of reason of State.

Of course, Perkins does give a great deal of attention to the disposition of the "inward affections"—to feelings of repentance, faith, conviction of sin, and so on. Genuine conversion begins with a "mustard seed" of faith; it begins with meditating, endeavoring, striving, asking, seeking, knocking.[136] "God accepts the endeavour of the whole man to obey, for perfect obedience itselfe."[137] ". . . The desire of reconciliation with God in Christ, is reconciliation itselfe:[138] the desire to beleeve is faith indeed: the desire to repent, repentance itselfe."[139] It is, in fact, the presence of these intentions which provides the "infallible certainty of faith" to troubled consciences,[140] because salvation is defined with reference to the will or conscience that strives to serve

136. I, 642.
137. I, 641; cf. I, 538.
138. Still, even within these statements there is an ambiguity in Perkins's words. He says further along on the same page: "A desire to be reconciled, is not reconciliation in nature (for the desire is one thing, and reconciliation another) but in Gods acceptation" (I, 639).
139. I, 639.
140. Perkins's interest in this "infallible certainty" is quite intense. It is, after all, what convinces one of his new humanity.

God. That alone is good that stems from "a pure heart, good con-science, and faith unfained . . ."[141]

However, to argue that because of this emphasis upon the regenera-ted conscience Perkins is unconcerned with action is totally misleading and fails to grasp the dimensions of the pattern of order at work here. Again and again, Perkins lays it down that the elect "must be plentifull in all good works . . ."[142] "Thus beleevers in Christ are great offend-ours, when reformed religion, and unreformed life are joyned to-gether, as often they are."[143] He who is justified in Christ is also sanctified to the practice of holy works in his life, for justification and sanctification are inseparably related.[144] Conscience and obedience must be joined together in the Christian's life for, says Perkins, repent-ance, humiliation, and faith are nothing unless they lead to "new obedience unto God in our life and conversation."[145] The repentant person "must not live in the practice of any owtward sin."[146] Perkins is in no way unconcerned with action; his point is that *no good action is possible without the active determination of the free and voluntary conscience.* In fact, only when that is present will actions occur that produce right relations or good order. So long as man lives in the sinful world, conscience will not automatically coincide with perfect obedience[147]—that, as we have seen, will take place only in the King-dom of God. But the redeemed man here and now strains in this direc-tion, he struggles so to stand before God that "each one is a sufficient governour of himselfe, and yet all subject to God . . . " He endeavors, in a word, to will the command of God and thereby to fulfill the order of God.

The inseparable relation of intention and action[148] is portrayed sharply in Perkins's all-important treatment of the "secular" calling of a

141. I, 560.
142. I, 292.
143. II, 212.
144. III, 57*.
145. II, 16; cf. III, 31*.
146. II, 16; III, 8*, Perkins remarks: "Here it is plaine that men must not be con-
     tent to keepe their faith close in their hearts, but they must exercise the
     fruits of it in the world: and then both these together will make a man truly
     commendable."
147. This tension between striving and attainment Perkins shared fully with
     Calvin, though in general Perkins dwelt more extensively on the point than
     Calvin did.
148. Very significantly, Perkins remarks: " . . . this is evidence of a good con-

Christian. Here we come again to the familiar connection between ecclesiological and economic action. In his *Treatise of the Vocations, or Callings of Men, with the sorts and kinds of them, and the right use thereof*, Perkins defines a vocation or calling as "a certaine kinde of life, ordained and imposed on man by God, for the common good."[149] God is the author of every "lawful calling" which is a particular office or function in the world allotted exclusively for the enrichment of the whole social order: "men should be [God's] instruments, for the good of one another."[150]

> For the Church and Commonwealth are as a mans body, wherein every member hath his severall offices, for the good of the whole body: and indeed everyman should have not onely a generall calling of a Christian, but a particular calling also, wherein he must imploy himselfe for the common good: it is against the Word of God and the light of Nature, that any man should live having nothing to do.[151]

According to Perkins, the calling of God has two aspects, a "general" and a "personal" one. In the first, the Christian is called to membership in the Church, in which he becomes a "living stone" entrusted with the "duties of edification." As such he brings "free-will offerings" of prayer, service, and possessions, in order to "procure the good of the whole mistical body of Christ."[152] One fulfills this calling by a daily renewal of repentance and faith and a fresh "indeavour to performe new obedience in respect of all [God's] commaundments."

"A personall calling is the execution of some particular office, arising from the distinction which God makes betweene man and man in every societie."[153] The election of a Christian is embodied in the specific secular task he is given to do, and God's true order is manifested in the integration and harmony of all the differentiated functions, or the "diversity of gifts" that the elect collectively possess. A personal calling is honest and lawful if it upholds and serves the three basic societies—

science, when a man shewes himselfe a Christian in his calling at home, and conversation [employment] among his brothers" (III, 149). We emphasize this over against Mosse's line of argument. The autonomous conscience exercises itself "religiously" and "secularly."

149. I, 750.
150. I, 757.
151. III, 91.
152. I, 752-754.
153. I, 754.

the Church, the commonwealth, and the family. It is "fit" for an individual if he has the necessary talents and capacities, if he receives "allowance from men," and if it seems, from his point of view, "best for him." The Christian must be discouraged from changing occupations,[154] though a basis for change does exist when private necessity and the common good so dictate.[155] Particular accoutrements vary with each personal calling, which means that one is compensated "according to our abilitie," though men must seek no more than is "necessary" and "sufficient" to their station.[156] While the acquisition of profit is by no means bad in itself,[157] a calling must be profitable not only to the individual but to the commonwealth as well.[158] Therefore, riches must be attained and employed in moderation, and wealthy men may be honored only insofar as they are "made instruments to upholde and maintain vertue."[159]

That is to say, wealthy men must labor usefully. Hill misleadingly quotes only part of what Perkins actually says:[160] "Men are to bee honoured for their riches." In the passage itself, Perkins significantly modifies this statement: "I meane not for riches simply but for the right use of riches; namely as they are made instruments to uphold and maintain vertue." Riches in and of themselves are of no value—only as they are signs of unrelenting labor. That is why Perkins stands so strongly against the idle gentry—"such as live in no calling, but spend their time in eating, drinking, sleeping and sporting . . . "[161]

Of course, there is in Perkins a tendency to equate prosperity with the sign of God's blessing—that is, as the mark of, or reward for, voluntary industriousness. If one does a job well, he can, in general, be sure of prosperity,[162] for that kind of activity or obedience is precisely the

154. I, 756.
155. I, 775.
156. Perkins says that the rule for determining what is sufficient must be "the example and judgement of the godly, and grave men of our estate and order" (I, 768).
157. Perkins is by no means unconditionally in favor of usury, though he argues that under certain circumstances it is acceptable, III, 163-164*. Accordingly, he clearly perpetuates a trend begun by Calvin. See Bibliographical Essay D, p. 258.
158. I, 764.
159. II, 150.
160. *Op. cit.*, 229.
161. III, 163-164.
162. I, 772.

direction of the will of God.[163] The way in which this motif fits into the pattern of order is clear: economic well-being for all is one of the ends of God's order, and voluntary obedience is the means by which it is achieved. However, Perkins allows that God may be "trieing" man by subjecting him to poverty. Therefore, he argues, men must not "profane their lives and callings" by seeking to "get honours, pleasures, profites, worldly commodities, etc. for thus we live to another end than God hath appointed, and we serve ourselves, and consequently, neither God, nor man. . . . Men should be his instruments, for the good of one another."[164]

As endeavor and striving in a Christian's life are signs of regeneration, so unrelenting industry in one's personal calling is evidence of the precise apprehension of God's call. "Labour in a calling is as precious as gold or silver."[165] A man may lose a hand, but skill and diligence can never be lost. In other words, a man achieves his humanity through his specific, voluntary, and intense activity in the order of God. The free and spontaneous activity he displays in his function is at once the measure of his individuality (his individual election) and the measure of his participation in God's order: he who hears the order fulfills the order.

That is why Perkins heaps such opprobrium upon the "slothful" and the "idle." Such people are the very incarnation of evil, that is, of disobedience and disorder. "Idleness," says Perkins, "is the shop of the divell."[166] "Slouth and negligence in the duties of our callings, are a disorder against that comly order which God hath set in the societies of mankinde, both in church and commonwealth . . . and, indeed, idelnes and slouth are the causes of many damnable sins."[167] Perkins lists four categories of "useless" people: (1) rogues, beggars, and vagabonds; (2) monks, friars, and Papists in general, whose 52 holy days have meant that they "spend more than a quarter of a yeare in rest and idlenes";[168] (3) gentlemen "enriched with great livings and revenewes," who "spend their days eating and drinking" and serve neither Church nor commonwealth; and (4) serving men, who, in their eating

163. I, 766; cf. 757; III, 5.
164. I, 756-757.
165. I, 751.
166. I, 752.
167. *Ibid.*
168. It is interesting to observe how Perkins shares Cartwright's aversion to holy days for precisely the same reasons: they produce idleness.

and drinking, yield nothing. No doubt because there were so many of them at the time, Perkins is especially hard on the "sturdy beggar":[169]

> It is a foule disorder in any Common-wealth, that there should be suffered rogues, beggars, vagabonds; for such kind of persons commonly are of no civill societie or corporation, nor of any particular Church; and are rotten legges, and armes, that droppe from the body. Againe, to wander up and downe from yeare to yeare to this end, to seeke and procure bodily maintenance, is no calling, but the life of a beast: and consequently a condition or state of life flat against the rule: That every one must have a particular calling. And therefore the Statute (Anno 39, Eliz.) made in the last Parliament for the restraining of beggars and rogues, is an excellent Statute, and beeing in substance the very law of God, is never to be repealed.[170]

Giving alms to these idlers was, from Perkins's point of view, the severest infringement of God's law. At all costs, those who were able must be "set on work," they must be urged, guided, and if need be coerced to take their rightful place in God's scheme of things. So long as they are unemployed, so long as they do not eagerly and actively do what God has bid them, they remain the "plague of our times."

The point of central significance to our study is that the general or, roughly, ecclesiological activity of the Christian, and the personal or "secular" (especially economic) activity are intertwined in Perkins's thought. "The generall calling of Christianity, without the practice of some particular calling, is nothing els, but the forme of godliness, without the power thereof. And therefore both callings must be joyned, as

---

169. The enclosure movement and inflation due to a sharp rise in prices were among the important economic causes for the increase of beggars in sixteenth-century England. See, for example, Hill, *op. cit.*, 219 ff.; J. B. Black, *Reign of Elizabeth, 1558-1603* (Oxford, 1952), 222-225; E. M. Leonard, *Early History of English Poor Relief* (Cambridge, 1900).

170. I, 755. Perkins's emphasis upon restraining the "sturdy beggar" did not preclude an attitude of charitableness toward the needy poor. W. K. Jordan in *Philanthropy in England, 1480-1660* (New York, 1959) uses Perkins as the leading example of the English Calvinist position on philanthropy: for him, says Jordan, "the fact of wealth and the necessity of charity are inseparable, for almsgiving [affirmed Perkins] 'is the best kinde of thrift or husbandry . . . it is not giving, but lending, and that to the Lord, who in his good time will return the gift with increase,'" 152. Jordan continues: "The Calvinist not only said that but he believed that we are but stewards of wealth for which we are accountable to God. . . . This view of charitable obligation was remorselessly and deeply etched into the English conscience by a host of Calvinist divines . . . "

bodie and soule are joyned in a living man."[171] As we have seen throughout the treatment of the Calvinist Puritan pattern of order, the Church—as the present embodiment of the new order—strains toward the creation of a new society. He who is a "living stone" in the building of the Church is, by definition, a member of that new society. By genuinely taking his assigned place in the Church and by participating willingly and eagerly, he is also taking his place in the society which is to be. Therefore, evidence of a repenting, endeavoring, willing conscience in the Church will be matched by an energetic, industrious diligent conscience in the world, and vice versa.[172] For Perkins, a Christian can have "a sure testimony of his election" whichever perspective he gauges his life from. It is all the same, since true repentance, etc., in the Church demands social expression, and true industry, etc., demands faith in the grace of God. Election means voluntary participation in and obedience to the order of God; therefore, he who so participates *is* elect. He shares already in that new heaven and new earth toward which all things press. For him was the world created, and to him belongs the rightful dominion. He sets the ultimate standard for social life—he is, in short, a member of the new elite.

Above all, he stands directly before God, free to pursue the "speciall duties of [his] lawful calling" (in Church and world) without lesser earthly control or domination. Such freedom is his inheritance, it is the hallmark of his new life. The new society is regulated and harmonized by the consensual self-integration of all the varied functions of the elect. In fact, says Perkins, the new order is like a city, which is a "place of freedom," that is, "a place where generally are all necessaries and comforts for mans life: one part of the countrey hath this commodity, another that; but in the city are all, either brought unto it, or of itselfe."[173] Because of the wide range of possibilities, due to the high degree of diversity and differentiation, a city's life is to a large degree regulated by the free choices and decisions of its members. So, precisely, is the new order. The Christian's whole existence is a struggle to become a "freeman of heaven, and never rest till he know he be."[174]

The importance of these passages to our argument cannot be overestimated. Here is an unqualified exaltation of the city. It is chosen by Perkins to describe the character of the Kingdom or the "City" of God.

171. I, 757.
172. Perkins urges that true religion be spread into every calling (III, 246*).
173. III, 79*.
174. III, 80*.

And it is chosen with reference to its economic significance, that is, with reference to the division and interdependence of labor. In discussing Richard Baxter's thought, Weber called attention to the importance of the idea of division of labor in the Puritan moral scheme. "Baxter expresses himself in terms which more than once directly recall Adam Smith's well-known apotheosis of the division of labor. The specialization of occupations leads, since it makes the development of skill possible, to a quantitative and qualitative improvement in production, and thus serves the common good, which is identical with the good of the greatest possible number."[175] The sentiments we are citing from Perkins anticipate Baxter on this point.

It is, then, in this intricate setting that the supremacy of the conscience and the freedom of the will are to be seen. The exalted role they play in Perkins's thought has the most central implications for the agencies of social control, that is, for legal and political institutions.

> ... Now the courts of men and their authorities are under conscience. For God in the heart of every man hath erected a tribunal seat, and in his stead hee hath placed neither saint nor angel, nor any other creature whatsoever, but conscience itselfe, who therefore is the highest Judge that is or can be under God; by whose direction also courts are kept, and lawes are made.[176]

The revolutionary thrust of these words cannot be missed, even though Perkins hastens to add that the "wholesome lawes" of man made by the magistrate and implemented by the courts are certainly binding and may not be disobeyed with impunity. The positive law of the commonwealth is directly commanded and supported by God as "bones and sinews," as "props and pillars" to uphold the commonwealth. The magistrates have a mandate from God rigorously to enforce these laws through corporal punishment.[177] But they are enacted with respect to "things indifferent," to "owtward life," while the laws of God, such as parts of "Gods worship," moral behavior, and also business dealings, transcend human laws.[178]

It can hardly be accidental that Perkins singles out business dealings as a realm for special Christian responsibility over and above prescriptions of the law. "For it is the dutie of every Christian man, to remember in all his bargains and dealings, that his manner of dealing, must not

175. *The Protestant Ethic*, 161.
176. I, 530, 529.
177. I, 530, 529.
178. II, 437; II, 190.

onely be warranted by the lawes of the land, but even by Gods Word also: and this is to be known and taken for a generall rule in all this treatise."[179] Business activity is a special field of Christian freedom. Here is an area that transcends the normal province of human law. These dealings stand directly under God's Word, that is, under the rubric of voluntary agreement. Lacking incentive, men ought, says Perkins, to be coerced by the magistrate to fair business practice. "But it is better," he says, "to do it of themselves, then to be compelled to do it by authoritie: for every vertue and good worke, the more free and voluntarie it is, the more acceptable it is to God, and more commendable before men ..."[180]

According to Perkins, human or positive law is law in its "extremitie." It appears to him as set, unbending, coercive. It needs a varying, unpredictable "mitigation" or "equitie," which can only be supplied by the law of God. "Equitie is Christianitie," he says, which "was before there were any lawes of men."[181] He therefore concludes that positive law "must be according to the rules of Christianitie," that is to say, according to that life in which men regulate themselves on the basis of free, conscience-felt mutuality and not on the basis of hard and fast coercive rules.

The laws of the land, therefore, must be framed according to the equity of God, which is the end of the law. While they have a restricted degree of autonomy, they are not ultimate but decidedly subordinate to the purposes of God:

> Men in making lawes are subject to ignorance and errour: and therefore when they have made a law (as neere as possibly they can) agreeable to the equitie of Gods law, yet can they not assure themselves and others, that they have failed in no point or circumstance. Therefore it is against reason, that humane lawes being subject to defects, faults, errours, and manifold imperfections, should truly bind conscience, as Gods lawes doe, which are the rule of righteousnesse. All governours in the world (by reason that to their old lawes, they are constrained to put restrictions, amplifications, and modifications of all kindes, with new readings and interpretations) upon their daily experience see and acknowledge this to bee true ...[182]

179. *A Treatise of Christian Equity and Moderation,* II, 440. See Bibliographical Essay D, pp. 256 ff.
180. II, 440.
181. II, 441.
182. I, 529-530. For purposes of comparison, this passage is astoundingly at odds

Human laws can bind neither the context of the regenerated conscience, that is, the Church (which is ruled directly by Christ) nor, as we have seen, the conscience itself.[183]

An individual citizen may even disobey the law of the land if *in his judgment* the end of the law (the purpose of God) is advanced by his action! For example, says Perkins, a person is quite justified in opening the gates of the city to allow citizens in, even though the magistrate has declared absolutely that no man shall open them, because he has not hindered the *end of the law,* which is to protect citizens' safety. This example is exceedingly instructive. Who is it, in Perkins's scheme, who grasps the end of the law? Who is it who perceives that toward which all laws drive? It is, of course, the genuine Christian. In effect, he stands above the law with a special capacity to judge it, because he stands in a new order toward which all earthly law points and in which it is fulfilled.[184] In the new elite, he has become a law unto himself.

The agencies of legal and political order are certainly subordinate and subservient to the purposes of God, but they do perform a positive function, as with Calvin and Cartwright. The magistrate, because of his

with official Anglicanism and with the general position of the common lawyers; for example, of Coke. From both their respective points of view (which we shall later try to show have deep similarities), such condescending comments about human law could only be regarded as heresy. With very minor exceptions, for Whitgift, Hooker, and Coke, the laws of the land—the "old lawes," as Perkins calls them—are themselves the rule of righteousness, are themselves God's law. The Calvinist Puritan emphasis upon the distinction between human and divine law, or old and new order, is here sharply opposed to the Anglican identification of human and divine law.

183. It must, however, be pointed out that while Cartwright perhaps more consistently rejects all possibility of ecclesiastical courts, Perkins concedes the need for the "reprehending and punishing of all those sinnes which the civill court reacheth not unto" (III, 293*). Still, this reference would seem simply to emphasize Perkins's lenient view of the existing ecclesiastical structure and his readiness to compromise, particularly because I found no other reference or justification for ecclesiastical courts than this one. One passing reference can hardly be compared to Whitgift's extensive and ardent defense of Church courts. For him they mean something because they fit vitally into his point of view.

184. Porter in *Reformation and Reaction* (Cambridge, 1958), 144, remarks that in the 1580's one of the most popular Puritan themes in the Cambridge pulpits was that "any sentence given by a judge is to be examined of every private man, by the Word of God"; "it deserveth not obedience, if by them it be not found to be thereunto agreeable ... " This is the obvious context for Perkins's thoughts along these lines.

use of coercion, can never accomplish the final end of God; but at the same time he must subject his office to God, and serve him insofar as he can. His essential task is to drive men in the direction of election, toward a conscience and will that are voluntarily obedient to God. "True it is, the will cannot be compelled; and true it is likewise, that the Magistrate doth not compell any to beleeve: for when a man doth beleeve, and from his heart imbrace true religion, he doth it willingly: notwithstanding meanes are to be used to make them willing, that are unwilling, and the meanes is to compell them to come to our assemblies, to heare the word, and to learne the grounds for true religion . . ."[185] Perkins states elsewhere (III, 365*) that punishment is not for revenge, but "to bring . . . to amendment, and to make . . . obedient to the will of God." The will cannot be compelled and yet it must be compelled. This is the same tension we have seen throughout our study between coercion and freedom. Accordingly, idolaters, blasphemers, witches, and the like must be put to death unless they reform, for a will hardened against God is the very definition of disobedience and the source of all disorder.[186] They it is who threaten the foundations of the order of God, and therefore of the society of man. The "moral law"—the first table of the Decalogue—must, for this reason, be rigorously enforced by the authorities.

By the same token he who is idle and slothful, who will not voluntarily assume the duties of a calling, and who is of no use to society, is no better than a thief. "The Magistrate is to punish him for his idlenesse, and compell him to labour."[187] Like the heretic and blasphemer, he threatens the order of God at its heart. A conscience and a will hardened against the call of God are intolerable. They must either be broken or eliminated.

Having examined the theological and ethical attitudes toward order in Calvin and two representative Elizabethan Puritans, we are now in a position to make a preliminary assessment of ascetic Protestantism as Weber understood it. In the first place, we have demonstrated the striking consistency between Calvin and early English Puritanism, albeit in a manner somewhat different from Weber. There are the same tensions, the same tendencies, latent and manifest, in the Puritans that one finds in Calvin. Weber's intuition at this point was certainly far nearer the

185. II, 412.
186. II, 251-252.
187. II, 145.

mark than most of his critics recognize.

In the second place, and far more important, there is a reasonably stable basis in Calvinist Puritanism upon which to legitimate the central characteristics of Weber's rational-capitalist social order.

(1) The Calvinist Puritan pattern of order contains pre-eminently a principle of differentiation between the command and structure of God and the command and structure of the world. This principle entails the *institutional establishment* of an independent sphere of behavior—the Church—whose patterns are shaped in response to the new order. Accordingly, social and political traditions are devalued in the sense that they are robbed of all automatic sanctity; in fact, they are theoretically subordinated to the overriding claims of the coming order. In Cartwright something emerges that was latent in Calvin and Perkins and is of the greatest consequence to seventeenth-century Puritanism: the notion of Church patterns as the model for social and political life or, in other words, as a standard "by which everything must be tested anew." Not only was the whole range of Church activity to be re-examined in the light of this standard, but family, economic, and social patterns as well. This sort of rationalization or resystematization of conduct could take place at all only because a distinct institution arose which was not dominated by the established authorities.

(2) The new order of Christian existence is interwoven with economic modes of expression in Calvin and Perkins, and to a lesser extent in Cartwright. The Calvinist discipline, which requires vigorous, self-initiated action in the context of the Church, quite specifically spills over into vocational conduct. The images of "striving," "progressing," "achieving," so central to the ethical thought of Calvin and Perkins have economic consequences. Furthermore, by differentiating the new order from the old political-legal order, the Calvinist Puritan system, ideally at least, sets economic behavior free from the all-encompassing control of the State. Vocational activity becomes by implication a special realm of Christian freedom. There, as in the Church, the Calvinist acts out in an ultimate way his role as the instrument of God's coming Kingdom.

(3) Christian action is, above all, voluntary, free-willing, consensual action. That is to say, one's "given" nature, status, and mode of conduct are in no sense absolutely binding. On the contrary, though not all bad, "nature" is shot through with disobedience and disruption, in short, with "sin." So conceived, the existing conditions of social life that provide order—political-legal coercion, involuntarily ascribed pat-

terns of status and vocation—are all called into question, are all modified by the claims of the new order. And, most significantly, they are
modified not only in theory, but in fact by the existence of the
Church, which provides a concrete base of operations for a voluntary
mode of conduct. As we have noted time and again, "voluntary labor"
is put in an ultimate context of meaning and purpose that stands apart
from the temporal goals and purposes of the political-legal order.

(4) As we saw, Calvin urges the universal application of God's command "without regard for persons." There is "no obedience to God,
when it is not rendered equally according to his command. . . . Let
there be, therefore, a uniformity." This sentiment was put to work in
Puritan reflection about Church life. In the new order, status is leveled
and preferential treatment done away with. Certainly in theory and to
some degree in fact, this set a standard for the reordering of Puritan
congregations. As a result, the ideals of these congregations often stood
in tension with existing patterns of stratification.

(5) Finally, tasks become "functionalized" in the Calvinist Puritan
system. That is, all tasks are assigned and rather carefully specified on
the basis of their instrumental value in contributing to the common
good. In Cartwright's classic terminology, authorities must not be called
"simply governor or moderator but governor or moderator of that action and for that time and subject to the orders that others be and to be
censured by the company of the brethren as well as others if he be
judged any way faulty." Function, then, is determined with specificity
and flexibility, subject to general, impersonal rules ("the orders that
others be"), as well as to the consensual agreement of the whole
community.

Our point is that these five characteristics of ascetic Protestantism
form an interrelated complex of normative patterns which is anything
but incidental or tangential to the central theological, ecclesiological,
and ethical thought of Calvin and Elizabethan Puritans. Nor is any one
of these characteristics properly described as a later accretion, as so
many critics have mistakenly argued. Rather, these ingredients of the
Calvinist Puritan pattern of order are part and parcel of a general
religious frame of meaning and coherence.

It is true, of course, that these characteristics are heightened to
varying degrees of intensity throughout the Calvinist experience. I have
called attention to this fact at several points and attributed it, in large
measure, to the historical circumstances that Calvinism encountered as
it attempted to work out its way of life. My general hypothesis for

Calvinism (for which this study can give only partial validation) is (a) that the kind of practical accommodation achieved with the political-legal authorities will determine to a great extent how intensely and how novelly the characteristic of ascetic Protestantism will be expressed, and (b) that the kind of political accommodation depends in large measure upon historical circumstance.

I am suggesting that if the political order is successfully subordinated to the theological purposes of Reformed faith, as was the case in Geneva, early New England, and Scotland, the distinctiveness of the new order—including its ingredients of voluntarism, universalism, modification of political control, and so on—will not be so intensely or novelly expressed (though they will not by any means be altogether eliminated either). This point, of course, must be insisted upon. Our whole effort is intended to show that Calvinism is not "merely" the function of a social situation—a phenomenon that looks one way in one situation and quite the opposite in another. It is a coherent phenomenon that moves in determinate directions depending, in part, on the social situation. It is therefore very interesting that, for example, in "theocratic" Massachusetts Bay, where the accommodation between the government and Reformed religion was close, the Puritans were so concerned to maintain a proper differentiation between Church and State. "The relationship between church and state was one of the things that the Puritans knew they must get right. . . . In Massachusetts the Puritans drew a firmer dividing line between the two than existed anywhere in Europe. . . . The church had no authority in the government and the government was particularly careful not to allow the actions of any church to affect civil and political rights."[188]

On the other hand, if such subordination proves impossible, as in pre-Revolutionary England, the differentiation between the new order and the established society will be emphasized and along with this the various ingredients of the new order will be magnified in importance. In other words, to differentiate the social order is to encourage the characteristics of ascetic Protestantism, while to modify the differentiation means correspondingly to modify these characteristics.

It seems clear that Elizabethan and pre-Revolutionary Puritanism was caught precisely between the poles of differentiation and subordination, a perplexity in the Calvinist system that I have entitled the dilemma of earthly power. Following the inclination of their Genevan

188. E. S. Morgan, *Puritan Dilemma* (Boston, 1958), 163.

master, Cartwright and the Presbyterian Puritans leaned heavily on the side of subordinating the political-legal realm to the interests of Reformed religion. Geneva was their model. However, their campaign was not so successful as Calvin's had been. For good historical reasons, they faced a political situation that was far too intractable in the sixteenth century and far too volatile in the seventeenth. Try though they would, they simply could not satisfactorily harness the powers that were. Consequently, as the struggle between the new order and the old intensified, the distinctions and the differences between them became more and more emphasized as well. Under the stress and strain of conflict, the revolutionary characteristics endemic all the time in Calvinist Puritanism came to the fore and were thenceforth irrepressible.

So it was that the Presbyterians, in the very activity of men like Cartwright, sowed the seeds of their own undoing. The middle and especially left-wing Puritans, who made things so difficult for the Presbyterians around the time of the Revolution, only read a more radical lesson in the demands of the new order than had their more conservative brethren. There was no hedging in these groups. The context of Christian freedom was set unmistakably outside the jurisdiction of the sword and, concomitantly, the voluntary, consensual, and universal (or "leveling") dimensions of the true society gained dramatic prominence.

While there was probably much original sense in it, Milton's famous aphorism, "new presbyter is but old priest writ large," has led to intolerable confusions in understanding the pattern of Puritanism. The struggle for social dominance, so obvious in much of English Puritanism, is a very special sort of struggle, embodying a very special sort of concern and objective. The concept of order in Calvinist Puritanism is not in any fundamental sense like that of established Catholicism or Anglicanism, even though they all seek dominance of a kind. On the contrary, the struggle of Puritanism is for a system of social arrangements that ultimately attenuates all forms of involuntary domination—political-legal coercion, conventionally ascribed status and role, and so on. Indeed, in a unique way within the Christian tradition,[189] it very

189. Many radical, sectarian Christian groups of course constitute an exception to this generalization. Often in forms more extreme than Calvinism, they developed democratic, equalitarian polities that stood in self-conscious tension with established social life. Indeed, Calvinism embodies certain "sectarian" tendencies, as mentioned already. But certainly in comparison with mainline, institutionalized Roman Catholicism, both of the Middle Ages and of the Counter Reformation, and with Lutheranism, Zwinglianism, and Angli-

self-consciously lays out an ecclesiological pattern that engenders this inclination. Yet, at the same time, it is not adverse to enlisting the services of political authority in promoting and defending its new order. To be sure, this peculiar conception of Church and world, and of the relations between them, involves the Calvinist in some wondrous ambiguities. Nevertheless, they are ambiguities for which there are good and sufficient reasons in a distinctive pattern of thought. Leave the distinctive pattern of thought out of account and the whole significance of Puritanism is missed.

Some attention to the way official Anglicanism went about solving the problem of order will make it obvious that the new presbyter was anything but old Anglican priest writ large.

canism, Calvinism is distinguished by its emphasis upon designating the Revolutionary new order in ecclesiological form.

5. The Old English Order
and Its Anglican Defenders

It must be observed, that the contempt of human laws implies injury offered to the majesty of God, insofar as he deemed it necessary that man should obey to men; and that every soul should be subjected to the higher powers; to such an extent that whoso despiseth a man endowed with power, despiseth not man, but God ... I say that disobedience is the greatest and most infamous crime which carries with it many other faults, and opens a door to all profligacy. Therefore the prince's first care must be, for the glory of God, in whose place he stands, to maintain obedience.

—Stephen Gardiner, Bishop of Winchester,
Contemptum humanae legis

"The one definite thing which can be said about the Reformation in England is that it was an act of State." "The reformation was to be regarded as a return to the past, a vindication of the rights of the Crown against usurped jurisdiction."[1] In these two sentences Sir Maurice Powicke summarizes the twin pillars of the Anglican establishment and two of the fundamental components of its pattern of order: the supremacy of the State over the Church and the legitimation thereof "by divers sundry old authentic histories and chronicles."[2] It was these pillars, as indispensable to each other as they were to the support of the old English order, that were manfully defended by divines from

1. Sir Maurice Powicke, *The Reformation in England* (New York, 1961), 1, 51 respectively.
2. Act of Parliament, February 1533.

132

Gardiner to Laud against the successive onslaughts of Roman Catholics and Puritans.

With respect to the first, the supremacy of the State, Powicke demonstrates that from as early as the Constitutions of Clarendon in 1164 the control of real property and the rights of advowsons and benefices rested in the hands of the English crown and the barons. There was a strong tradition favoring lay economic control over the Church, even though religious harmony had been maintained between England and Rome. Moreover, the Statutes of Praemunire were interpreted increasingly by the English kings in favor of royal supremacy over private or foreign jurisdiction in legal affairs. The comparative ease and naturalness with which the dissolution of the monasteries (1536-40) was accomplished, as the result of lay control over monastic property, further exemplifies the inherent weakness of Rome's hold on late medieval English institutions. In other words, the transfer of complete power over ecclesiastical matters to Henry VIII in 1532 was, from the English point of view, not nearly so novel as one might think. The inseparability of Church and State had deep roots in the English mentality.

In fact, as Powicke makes clear, the Reformation occurred *not* because of the development of a national religious consciousness and a national Church over against papalism, but rather because Englishmen as a whole were "very insular and English."[3] They were—including the ecclesiastics—conscious of what they understood to be their hallowed institutions and traditions.[4] Englishmen owed allegiance to a society whose self-contained integrity was the product, they thought, of "ancient ordinances, rites, and long approved customes, of our venerable predecessors," as Richard Hooker was to put it. It was a society in which the law and order of God was barely distinguishable from the law and order of man. Indeed, for all intents and purposes, one *was* the other. For this reason, the clergy quite readily subordinated themselves to the control and limitation of the common law.[5] For a variety of reasons, Henry VIII saw fit to appease the common lawyers at the decided expense of the civilians (the study of canon law was forbidden). In a proclamation in 1546 Henry laid it down that nearly all pleadable cases could only be undertaken by a common lawyer trained

3. *Op. cit.*, 14.
4. F. W. Maitland, *The Constitutional History of England* (Cambridge, 1961), 21.
5. Charles Ogilvie, *King's Government and the Common Law* (Oxford, 1958).

in an Inn of Court. The Reformation appeared to be a vindication of
the divine authority of the English past. It returned to the country its
time-honored, religiously sanctioned old order, rid once and for all of
"foreign domination" by the Pope.

The king, of course, was regarded as the central focus of traditional
English institutions. By no means should he rule arbitrarily, nor was he
a law unto himself. Bracton had long since laid it down as an axiom of
English political life that "Rex non debet esse sub homine, sed sub Deo
et lege." He was to rule as the Crown-in-Parliament, and Parliament
was, in turn, a law court.[6] The king must govern in relation to and in
accord with the laws of the land, whose validity had been established
"time out of mind." But a serious conflict between king and law was
scarcely contemplated up through the reign of Elizabeth, nor was a
serious conflict between State and Church. So continuous, so harmonious, so balanced was English society conceived to be that any suggestion of doubt regarding "traditionally" defined authority, status, and
function, any proposal for basic *re*organization or *re*order was by
nature taken as antisocial. As the judicious Hooker had it, "there are
few things known to be good, till such time as they grow to be ancient."

However, if there were deeply rooted historical factors that facilitated and lubricated the emergence of the English Reformation, it was,
nonetheless, a revolution. So long as the Church of England owed its
primary religious allegiance to the Pope, so long as it remained a branch
of the Roman Church, the full development of self-consciously independent institutions was impossible. The Church's doctrines and practices were controlled by the Curia, and the Church had its own legislature and courts, shaped and informed not by common law but by
Roman canon and civil law. English kings could by no means disregard
papal power and influence, as Henry II learned after the murder of
Archbishop Becket. In fact, England had in large degree been unified
and stabilized as a nation by the work of Roman Catholic missionaries,
and its traditions and laws bore the unmistakable stamp of that activity.
The earliest written law, says Maitland, "is already Christian, and so
close is the connection between law and religion, that we may well

6. See, for example, G. L. Haskins, *Growth of English Representative Government* (New York, 1960) or G. H. McIlwain, *High Court of Parliament* (New
Haven, Conn., 1935) for elaborate discussions of the legal nature of Parliament at this time.

believe that it has already undergone a great change."[7] Roman Catholic authority was a force to be reckoned with.

This authority had served as a unifying and stabilizing factor so long that its elimination raised in the profoundest and most far-reaching way the question of social authority. If the break with Rome was the result in part of an indigenous English self-consciousness, it had the effect of intensifying that self-consciousness, of driving Englishmen, when necessary, to manufacture the foundations for social life out of their own traditions. The dramatic need for a new authority set them in search of self-authenticating institutions, urged on them the belief that no segment of their common life, including the Church, needed to rely upon anything but their own sovereign past.

It is, we are claiming, the English Reformation that stimulates and focuses the creation of what has aptly been called "an ideology of historical consistency" or "a fiction of continuity."[8] This same ideology, this same fiction, which plays so significant a role in subsequent conflicts of authority in the sixteenth and seventeenth centuries between crown, Parliament, and law, had a ready ally in the religious pattern of order emerging at the time in the Anglican Church. It is no accident that in raising the question of the foundations of religious authority, the English Reformation raised simultaneously the question of authority in law and politics. Certainly no assessment of the "old English order" can be adequate without an evaluation of the religious thought that buttressed it.

JOHN WHITGIFT (1533?-1604)

In 1576, in response to Elizabeth's command that Puritan preachers be diminished and the "prophesyings" stopped, Archbishop Edmund Grindal stood bravely by his Calvinist convictions and informed the queen in a long letter that she was not the ultimate earthly authority over the Church of God. "Remember Madam," he wrote with no little temerity, "that you are a mortal creature. . . . ; and although you are a mighty Prince, yet remember that He which dwelleth in Heaven is mightier." The letter infuriated Elizabeth, and Grindal was promptly suspended from his duties and confined to his home, where he died in 1583. His death terminated the direct influence of the fraternity of

7. Maitland, op. cit., 2.
8. Professor Harold J. Berman used these expressions in private correspondence.

Marian exiles within the Church of England.[9] An era of undivided
official loyalty to the crown and to the society it symbolized was
dawning. It would last until the decapitation of Laud.

John Whitgift epitomized that era. He was, according to Dawley, his
biographer, the typical English churchman.[10] He assumed the office of
Archbishop of Canterbury in 1583 after a rather active career as Master
of Trinity College, Cambridge, and Regius Professor of Divinity. During
that time he became accustomed to debating with Puritans, developing
a particular dislike for them and all they stood for. It would have been
as impossible for him to utter the words of Grindal above as to espouse
any of the characteristic elements of the Calvinist Puritan system of
thought. By no stretch of the term could he be called a "Calvinist."
Despite the Lambeth Articles in 1595, which were a superficial victory
for certain Calvinist doctrines, "high" Calvinism was decidedly on the
wane within the Anglican Church, and Whitgift wherever possible
suppressed its influence. Dawley remarks that the "anti-Calvinistic
party in Cambridge were invariably the recipients of his patronage and
ecclesiastical favors."[11]

Whitgift was in all respects a dedicated son of the Henrician and
Elizabethan settlements. No sooner had he assumed office than he published six articles to which the clergy were required to give unqualified
subscription. The first underlines his devotion and summarizes his position: it demanded the ecclesiastical supremacy of the crown.[12] Nor was
he inclined to leave subscription up to the individual. He quickly converted the High Commission into a smooth, efficient investigatory
agency whose main weapon was the notorious oath of *ex officio*.[13] Its
success in rooting out Puritans was impressive, and it was mainly
responsible for the enfeeblement of Puritanism toward the end of Elizabeth's reign. Such methods, on the other hand, provoked the gentle
Burghley to describe Whitgift's High Commission as "too much savoring
of the Roman Inquisition." It is doubtful that Whitgift was as tolerant
and forbearing as some have claimed.[14] He was too ardent a defender of
the old order.[15]

9. Neale, *op. cit.,* I, 372-373.
10. P. M. Dawley, *John Whitgift and the English Reformation* (New York, 1954),
     x.
11. *Op. cit.,* 214. See Bibliographical Essay D; pp. 253.
12. See H. S. Betteson, *Documents of the Christian Church* (London, 1944), 330.
13. See fn. 68, pp. 98-99.
14. For instance, Dawley, *op. cit.,* 186, or Rowse, *op. cit.,* 475.
15. For a somewhat more realistic appraisal, see Neale, II, 21-23; Black, *op. cit.,*
     162; Powicke, *op. cit.,* 131.

Whitgift is not a systematic theologian, nor does he make very positive statements about the affirmations of the Anglican Church. His writings are primarily defensive and negative, and his thought is incomplete apart from Hooker, who fills in the gaps and shores up the underpinnings. But the unmistakable outlines of his pattern of order are there: he paves the way for Hooker: "with Whitgift on one side and Hooker on the other [the Church of England's] essential characteristics become established."[16] Summarizing the relationship of Whitgift and Hooker to the Anglican Church, Dawley states:

> Possibly the uniquely distinctive feature of the Reformation experience of the English Church was the achievement of a synthesis between the Christian elements in the Renaissance awakening and the truth that was preserved and transmitted through the mediaeval order. In that invigorating synthesis Anglicanism finds its justification. In its appeal to Scripture the evangelical spirit of John Colet triumphed over the narrow biblicism of Thomas Cartwright. In its appeal to tradition a faithfulness to history, informed and controlled by the claims of reason, opened to Richard Hooker not only the whole range of classical and patristic learning, but the creative insights of the mediaeval schoolmen as well. The line of spiritual continuity is clear—from Colet to Cranmer to Jewel to Hooker, and then to the Caroline divines. . . . But the character of the new tradition was determined by the continuing shape of the old Church out of whose life it came. There is another succession—from Warham to Gardiner to Parker to Whitgift—the line of institutional continuity, the identity of the Church of England with its own past. In the long run it was the continuing life of the ecclesiastical institution that mattered most. . . . It is well to remember that what came to maturity in the massive learning and simplicity of spirit of Richard Hooker is the constant potential of the ecclesiastical institution to which John Whitgift devoted his life."[17]

While I would hold aloof from Dawley's lyrical attitude toward the Church of England, the deep relation he finds between the institutional structure of the Church and Anglican theology must be emphasized; the two are quite inseparable.

Whitgift stands sharply over against the Calvinist Puritan position. Whereas for Calvin, Cartwright, and Perkins, God's command breaks through the structures of worldly order and calls for a new order with a

16. Rowse, *op. cit.*, 388.
17. Dawley, *op. cit.*, 193-194.

new kind of obedience, for Whitgift God's command emerges from the structure of things as it already exists. The command of God can in no way be discontinuous with the way things are, nor can the reverse be true. On the contrary, the divine command issues in the existing order and the existing order gives form and content to the command. In terms of our general analytical scheme, both dimensions of order, command and structure, are identical.

Whitgift allows one qualification: the identification obtains only when the existing order is under the rulership of a "Christian prince." In fact, the Christian prince may defend Christians of another nation from the "imposition of idolatry." Presumably, he may declare war on such a nation, for "his own kingdom is threatened by the idolatry of foreign powers."[18] However, Whitgift offers no criterion by which the character of the prince's religion can be measured or judged to tell when he is properly "Christian" and when not. The prince's ultimate authority rests in the fact that he is *established by tradition.* By the same token, Whitgift offers no criterion by which the citizen can make sure that obedience to the prince is "not against the word of God."[19] It is the magistrate who determines what is and what is not in keeping with the Word of God: he has the last word over affairs ecclesiastical. Therefore for England, Whitgift is quite certain that God's command agrees with the existing order. When the Puritans claimed that they would in fact do nothing against the Word of God, even if it meant disobeying the queen, Whitgift significantly answered that they could not make such a judgment. If they did, they were setting themselves over against the established authority of the queen; he had them coming and going. So far as action is concerned, the Word of God and the word of the queen are identical.

Whether Whitgift took adequate account of the possible conflict between God and ruler is a fair question, but one that he would not have understood. For Whitgift, it is completely unthinkable to contemplate a differentiation between established order and God's order, between earthly political authority and divine sovereignty. *Order is one.* The supremacy of political and legal institutions in his thought does not mean that God's rule is subordinated to them, it simply means that there is no essential difference between them. The framework of obedience (of social action) is, therefore, *conformity to*[20] "the laws estab-

18. Strype, *Life and Acts of John Whitgift,* III, 167-168.
19. *Ibid.,* III, 74.
20. Whereas the Calvinist Puritans may be said to express obedience generally in

lished," "to the practice of all well-ordered states and churches."[21] For this reason, "innovations are [by definition] scandalouse and dangerous."[22] There is absolutely *no* new order.

On the anniversary of Elizabeth's coming to the throne, November 17, 1583, Whitgift preached a sermon on obedience to the powers that be. He closed with these characteristic words:

> Let us provoke one another to love and peace, because the days are evil, and the time short. And so shall our God, the author and giver of all peace, bless us with it in this world, and with an everlasting peace in the world to come.[23]

Undisturbed peace and harmony is the goal of Whitgift's life and the keynote of his theology. The Gospel of Christ is above all a "peaceful" Gospel. Quoting Brentius, he says: "For Christ came not to trouble civil laws, and the ordinary governments of the kingdom of this world, but rather that, these being preserved, his gospel might be preached quietly."[24] The Word of God, embodied in Christ and recorded in the Bible, does not conflict with the existing structure of things; it is, at most, supplementary to it. It deals primarily with salvation and everlasting life, affairs that are "invisible" and "spiritual" and therefore, according to Whitgift, incapable of institutionalization. The Word of God is addressed to the internal conscience and heart of man, to be sure, and those who rightly respond are counted among the elect of God; they constitute the invisible Church which is destined for everlasting life. But their response embodies no new form of social behavior. It amounts, rather, to *obedientiam actionis* to the command of the magistrate as against giving him merely "cap and knee."[25]

> There are two kinds of government in the church, the one invisible, the other visible; the one spiritual, the other external. The invisible and spiritual government of the church is, when God by his Spirit, gifts, and ministry of the word, doth govern it, by ruling in the hearts and consciences of men, and directing them in all things necessary to everlasting life, and it is in the church of the elect only. The visible and external government is that which is executed by

terms of *re*forming, the Anglicans may be said to express it in terms of *con*-forming. This all-important distinction characterizes, of course, the essential conflict between them.

21. Strype, *op. cit.,* III, 127.
22. *Ibid.,* III, 125.
23. *Ibid.,* III, 81.
24. *WW,* I, 155.
25. Strype, *op. cit.,* III, 73.

man, and consisteth of external discipline, and visible ceremonies practised in that church, and over that church, that containeth in it both good and evil, which is usually called the visible church of Christ.[26]

So far as actual social order is concerned, it is the visible Church that is of exclusive importance in Whitgift's scheme. From first to last, it stands under the earthly prince, established by and responsible to his command.[27]

> I am persuaded that the external government of the church under a christian magistrate must be according to the king and form of government used in the commonwealth; else how can you make the prince supreme governor of all states and causes ecclesiastical? Will you so divide the government of the church from the government of the commonwealth, that, the one being a monarchy, the other must be a democraty, or an aristocraty? This were to divide one realm into two, and to spoil the prince of the one half of her jurisdiction and authority. If you will thereof have the queen of England rule as monarch over all her dominions, then must you also give her leave to use one kind and form of government in all and every part of the same, and so to govern the church in ecclesiastical affairs as she doth the commonwealth in civil.[28]

> I perceive no such distinction of the commonwealth and the church that they should be counted, as it were, two several bodies, governed with divers laws and divers magistrates . . . [29]

Furthermore, the Christian prince retains "supreme authority . . . in deciding of matters of religion, even in the chief and principal points."[30] So ultimate is the power and authority of the crown in ecclesiastical matters, that offices and practices in the Church's life are under its direct determination. "The bishops of this realm," he states, "do not . . . nor must not claim to themselves any greater authority than is given them [by statute]. For if it had pleased Her Majesty, with the wisdom of the realm, to have used no bishops at all, we could not have complained justly of any defect in our church."[31]

26. *WW*, I, 183.
27. The queen's authority in the Church, says Whitgift, is "given unto her by the laws of God . . . " (*WW* II, 239).
28. *WW*, II, 263-264; I, 392.
29. *WW* I, 21.
30. *WW*, III, 306.
31. Strype, *op. cit.*, III, 222. Cf. J. W. Allen, *op. cit.*, 177.

It becomes clear why Whitgift regarded as "absurd"[32] the Puritan notion that the basis for Church order was to be found in the Word of God—that is, in a special Word demanding special obedience. In relation to the crown's command, the Word of God is not special. To make such a claim was the central flaw in the Puritan position. Scripture, according to Whitgift, simply does not supply a system of Church order, or any other kind of order. That is not its function. If it has a function with respect to behavior, it refers man to the magistrate as the source of order.

Against Cartwright's suggestion that sacraments are sufficient bonds of unity among Christians without coercion, Whitgift retorts: "such is the crooked and rebellious nature of man" that "therefore hath God also appointed magistrates, and given them authority to make orders and laws to maintain the peace and unity of the church, that those, which of conscience and good disposition will not, by such laws and orders may be constrained at the least to keep the external peace and unity of the church."[33] Indeed, coercion or constraint, the indispensable handmaidens of earthly political-legal authority, are very much in place in the regulation of the Church's life:

> God useth corporal punishments as a means to drive even the elect to the hearing of the word of God, and to honesty of life. He useth it also to bridle the wicked, that by their examples other men might learn to beware, and that they themselves also may be kept in order. . . . Indeed, if these reasons of yours [Cartwright's] were of any force, the magistrate might put up his sword, especially in ecclesiastical matters . . . [34]

If any man be truly converted, even though he is prodded by the sword, his conversion, says Whitgift, is of God.

That the elect ought to be directed in their Church activity by the "corporal punishments" of the magistrate is, despite certain "concessions to necessity," directly opposed to the conclusions of the Calvinist Puritan point of view. The central point to be stressed in this contrast between Calvinist Puritanism and official Anglicanism is that in the former there exists the notion of a sphere of relations that is consciously set over against the civil order, one whose internal order is regulated by a polity *intentionally different from* and, so the Calvinists believed, *supe-*

32. McGinn, *AC*, 378.
33. *WW*, II, 62.
34. *WW*, III, 437.

rior to civil polity. This polity institutionalized, to an extent at least, the democratic methods and ideals inherent in the Calvinist conception of a "community of wills." That Calvinism subordinated the State to the Church did not simply mean that ecclesiastical dictators replaced secular ones. It meant that a new ideal sphere of relations, admittedly only partially implemented, became the model for all social life, and that this new order robbed the civil system of its ultimate legitimation. As we have mentioned, Calvinism was never very precise as to the practical relations between the two orders, and there was in Geneva often a confusing jumble between them. At the same time, the Calvinists were passionately conscious of two orders that could never finally (or eschatologically) get on together. Whitgift's position, on the other hand, gave complete, unambiguous justification to the civil system as the pattern for ecclesiastical organization and regulation. The methods and patterns of the one were automatically the methods and patterns of the other.

This, of course, is the reason why Whitgift supports ecclesiastical courts that are able, when necessary, to employ coercion and punishment. Against Cartwright, he urges that the queen has seen fit to establish such courts, and that is reason enough.[35] She can, in other words, extend the capacity of adjudication and law enforcement to whomever she pleases. "The prince executeth his laws by himself; and he also executeth them by an other, to whom he hath given that authority for the fuller and better execution of them: in this number are the bishops; for the authority they have in such matters they have from the prince; and therefore their executing of it is not to divide stake with the civil magistrate."[36] We have already referred to Whitgift's enthusiastic implementation of this notion in the High Commission. As he makes extremely plain, he will admit no "distinction of ecclesiastical and profane laws."[37]

The profound battle lines between Whitgift and the Puritans become particularly clear and dramatic in the exchanges over Church polity. The exciting level of discourse achieved when the question of consensual participation is raised marks a high point in what is often tedious reading. In reaction to Cartwright's proposals for the election of Church officers, Whitgift flings back at him: "You seek freedom from all laws of princes, and imagine that such perfection may be in men,

35. McGinn, *AC*, 339.
36. *WW*, III, 439.
37. *WW*, I, 389.

that they shall not need to be governed by civil laws, but every man to
be a law unto himself."[38]

> And indeed when are there more unworthy men chosen to offices,
> when is there more strife and contention about elections, when do
> partial and sinister affections more utter themselves, than when an
> election is committed to many?[39]

> The reason of the law is because, it being almost an impossible thing
> for all men in such a body to agree in one, and there being amongst
> men for the most part (as it were) a natural inclination to dissent
> and disagree one from another, there should never any law or order
> be made, if every singular man's consent should of necessity be
> had.[40]

In a sermon he remarks: "Where many rule there is no order; where
there is no order everything is in confusion.[41] Order is never to be produced by many; it is produced by one. It is imposed from without and
may only be conformed to.

The same applies to Cartwright's argument in favor of equality and
consensus among the bishops of the Church. "For if the bishops were
divided among themselves, and at variance, and had no superior, who
should compound the controversies?"[42] For the Puritans, disorder
could never be the end result of free exchange among the elect. For
them, voluntary activity creates true order; for Whitgift, it creates dissension and atomization, with every man tending where he lists. Like
everyone else, a bishop must be "subject to orders and laws."[43]

Whitgift incisively perceives the direction of the Calvinist Puritan
pattern of order. He sees that once the new order of God is allowed to
express or institutionalize itself in the Church, and that order is thereby
split into "old" and "new," the implications are clear: the new order
will (logically) overtake the old. Puritan views of order, "when they
come among the people, will be easily transferred to the state of the
commonweal . . . "[44] In this Whitgift proved to be a wise prophet,
though one horrified by his own premonitions. The devaluation of
political and legal dominon, the emancipation of segments of society

38. *WW*, II, 19.
39. *WW*, I, 130; cf. 372.
40. *WW*, I, 371.
41. Strype, *op. cit.*, III, 72.
42. *WW*, II, 211.
43. *WW*, II, 366.
44. *WW*, II, 239.

from its overruling control, were prospects that aroused in him the
stiffest possible resistance.

In the debate with Cartwright over holy days, Whitgift's opposition
to all forms of voluntary activity shifts, significantly, from the ecclesiological sphere to the economic. He boldly defends governmental control
of economic activity: the magistrate has "power and authority over his
subjects in all external matters, and bodily affairs; *wherefore he may
call them from bodily labour or compel them unto it, as shall be
thought to him most convenient* . . . "[45]

> In things indifferent private men's wills are subject to such as have
> authority over them; therefore they ought to consent to their deter-
> mination in such matters, except they will shew themselves to be
> wilful; which is a great fault, and deserveth much punishment. . . . In
> bodily business he is to be governed by magistrates and laws. This
> doctrine of yours is very licentious, and tendeth too much to carnal
> and corporal liberty . . . [46]

The Puritans also declared that the magistrate has power and authority
over "external matters," "bodily affairs," and "things indifferent." But
the question is what constitutes these things. According to the Puritan
scheme, voluntary and consensual action in the Church and business are
most certainly *not* things indifferent.[47] For Whitgift, on the other
hand, *all action as such* is external and indifferent and therefore subject
to royal regulation. For him it is invisible inwardness that constitutes
the realm of true religion.

In the analysis of Whitgift we must not, however, overlook the other
all-important dimension in his thought. If he emphasized that all earthly action, including religious, was determined by the magistrate, he was
no Hobbesian or Austinian in his conception of governmental decree.
The king does not rule arbitrarily; he is no law unto himself. He rules in
keeping with the tradition and the established laws of the land. In a
circular way, his command emerges from the way things have always
been and harmonizes the present with the past. The command of the
prince always recapitulates the old order (the "traditional" structure of
social relationships).

As a result, the organization of the Church, with its hierarchy of
rank and authority, does not depend only upon the command of the

45. *WW*, II, 570, my italics.
46. *WW* II, 570-571.
47. That is, of course, why the debate between the two sides takes place at just
these two crucial points.

prince but also upon the strength of tradition.[48] It is for this reason that Whitgift undertakes to debate with Cartwright on questions of Church history. He was naturally not content simply to argue that the Church came into being by the fiat of the prince. He constantly cites the fathers in justification of the Church of England.[49] "Stand not so much in your own conceit," he counsels Cartwright, "this order [of the Church of England] is most ancient in the church, it is confirmed by the best and noblest councils, it is allowed by the best-learned fathers, it hath the pattern from the practice of the apostles ... it is the most meet for this state and kingdom ... "[50] Rank and authority are the basis for proper order within the Church as within the commonwealth. To allow these distinctions in the latter and not in the former would be to contradict both the "very ancient histories" and the "great learned fathers" and interests of "reverence, duty, and obedience."[51] It may even be a contradiction of the natural structure of reality—"the celestial spirits are not equal: the stars are not equal: the apostles themselves were not equal ... "[52]—though Whitgift does not often enter the realm of natural and metaphysical speculation.

As McGinn points out,[53] Whitgift does, however, affirm that in the "spiritual realm" all men are equal. The point of difference between Whitgift and the Puritans was that for the Puritans the new transformation had begun to take place, had begun to be institutionalized, while for Whitgift spiritual equality remained an other-worldly phenomenon. In this connection, Dawley's comments about the reception of the "Renaissance awakening" in the Church of England[54] are very pertinent. It is quite clear that there is more at work in Whitgift and Hooker than Renaissance humanism. Yet, with Renaissance writers as well as with Whitgift and Hooker, man's ethical obligation is to conform to what is; the "golden age" and the "spiritual realm" are transcendentalized, or rendered incapable of institutionalization. This similarity would

48. It is well to remember that the distinction drawn here between "the command of the prince" and "the strength of tradition" would have made no sense to Whitgift. *One is the other*; Whitgift is forever interchanging these dual authorities at random.

49. *WW*, I, 214-215, 252-257.

50. *WW*, II, 262.

51. *WW*, II, 190.

52. *WW*, I, 158. "Equality of persons engendreth strife; which is the cause of all evil" (Strype, *op. cit.*, III, 72).

53. *AC*, 293.

54. See above, p. 136.

indicate that the assimilation of Renaissance thought was profound.

It boils down to what we have seen all along: "the province (if it be christened) is the church."[55] The order of one is the order of the other. On the basis of the traditional "laws of God and man" (which are, at bottom, the same), Whitgift is quite confident that "we have the true doctrine of the word of God, and the right administration of the sacraments; and therefore to make contention in this church, and to disturb the quietness and peace, cannot be but mere schismatical, I will say no more."[56]

Furthermore, the prince himself is a "lawful magistrate" and a "lawful authority." In response to Cartwright's charge that a monarchy tends toward being excessive and tyrannical, Whitgift replies that the king of England governs "with equity and reason . . . *according to the laws that are prescribed for him to rule by.*[57] "There is neither prince nor prelate in this land that ruleth 'after their pleasure and lust,' but according to those laws and others that are appointed by the common consent of the whole realm in parliament, and by such laws of this monarchy as never hitherto any good subject hath misliked . . ."[58] Whitgift here wholeheartedly reaffirms the words of Bracton: the king rules *sub Deo et lege.* The laws of the realm completely correspond to and express the sense of order that exists in every "good" individual subject. That concurrence is made plain in the "common consent of the whole realm in parliament." The king's right to command does not contradict but confirms and fulfills the traditonal order of proper social relationships, as any good subject has always seen.

Emphatically, the subjects do *not* possess within themselves the ultimate sovereignty to determine the law. On the contrary, the multitudes of citizens, "be they never so godly," are naturally prone to error and confusion, if left to themselves.[59] To live in harmony, they must conform to the "fundamental law"[60] that stands above and outside and behind them. Good subjects are those who express their liking of the law in Parliament. Their consent simply reaffirms the supremacy of the already existing law. Of course, it would never have occurred to Whit-

---

55. *WW,* II, 204.
56. *WW,* II, 243.
57. *WW,* II, 239.
58. *WW,* II, 240; my italics.
59. *WW,* II, 241.
60. Whitgift himself does not use this term, but it is appropriate to describe what he had in mind, as will become clear in Chapter 6.

gift that a real conflict between parliamentary confirmation and the law of the land were possible, so continuous, unified, and circular did the process of law and consent appear to him. But when he is pressed by Cartwright on this issue,[61] he holds firm to the objectivity of the law. You cannot create law on the basis of men's consent, for men have a "natural inclination" to dissent and disagree. Just because of that inclination, overreigning law is necessary, and *"it is therefore sufficient . . . if the laws, statutes, and customes of the place be observed."* [62] Obedience to the laws of England and to the crown which they authorize is the sum and substance of "true obedience" for Whitgift.[63]

The lines of dispute between Whitgift the Anglican and Cartwright the Puritan could hardly be sharper or more profound. It begins to be clear how utterly superficial are all views to the contrary. We see emerging before us a theological-ethical conflict between a *pattern of conformation* and a *pattern of reformation,* corresponding respectively to the types of "old order" and " new order" which we have been using throughout this essay. For Whitgift, that which is new is scandalous—it contradicts the essence of God. For Calvin, Cartwright, and Perkins, God has, is, and will make everything new.

RICHARD HOOKER (1554-1600)

Hooker's *Laws of Ecclesiastical Polity* is in every respect an extension and a refinement of the pattern of conformation. His lengthy fifth book he dedicates, significantly, to Whitgift. On the first page of that dedication he writes what may be taken as the core of his monumental *Laws*: "For surely I cannot find any great cause of just complaint, that good laws have so much been wanting unto us, as we to them."

Richard Hooker lived a brief and rather uneventful life. As Christopher Morris remarks in his introduction to the *Laws*,[64] Hooker might rather be the name of a book than a man. His appointment as master of the Temple in 1584 marked the beginning of the one exciting phase of his life, for it was as chaplain of the Inns of Court that he encountered head on two of the bodies of opinion which shaped the writing of his *Laws of Ecclesiastical Polity*: Puritanism and English law.

Puritanism he met in the person of Walter Travers, who was then

---

61. See *WW*, I, 370-377.
62. *WW*, I, 371; my italics.
63. *WW*, III, 586-596.
64. *Op. cit.*, I, v.

lecturing at the Temple Church. Hooker and Travers engaged in count-
less heated theological exchanges which became increasingly painful to
the new master. His report of these exchanges is worth quoting because
it reveals both his gentle character and his way of looking at Puritanism.

> I take no joy in striving, I have not been nuzzled or trained up in it. I
> would to Christ they which have at this present enforced me here-
> unto, had so ruled their hands in any reasonable time, that I might
> never have been constrained to strike so much as in mine own de-
> fence. . . . But sith there can come nothing of contention but the
> mutual waste of the parties contending, till a common enemy dance
> in the ashes of them both, I do wish heartily that the . . . strict
> commandment of Christ unto his that they should not be divided at
> all, may at length . . . prevail . . . to the burying and quite forgetting
> of strife, together with the causes which have either bred it or
> brought it up; that things of small moment never disjoin them,
> whom one God, one Lord, one Faith, one Spirit, one Baptism, bands
> of great force, have linked . . . finally that no strife may ever be
> heard of again but this, who shall hate strife most, who shall pursue
> peace and unity with swiftest paces.[65]

Like so much of his writing, these words echo the sentiment of Whitgift,[66] who early recognized in this quiet, retiring individual a formid-
able champion of the Establishment. For good reason, Whitgift made it
possible for Hooker to produce his great work[67] in semi-seclusion.

65. John Keble (ed.), *Works,* (3 vols., London, 1888) III, 596 (referred to henceforth as III are all references to Books VI-VIII).

66. As J. W. Allen, *op. cit.,* 185, remarks, "He owed far more to Whitgift than to
any writer of the Continent. Hooker, in fact, was intensely and typically English."

67. As is well known, Books I-V are reliable. I am using the Everyman edition of
these (designated I for Books I-IV and II for Book V). I use Keble (III) for the
other three, which were regrettably mutilated when only in manuscript form,
and were finally published posthumously. Of VIII (upon which we draw most
amòng these rather unreliàble books) Allen says: VIII "may at least be taken
as substantially representing Hooker's thought and contains much that one
feels almost sure was written by him as it stands" (*op. cit.,* 184). It has been
suggested that the title *Of the Laws of Ecclesiastical Polity* is somewhat
misleading to the modern reader and might better have been changed to
include *and Civil Polity;* but such a suggestion would have baffled Hooker. He
might have called it one or the other, not both. The whole point of the work
is that at bottom both polities are the same, subject to exactly the same logic.
To separate them into two independent spheres of order, as the Roman Catholics and the Puritans wished to do, represented to Hooker a specter of social
disruption. All action was, in the final analysis, embraced within the unity and
competence of the law of the land.

Living and working within the walls of the Temple for seven years, Hooker was naturally in constant contact with the legal thinking of his day. It is said, for instance, that Edward Coke was frequently among his congregation at the Temple church. The way in which he was to attack Puritanism was clearly influenced by these legal contacts. As Marshall says, "he was thinking in terms of the legal problems of the time, and . . . he was helping to crystallize the fluid legal thought of his age."[68]

In the name of the old law and order of England, Hooker sought brilliantly to demolish the Puritans once and for all. He argued—not without reason—that "the world by receiving [their message] should be clean turned upside down."[69] Stability and coherence were England's only if she guarded the hallowed legal traditions bequeathed to her by the past. And, for Hooker, the lawyers were the yeomen of that bulwark. It remained to be seen, however, whether even the masterful Hooker could entirely quarantine the lawyers from the new order heralded by those "patrons of liberty."

No better or more eloquent summary of Hooker's position exists than the famous concluding paragraph of Book I of the *Laws*:

> Of Law there can be no less acknowledged, than that her seat is the bosom of God, her voice the harmony of the world: all things in heaven and earth do her homage, the very least as feeling her care, and the greatest as not exempted from her power: both Angels and men and creatures of what condition soever, though each in different sort and manner, yet all with uniform consent, admiring her as the mother of their peace and joy.[70]

"The being of God is a kind of law to his working;"[71] the seat of the law, as he says, "is the bosom of God." "God doth determine of nothing that it shall come to pass, otherwise than only in such manner as the law of his own wisdom hath set down within itself."[72] God can will nothing irrational, unjust, or bad; he acts according to a higher universal rational law from which, as the above summary makes clear, it is difficult to distinguish him: "They err therefore who think that of the will of God to do this or that there is no reason besides his will."[73] As with

68. Marshall, *op. cit.*, 49.
69. I, 132.
70. I, 232.
71. I, 150.
72. II, 513.
73. I, 153.

Whitgift, and in diametrical opposition to the Calvinist Puritan pattern of order, the identification of command and structure in Hooker's thought could hardly be plainer. There is no possible separation between the two dimensions of order, that separation by which Calvin, as we have seen, differentiated between the old (fallen) structure of things and the new command of God, between the old command of political-legal power and authority and the new pattern of social relationships. For Hooker, order is one: command emerges from structure and refers back to it again. God's "eternal decree is that we term an eternal law":[74] "the counsel of God, and the law of God . . . being one."[75]

A law, according to Hooker, is "any kind of rule or canon, whereby actions are framed."[76] All action, even that of God, is prescribed and regulated by law. Eternal law controls the universal order and being of things, and is immutable. Hooker concedes that all things do not conform to eternal law "as they ought to," but even actions that are "repugnant unto the law which God hath imposed upon his creatures" do at least work according to the "first law eternal," as distinguished from the "second law eternal."[77] This distinction is, significantly, not elaborated, and it is plain that the similarities between the two laws are more important than the differences, for Hooker remarks: "it is not hard to conceive how they *both* take place in all things."

The eternal law is the law of being, by which everything that is unavoidably moves toward goodness or perfection.[78] Evil or disobedience is failure to conform to ever higher perfection; it is being satisfied with the lesser good. Nevertheless, "because there is not in the world any thing whereby another may not some way be made the perfecter . . . *all things that are, are good.*[79] All action is good, for no action is possible that does not to a greater or lesser extent conform to the eternal law of being. In some cases, it is simply not good enough.

The essential goodness of existing patterns of action, their assumed harmony with the order of things, is a crucial point in Hooker's pattern

---

74. I, 150.

75. I, 154.

76. *Ibid.;* cf. I, 150.

77. I, 155.

78. I, 164. The Thomistic background of this thought is clear, and in many ways Hooker retains Thomistic categories, as is well known. But, as we shall see below, there are important respects in which Hooker's pattern of order is hardly very meaningfully referred to as "Thomistic."

79. I, 164; my italics.

of order. As we shall see more fully later, all human beings, by virtue of what they are, act with respect to "an infallible knowledge . . . whereby both general principles for directing of human actions are comprehended, and conclusions derived from them; upon which conclusions groweth in particularity the choice of good and evil in *the daily affairs of this life.*"[80] In sharp distinction both to the Roman Catholics, particularly Thomas, and to the Puritans, Hooker holds that all the activity of this life is and ought to be carried out in relation to the given structure of things by which "constant Law and Order is kept."[81] Consequently, he gives the Thomistic category of "divine law" or "supernatural law" an important twist. Like Thomas, Hooker argues that the law of being impels man toward that infinite felicity and bliss found in the contemplation of God, who is the "end of all our desires . . . the highest degree of all our perfection."[82] Also, as for Thomas, a Fall occurred which deprived man of the attainment of the felicity he sought and subjected him to "sundry imperfections" or, quite precisely, to disobedience to the eternal law of perfection. Christ by his obedience and death makes it possible for man once again to enter that "sea of Goodness whereof whoso tasteth shall thirst no more." By grace and mercy to the elect, he opens the door to life everlasting in the Kingdom of God.

But for Hooker, unlike Thomas, this gracious gift remains absolutely invisible and transcendent. It in no way alters or adds to the patterns of action of this life. For Thomas, God revealed a divine law in Christ and in Scripture, which implied certain patterns of perfection or "theological virtues" that in turn become to some degree at least embodied and expressed in the Church's life. For Hooker, on the other hand, such revealed law remains fully supernatural. It is incapable of institutionalization. The supernatural virtues—faith, hope, and charity—are described by Hooker exclusively in mystical-contemplative language.[83] Scripture, which is the means whereby divine law is revealed, has to do solely with salvation and everlasting life, internal affairs of the heart and conscience which are known only to God.[84] It would be intolerable to think, says Hooker, that the redemption of Christ had anything to do with "outward actions"; rather, it is "by the secret inward influence of his grace"

80. I, 280; my italics.
81. I, 152.
82. I, 203.
83. I, 209.
84. II, 342-343.

that he gives "spiritual life and the strength of ghostly motions . . . "[85]
Divine law is in a strict sense "ghostly" law. It is concerned with a
distinctly transcendental world.[86]

Hooker's view of the Incarnation of Christ itself makes this plain. As
deity, Christ possesses "gifts and virtues" that "make him really and
habitually a man more excellent than we are, they take not from him
the nature and substance that we have, they cause not his soul nor body
to be of another kind than ours is. Supernatural endowments are an
advancement, they are no extinguishment of that nature whereto they
are given."[87] Christ adds his virtues to human nature by "inherent
copulation," but in no way alters that nature by which the outward
affairs of daily life are determined.

Those who are members of his mystical Body, the invisible Church,
and who enjoy his inward gifts and virtues are, even as the gifts they
enjoy, absolutely invisible to "our sense."[88] Only God can know who
his elect are; man has not the slightest inkling, for he has no criterion
by which to judge. Certainly, there is no kind of "gospel-like be-
haviour," such as the Puritans were alleging, which could serve as a
criterion.[89] The invisible Church has nothing to do with action in this
life. Furthermore, even the visible Church, which exists to testify to the
true religion brought by Jesus Christ, is distinguished not by its action
but by its *outward profession*: "Church is a word which art hath devised thereby to sever and distinguish that society of men which pro-
fesseth the true religion from the rest which profess it not."[90] "For,"
Hooker continues, "neither doth God thus bind us to dive into men's
consciences, nor can their fraud and deceit (against God) hurt any man
but themselves."[91]

> Touching parts of eminency and perfection, parts likewise of imper-
> fection and defect in the Church of God, they are infinite, *their
> degrees and differences no way possible to be drawn unto any cer-
> tain account.*[92]

85. III, 374.
86. "Transcendental" seems the best word to describe Hooker's attitude toward
the activity of Christ. It is not related to the world of action, that is, to the
world of "our sense."
87. II, 221.
88. I, 284.
89. II, 337-343.
90. II, 337; cf. III, 329.
91. II, 342-343.
92. II, 338; my italics.

Central to the Calvinist Puritan system, as we have seen, was the notion that precisely man's (inner) fraud and deceit "destroyed" the whole fabric of social order. Disobedience to God and social disorder are logical correlates. Just so, new obedience in the Body of Christ leads to a new social order. That is what the Church is; the realm of conscience and heart is unavoidably a social or external affair. To this, Hooker's position is strikingly opposed. For him the conscience is an internal-individualistic matter, with consequences only for everlasting life, something that is added (literally) over and above this life.

Therefore, whereas for the Puritans the distinction between the world and the Church, the old order and the new, was of paramount importance for action, to Hooker "the Church and the commonwealth are . . . one society, which society being termed a commonwealth as it liveth under whatsoever form of secular law and regiment, a church as it hath the spiritual law of Christ."[93] The visible Church, with which Hooker is most concerned in arguing against the Puritans, is "in nature and definition" distinguished from the commonwealth, but not, as the Puritans claimed, in "substance."[94] In a most significant passage, Hooker argues:

> We hold, that seeing there is not any man of the Church of England but the same man is also a member of the commonwealth; nor any man a member of the commonwealth which is not also of the Church of England; therefore as in a figure triangular the base doth differ from the sides thereof, and yet one and the selfsame line is both a base and also a side; a side simply, a base if it chance to be the bottom and underlie the rest; so, albeit properties and actions of one kind do cause the name of a commonwealth, qualities and functions of another sort the name of a Church to be given unto a multitude, yet one and the selfsame multitude may in such sort be both, and is so with us, that no person appertaining to the one can be denied to be also of the other.[95]

In relation to those patterns of regulation and relationship that characterize a given society or social order, the categories of Church and commonwealth are completely interchangeable—they are matters of definition, of "accident."[96] As Hooker's figure of the triangle makes clear, there is no real discontinuity between them.

93. III, 334.
94. III, 328-329.
95. III, 330; cf. I, 288-289.
96. III, 336.

Because Jesus Christ has opened the gates of eternal life and has founded the true religion, the Church is required to profess that fact and to provide the means whereby his redemption can, in a partial and inchoate way, be enjoyed. But these means of profession and mediation are primarily *sacramental*: "That saving grace which Christ originally is or hath for the general good of his whole Church, by sacraments he severally deriveth into every member thereof."[97] They are oriented toward a supplementary, or transcendental world, over and above "the daily affairs of this life." Ordinarily, the sacraments themselves are "signs effectual: they are the instruments of God, whereby to bestow grace; howbeit grace not proceeding from the visible sign, but from his invisible power."[98] They themselves are "moral instruments," making the hearts of men "like to a rich soil, fertile with all kinds of *heavenly virtues* . . . "[99] It is no accident that Hooker discusses the Incarnation and the redemption of Christ within the wider framework of the sacraments.[100] *The whole character of Christ's transcendental action for man is represented or signified in the action of the sacraments that is transcendental to earthly or social action.*

For this reason, Hooker consistently resists the Puritan emphasis that sacraments are fundamentally symbols or seals of a new form of social life among the participants in accord with God's Word. For the Puritans the new community was necessarily implied in communion with God, whereas for Hooker the sacraments are "instruments of grace unto every particular man,"[101] and therefore communion, for example, may be administered privately.[102] Hooker strictly defends the Anglican use of the singular "thou" in the admonition of the Lord's Supper against the plural form urged by the Puritans. This is no idle difference. Hooker is defending an internal-individualistic understanding of the meaning of Christ's redemptive act in opposition to the Puritans' directly social interpretation.

The kind of distinction Hooker makes between faith and action, between the realms of the transcendental and the worldly, is especially sharp when we come to the dispute with the Puritans over the action of the Church. He takes Whitgift's line of argument as completely obvious:

97. II, 236.
98. II, 506.
99. II, 505; my italics.
100. See II, 200-236.
101. II, 334-336.
102. II, 334-336.

that matters of faith, and in general matters necessary unto Salvation, are of a different nature from ceremonies, order, and the kind of church government; and that the one is necessary to be expressly contained in the word of God, or else manifestly collected out of the same, the other not so; that it is necessary not to receive the one, unless there be something in Scripture for them; the other free, if nothing against them may thence be alleged: Touching matters belonging unto the church of Christ this we conceive, that they are not of one suit. Some things it doth suffice that we know and believe; some things not only to be known but done, because they concern the action of men . . . *I somewhat marvel that they especially should think it absurd to oppose Church-government, a plain matter of action, unto matters of faith . . .* [103]

With this, we move into the center of the debate between the two camps, the area of the so-called things indifferent. For Hooker we are virtually in an other-worldly realm when we discuss matters of salvation and faith. So far as the Church is concerned, these are the ultimates, not outward actions in this life. For the Puritans we are squarely in the middle of inner-worldly action when we discuss salvation and faith. That is a big difference. The issue is not, as some have claimed, that the Puritans were simply overzealous and wooden interpreters of the Bible while Hooker was broad, tolerant, and reasonable in his outlook. Rather, it is a clash between two fundamentally opposed interpretations of life. The cleavage emerges with still greater clarity in Hooker's elaboration of the bases for social action.

In the "indifferent" affairs of daily life, the Church must follow its own discretion, based on the rulings of the magistrates and the laws of the realm, its own venerable custom, and the light of reason. Whatever combination of these various authorities finally determines the Church's patterns of behavior will be a matter of indifference[104] since they all possess a common unity in the one harmonious, all-pervasive fundamental law that is the ground of earthly action. Nor does this political, traditional, rational-natural law in any way conflict with the divine law: "That which doth guide and direct [man's] reason is first the general law of nature; which law of nature and the moral law of Scripture are in substance of law all one."[105] Order is one, and all its

---

103. I, 299-300; my italics.
104. Action is "indifferent" because there is no real alternative to the way patterns of action are; no real "difference" can be conceived from what is. For the Puritans, the difference between old and new was important in the extreme.
105. I, 326.

manifestations are, by definition, completely consistent with the eternal law and with each other.[106]

Above all, the objective structure of order that guides the Church's life, as well as the life of every human group, is given, whether by "necessity," "tradition," or "reason." The Church is subordinate to the prince "even in matters of Christian religion"[107] because supreme secular government is necessary in human affairs, and that which is given for the necessary or "natural" ordering of behavior must be of God.

> We are to note, that because whatsoever hath necessary being, the Son of God doth cause it to be, and those things without which the world cannot well continue, have necessary being in the world: a thing of so great use as government amongst men, and human dominion in government, cannot choose but be originally from him, and have reference also of subordination unto him. Touching that authority which civil magistrates have in ecclesiastical affairs, it being from God by Christ, as all other good things are, cannot choose but be held as a thing received at his hands; and because such power as is of necessary use for the ordering of religion, wherein the essence and very being of the Church consisteth, can no otherwise flow from him, than according to that special care which he hath to guide and govern his own people . . . [108]

By analogy, the same political and social structure ought to prevail in the Church:

> Sith therefore by the fathers and first founders of this commonweal it hath upon great experience and forecast been judged most for the good of all sorts, that as the whole body politic wherein we live should be for strength's sake a threefold cable, consisting of the king as a supreme head over all, of peers and nobles under him, and of the people under them; so likewise, that in this conjunction of states, the second wreath of that cable should, for important respects, con-

106. The distinction between natural law and rational law no longer exists in Hooker. Mosse, in *Struggle for Sovereignty*, 21, is certainly right in claiming that the law of reason is of central importance in Hooker, and that there is a crucial difference between medieval conceptions of natural law (for example, in Fortescue) and Hooker's point of view. This will become clearer as we proceed.

107. III, 342.

108. III, 380; cf. I, 188. As the focus of political order, it is the king (not elections by the people) who regulates political life (III, 422-425; 225). Elections are "unnecessary" since authority is given in the person of the king.

sist as well of lords spiritual as temporal: nobility and prelacy being by this mean twined together, how can it possibly be avoided, but that the tearing away of one must needs exceedingly weaken the other, and by consequent impair greatly the good of all?[109]

Hooker stands squarely on the side of the established social structure and justifies all the attendant inequalities within the Church against the "common conceit of the vulgar sort."[110]

Again it may justly be feared whether our English nobility, when the matter came in trial would contentedly suffer themselves to be always at the call, and to stand to the sentence of a number of mean persons assisted with the presence of their poor teacher, a man (as sometimes it happeneth) though better able to speak, yet little or no whit apter to judge than the rest . . . [111]

For we are not to dream . . . of any platform which bringeth equally high and low unto parish churches, nor of any constraint to maintain at their own charge men sufficient for that purpose; the one so repugnant to the majesty and greatness of English nobility, the other so improbable and unlikely to take effect that they which mention either or both seem not indeed to have conceived what either is.[112]

That religion is worthy, says Hooker,

which no way seeketh to make [the nobility] vulgar, no way diminisheth their dignity and greatness, but to do them good doth them honour also, and by such extraordinary favors teacheth them to be in the Church of God *the same which the Church of God esteemeth them, more worth than thousands.*[113]

Furthermore, in passages of the utmost importance for our purposes, Hooker emphasizes the necessity for secular and ecclesiastical control (at bottom, the same control) over economic activity:

Those things which the law of God leaveth arbitrary and at liberty are all subject unto the positive laws of men, which laws for the common benefit abridge particular men's liberty in such things as far as the rules of equity will suffer. This we must either maintain, or else overturn the world and make every man his own commander. Seeing then that labour and rest upon any one day of the six

109. II, 272.
110. I, 405.
111. I, 128.
112. II, 475.
113. II, 475; my italics.

> throughout the year are granted free by the Law of God, how exempt we them from the force and power of ecclesiastical law, except we deprive the world of power to make any ordinance or law at all?[114]

Like the social patterns, that system of economic life which already exists, defined as it is by the established authorities, is to be taken as fully in force. The "solemn proclamation" by these "patrons of liberty . . . that all such laws and commandments are void" and that "everyman is left to the freedom of his own mind in such things,"

> . . . shaketh universally the fabric of government, tendeth to anarchy and mere confusion, dissolveth families, dissipateth colleges, corporations, armies, overthroweth kingdomes, churches, and whatsoever is now through the providence of God by authority and power upheld.[115]

The regulation of the Church's daily actions by the necessary or given authorities is consistently complemented by an appeal to traditon. The polity and organization of the Anglican Church have been clearly "received and held for the space of many ages"[116] which is in itself "cause why we should be slow and unwilling to change, without very urgent necessity, the ancient ordinances, rites, and long approved customs, of our venerable predecessors. The love of things ancient doth argue stayedness, but levity and want of experience maketh apt unto innovations."[117] And it is no accident that what tradition obviously teaches for Church polity harmonizes so readily with the needs of secular politics. There is no law, accordingly to Hooker, which has not at some time or another instituted the "conjunction of power ecclesiastical and civil."[118] The inherent unity between tradition and necessity is very deep.

Finally, the Church has recourse to the third means for determining social action, namely, the law of reason. Hooker defines it as "that which men by discourse of natural Reason have rightly found out themselves to be all for ever bound unto in their actions."[119] As we would expect, he adds that the law of reason is "investigable by Reason, without the help of Revelation supernatural and divine."[120] At

114. II, 363.
115. II, 362, 363.
116. I, 425.
117. II, 29.
118. III, 250.
119. I, 182.
120. *Ibid.* As Munz, in his *Place of Hooker in the History of Thought* (London,

bottom, it is a law that is *universally binding,* one that manifests itself wherever reason is rightly employed with regard to social behavior. The Church relies upon it just as every other human group does: *the law of reason is the law of action.* Indeed, Hooker comes close to saying that the law of reason adjudges not only suitable action, but even the "things of God" which are recorded in Scripture. "Those things also we believe, knowing by reason that the Scripture is the word of God."[121] "For whatsoever we believe concerning salvation by Christ, although the Scripture be therein the ground of our belief; yet the authority of man is, if we mark it, the key which openeth the door of entrance into the knowledge of Scripture."[122] To be sure, as we have seen, God's revelation in Christ adds something above reason and nature, but there is no conflict or discontinuity between them. In the light of Hooker's pattern of order, how could it be otherwise? All is one grand unity and harmony. Reason will naturally concur with and confirm the demands of tradition and social necessity in Church and commonwealth.

The point to be emphasized is the one that has been emerging throughout our discussion of Hooker's view of the Church and of the place of religion. So far as action is concerned, the Church introduces absolutely nothing new. If there is a "politic use of religion," as Hooker calls it, it is simply an inward encouragement to obey "the laws whereunto [one] should be subject."[123] That is, churchly or religious behavior is completely defined by sources quite outside its own province. At most, religion urges a conformity to what is.[124]

We must, therefore, analyze these sources in the specifically political and legal context in which Hooker sets them. Basic to the entire system is the assertion that there exist "principles universally agreed upon" for the determination of human action. These are manifestations of what he interchangeably calls the law of reason or the law of nature.[125] "We

1952), correctly remarks: "The fine and important distinction which he [Hooker] derived from Thomas between reason and faith as two supplementary methods of finding natural law and divine law respectively, was wiped out" (62). Hooker, says Munz, established the "complete autonomy" of reason over the whole of life.

121. I, 319. Munz, *op. cit.,* 59, continues: "there was indeed nothing . . . that would prevent him from looking upon the dictates of reason as the direct commands of God, and thus from excluding . . . God from the government of society."

122. I, 267.

123. II, 19.

124. II, 12.

125. I, 179.

see . . . how nature itself teacheth laws and statutes to live by." [126]
Part of the requirements of this law of nature is that "we are naturally
induced to seek communion and fellowship with others,"[127] and,
further, that "societies could not be without Government, nor Government without a distinct kind of Law ... " In other words, natural or
rational law demands and leads to "laws politic" for the maintaining of
peace and public good. These latter human laws are made by and for
particular societies, and they are only good and binding insofar as they
express the universal approbation—both historically and contempo-
rarily—of a given society.[128]

> The most certain token of evident goodness [of laws] is, if the
> general persuasion of all men do so account it. . . . The general and
> perpetual voice of men is as the sentence of God himself. For that
> which all men have at all times learned, Nature herself must needs
> have taught; and God being the author of Nature, her voice is but his
> instrument. By her from him we receive whatsoever in such sort we
> learn.[129]

Vox populi is *vox dei* (as well as the voice of reason and nature), but
in a very special sense. It must be the "general *and perpetual* voice" of
men; it must be "that which all men have *at all times* learned."
Hooker's pattern of order works both ways; if the universal approbation
of laws by a society is necessary to make them acceptable, the existence
of a society living by laws to which it is accustomed signifies in itself
the legitimacy and acceptability (or the approbation) of those laws.
Antiquity betokens approbation. If the laws have been approved, that is
a good reason why they ought to be approved.

> And to be commanded we do consent, when that society whereof
> we are part hath at any time before consented, without revoking the
> same after by the like universal agreement. Wherefore as any man's
> dead past is good as long as he himself continueth; so the act of a
> public society of men done five hundred years sithence standeth as
> theirs who presently are of the same societies, because corporations
> are immortal; we were then alive in our predecessors, and they in
> their successors do still live.[130]

126. I, 187.
127. I, 188.
128. I, 194.
129. I, 175-176.
130. I, 195.

The remark quoted earlier takes on new importance in Hooker's system: "There are few things known to be good, till such time as they grow to be ancient."[131] Of course, Hooker concedes that certain human laws will, from time to time, need to be altered and even abrogated in order to adjust the past to the present.[132] But notice the logic at work: if the law has not been changed, there must be an important enough reason to make the reformation of laws a precarious enterprise at best:

> But true withal it is, that alteration, though it be from worse to better, hath in it inconveniences, and those weighty. . . . When we abrogate a law as being ill made, the whole cause for which it was made still remaining, *do we not herein revoke our very own deed, and upbraid ourselves with folly,* yea, all that were makers of it with oversight and with error? Further, if it be a law which the custom and continual practice of many ages or years hath confirmed in the minds of men, to alter it must needs be troublesome and scandalous. . . . What have we to induce men unto the willing obedience and observation of laws, but the weight of so many men's judgment as have with deliberate advice assented therunto; the weight of that long experience, which the world hath had thereof with consent and good liking? So that to change any such law must needs with the common sort impair and weaken the force of those grounds, whereby all laws are made effectual.[133]

So unitary, so consistent and self-contained is Hooker's view of society that in this passage he fails to distinguish between ancestors and contemporaries. *Past consent is present consent.* When old laws are altered, present decisions are changed, and vice versa. Such is the astonishing consistence with which Hooker argues his case. Laws that are "apparently good" are "things copied out of the very tables of that high everlasting law."[134] "Not as if men did behold that book and accordingly frame their laws; but because it worketh in them, because it discovereth and (as it were) readeth itself to the world by them, when the laws which they make are righteous." Good, established laws then, as now, order society because the all-pervasive law of reason is one: commands emerge from the given structure and relate that structure to the present.

131. II, 29.
132. For example, see I, 422.
133. I, 422; my italics.
134. I, 225.

Just because of this unity of order, contemporary universal consent represented in Parliament will not differ in any fundamental way from the law of reason. "The parliament of England," says Hooker, "is that whereupon the very essence of all government within this kingdom doth depend; it is even the body of the whole realm; it consisteth of the king, and of all that within the land are subject to him: for they all are there present, either in person or by such as they voluntarily have derived their very personal right unto."[135] Its assent is no less binding than if we ourselves "had done it in person."[136] The universal law of reason, which is historically expressed in this "perpetual voice of men" (voice of tradition), is also expressed in the "general voice of men" in Parliament. They are, of course, the same voice, both reflecting the same rational or natural law. As Hooker says, the laws that Parliament makes "do take originally their essence for the power of the whole realm and the church of England, than which nothing can be more consonant unto the law of nature and the will of our Lord Jesus Christ."[137] Any suggestion of conflict between the traditional law and Parliament would make no sense to Hooker. For that reason, we find neither a doctrine of the "supremacy of Parliament" nor a doctrine of "judicial review." He would have fully endorsed the remark of St. Germain in *Doctor and Student*: "It cannot be thought that a Statute that is made by Authority of the whole Realm, as well of the King and of the Lords Spiritual and Temporal, as of all the Commons, will recite a thing against the Truth." But his agreement would have stemmed from the basic assumption that tradition and consent are inseparable. For him, as for most legal and political thinkers of the Elizabethan era, Parliament was understood not as a legislature primarily, but as a law court—or as the "High Court of Parliament."[138] Haskins's description of the mentality of the times would, therefore, apply equally to Hooker: "the early idea that statutes were affirmations of existing law persisted long after that theory no longer described the facts."[139] Such

135. III, 408, 409.
136. I, 194.
137. III, 412.
138. III, 407.
139. Haskins, *Representative Government*, 100. There will be occasion to expand the importance of this assumed unity between law and consent when we come to Edward Coke. I am not at all convinced by Mosse's intimation that Hooker's view in general strengthened the hand of a "supreme Parliament" in the "struggle for sovereignty." It could just as easily be argued that he strengthened the lawyers' hand, in favor of "judicial review" (as McIlwain ar-

was the unity of order: the action of the present is the action of the past.

Furthermore, as no basic distinction within the perpetual voice (between past and present) can be tolerated, neither can any basic distinction or opposition within the general voice. Every individual or individual social unit inside the wider society must conform to the "public power" and the public law. "Because except our own private and but probable resolutions be by the law of public determinations overruled, we take away all possibility of sociable life in the world."[140] Such conformity is demanded by the nature of social existence. Therefore, according to Hooker, the Puritans introduce a fully divisive and antisocial element. The notion that the Church is a new community made up of free-willing members can lead to nothing but anarchy; it would throw into turmoil the whole neatly ordered legal universe. "By following the law of private reason, where the law of public should take place, they breed disturbance."[141] God is a God of peace and quietness, of unity and harmony, not of contention and dispute.[142] His order is duly established in perpetuity and in universality. Anyone who contends against that order, or in any way disputes with it is, by definition, a public enemy and one by whose message "the world . . . should be clean turned upside down."[143]

Lastly, the place Hooker assigns to the king with respect to the rule of law and social consent illustrates his unitary logic. Hooker is convinced that, aside from those nations ruled by conquest, every independent society originally "hath full dominion over itself" to determine the kind of polity it will live by.[144] There is no necessity that a monarchy should be designated, but once it has been appointed by the consensual decision of the society as, for example, in England, the law and God establish and recognize that monarchy.[145] "Every supreme governor doth personally take . . . his power by way of gift, bestowed of their own free accord upon him at the time of his entrance into his

gues). However, neither should be argued. Hooker's pattern of order made no room for such distinctions—indeed, when the tension between executive, legislature, and judiciary emerged, it placed a great strain on the monistic or unitary interpretation of social life at work here.

140. I, 228.
141. I, 229.
142. I, 122.
143. I, 132.
144. III, 343-344.
145. III, 346.

said place of sovereign government."[146] The king is therefore always in "subordination" and "subjection" to the good of the whole body of which he is the designated head. "Original influence of power from the body into the king, is cause of the king's dependency in power upon the body."[147]

What is important here is the term "original." The king was decided upon, he was established by common consent, and, as a result, the system of political authority which he represents is to be maintained. In direct opposition to the democratic tendencies of the *Vindiciae contra tyrannos,* Hooker argues that rulers ought by no means to be successively elected. Views that advocate such a thing are "strange, untrue, and unnatural . . . set abroad by seedsmen of rebellion. . . . Unless we will openly proclaim defiance unto all law, equity, and reason, we must . . . acknowledge, that in kingdome hereditary birth giveth right unto sovereign dominion."[148] In something as decisive as the political organization of a society, that which was the product of the general voice of the nation remains in force for the present and the future.

Because Hooker consistently assumes the identity of established consent with the universal law, his notion of the dependency of the crown upon the whole realm is another way of saying "Lex facit regem."[149] Not what the general voice does decide (the emphasis of the *Vindiciae*), but what it *has* decided for political authority, is binding and lawful. This view of Hooker's is significant not, as is usually emphasized, simply because it advocates the sovereignty of the law above the king but also, and in a more positive sense, because it establishes a king on the basis of past consent and, on the same basis, defines his power as completely in accord with the law of reason. Hooker can agree that "the prince is always presumed to do that with reason, which is not against reason being done, although no reason of his deed be expressed."[150] The past common consent by which the king was established is, it now appears, identical with the "rule of law." His subordination to the whole realm *is* at the same time his subordination to law. In other words, it is not the willing act of consent on the part of the realm that in itself determined a monarchical society. It was, rather, that that ancient "con-

146. III, 349.
147. *Ibid.*
148. *Ibid.*
149. III, 353.
150. III, 251.

tract" reflected or conformed to the pre-established rational or natural order of law.

One might, with equal validity, say that the pre-established rational or natural order of law reflects or conforms to the ancient "contract." The point of the argument is this very interchangeability: the law is determined by the realm, and the realm was determined by the law. Here, in essence, is the crucial identification of the command and structural dimensions of order. The way in which the realm is (has been) structured is the way in which the realm ought to be structured. "Realm" is, of course, simply another word for "structure" in our sense. Thus, to put the pattern of Hooker's thought in still another way, the very formation of the realm becomes the "right" prescription for its formation; circularly, however the realm set itself up, it ought to have set itself up. There is the simple assumption that what was contracted is "rational" or "natural" and what is "rational" or "natural" was contracted. Just as what ought to be for succeeding generations emerges from what already is, so what ought to have been for the "ancient realm" proceeded from the actual manner of its constitution. One is reminded here of Hooker's statement, "All things that are, are good."[151]

It may be suggested that this emphasis upon the consensual determinations of the ancient realm reveals an element of voluntarism. It is noticeable, however, that the act of deciding, of electing in itself—as the primary and continuing basis for true order—receives no attention from Hooker. What is central is what has been decided, and what is therefore given. As we have seen, Hooker rejects elections as the basis for political order. Social status and function are ascribed, the patterns of social life predetermined. In other words, there is nothing for the citizen to choose between. In the Calvinist Puritan system, a man was chosen out of an old order *into* a new one, so that he himself might choose obedience. To a certain extent, therefore, a new context of social action was institutionalized and set against the ascribed and prescribed patterns of the "given" society. In such a system consensual determination in the new order is important. In Hooker there is no such alternative context. The citizen simply conforms to what is; he does not reform anything. That is why all subsequent generations of the same society do not redetermine social order by their act of consenting, but rather declare, reaffirm, and reassert that which has been established.

151. I, 164.

The old order prescribed not solely the action of the king but also the patterns of action of the entire society. Above all, conformity and obedience to what is are needed, rather than the determination of something new. We repeat the lines from Hooker's dedication: "For surely I cannot find any great cause of just complaint, that good laws have so much been wanting unto us, as we to them."

Hooker's conception of a legal universe is, finally, emphasized by the importance he gives to the lawyers of the realm.

> Easier a great deal it is for men by law to be taught what they ought to do, than instructed how to judge as they should do of law: the one being a thing which belongeth generally unto all, the other such as none but the wiser and more judicious sort can perform. Yea, the wisest are always touching this point the readiest to acknowledge, that soundly to judge of a law is the weightiest thing which any man can take upon him."[152]

". . . Are we not," Hooker continues, "bold to rely and build upon the judgment of such as are famous for their skill in the laws of this land. In matter of state the weight many times of one man's authority is thought reason sufficient, even to sway over whole nations."[153]

"Laws are matters of principal consequence," and therefore the "wiser and more judicious" legal experts who are trained and educated in the law occupy a central (if not *the* central) position in the determination of action. Certainly it is no accident that in a system where law, including "every national or municipal law," is uppermost, that lawyers should be so highly regarded. Nor is it an accident that the pattern of order at work in this entire system should find such striking elaboration in the thought of the leading lawyer of the time, Sir Edward Coke.

152. I, 225.
153. I, 265; cf. I, 193; II, 36.

PART III.

LAW AND THE TENSIONS OF SOCIETY

6. Sir Edward Coke and the Conflict in Law and Order

Perhaps we should hardly believe if we were told for the first time that in the reign of James I a man who was the contemporary of Shakespeare and Bacon, a very able man too and a learned, who left his mark deep in English history, said, not by way of paradox but in sober ernest, said repeatedly and advisedly, that a certain thoroughly medieval book written in decadent colonial French was "the most perfect and absolute work that ever was written in any human science." Yet this was what Sir Edward Coke said of a small treatise written by Sir Thomas Littleton, who, though he did not die until 1481, was assuredly no child of the Renaissance. . . .

A lecturer worthy of that theme would—I am sure of it—be able to convince you that there is some human interest, and especially an interest for English-speaking mankind, in a question which Coke's words suggest: —How was it and why was it, that in an age when old creeds of many kinds were crumbling, and all knowledge was being transfigured, in an age which had revolted against its predecessor, and was conscious of the revolt, one body of doctrine and a body which concerns us all remained so intact that Coke could formulate this prodigious sentence and challenge the whole world to contradict it?

—F. W. Maitland, English Law and the Renaissance

Coke could cook law books.
But he couldn't cook by the books.
He could only cook books for Cokes.

—An anonymous contemporary rhyme

167

It has been demonstrated that the theological positions of Elizabethan Puritans and Anglicans were polarized into a deep-seated conflict over the problem of order. The question we must now pursue is whether the various characteristics of this conflict, as analyzed, show any significant similarity to the evidences of institutional change apparent in England during and after the late sixteenth century.

As noted in Chapter 2, Max Weber contended that the institutional developments during this period could be fruitfully examined by means of his typology of order. He believed that the manifest social tensions and disruptions could be understood as the collision of a patrimonial-traditional pattern with a legal-rational one. Moreover, he suggested that the Anglican-Puritan differences could be correspondingly analyzed. Weber had, in other words, a specific theory about what was happening to the institutions of English society as well as how religious-ethical systems of belief were related to the process.

Several things may be affirmed about the applicability of Weber's typology to English society of the period. In the first place, there is clear evidence of what Weber called "patrimonial traditionalism." Here was a society in which the allocation of social and political power—from the crown on down—was arranged in a hierarchical manner, pretty much along traditional lines. In Hexter's words, Tudor policy "was erected on old and deep-set ideas," and its object "was to maintain and support good order as good order had been understood for several centuries—social peace and harmony in a status-based society."[1] Moreover, there was firm sentiment in favor of a wide range of royal discretion in political, social, and economic affairs. Both Tudors and Stuarts fostered a system of economic nationalism or autarky,[2] a system characterized by widespread and arbitrary government intervention in the service of national interest and preservation. As Weber correctly pointed out, intervention often took the form of dispensing monopolies and special economic privileges on the basis of political considerations. This practice created a group of "Court-bound capitalists," whose mode of economic activity was in many ways diametrically opposed to Weber's rational capitalistic entrepreneur. Here, in short, was a society politically oriented in the extreme, a society that combined a deep allegiance to the past with a growing devotion to royal discretion and control.

1. Hexter, *Reappraisals in History*, 106, 108.
2. Lawrence Stone, "State Control in 16th Century England," *Economic History Review*, XVII (1947).

In the second place, it appears plausible that while the direction of institutional change from patrimonialism to legal-rationality is not so immediately apparent, there is firm evidence of at least the crude beginnings of a rational capitalistic society in late sixteenth- and early seventeenth-century England. According to the judgments of Nef and Lipson, there is, in this period, the emergence of an early industrial revolution. In their view, the important alterations in English industrial activity were accompanied by the decline of direct government regulation and intervention in economic affairs. Their interpretation is buttressed to a large degree by Eli Heckscher's classic study, *Mercantilism.* [3] The effects of this development were, willy-nilly, to begin to liberate the market from political domination, and to make some room for independent economic behavior. As Nef put it, "the early English industrial revolution . . . weakened the doctrine that human affairs are best ordered when controlled from above. It strengthened another more novel doctrine, that progress depends upon allowing free scope for individual initiative," or for "private enterprise," as he called it in another connection. This sort of situation made possible, incipiently at least, the "free market" and "voluntary labor," two characteristics of the greatest significance in Weber's understanding of modern rational capitalism.

In the third place, Weber's emphasis upon the role of the legal system in the development of a rational capitalist pattern was relevant to the English scene, if in a very complex way. Weber argued that modern capitalism "has need, not only of the technical means of production, but of a calculable legal system . . . in terms of formal rules." [4] It was his opinion that such a type of law is necessary to extrude all kinds of arbitrary "irrational limitations" that can be imposed upon the market. In certain important respects, the common law courts during the early seventeenth century "proved a great hindrance to the further development of industrial regulation." [5] That is, profound and telling antagonism existed among the common lawyers toward the interventionist, monopolistic policy of the crown, as well as toward some other forms of restriction and control. Up to a point, the courts were responsible for standardizing many of the procedures on corporate ac-

---

3. See Bibliographical Essay B, esp. pp. 240 ff., for a summary of relevant materials on economic history.
4. Weber, *The Protestant Ethic,* 25.
5. Eli Heckscher, *Mercantilism,* trans. M. Shapiro (2 vols., London, 1935), I, 285.

tivity and for developing a few formal criteria by which to discriminate between admissible and inadmissible kinds of market restriction.

Hŏwever, having affirmed these three points about the application of Weber's typology, we must still proceed with utmost caution. The precise relation between the legal system and the broader tensions in English society is very involved. Weber himself, out of his own historical work, recognized the vast complexities. According to Max Rheinstein,

> there are many indications that Weber at some stage of his work regarded it as possible that a peculiar relationship existed between the logically formal rationality of legal thought and the purposively rational kind of economic conduct and thus with modern capitalism. But Weber's own work shows that this connection is not one of absolute correlation. In England where capitalism developed earliest, logically formal rationality never came to dominate legal thought to the same degree to which it was developed in Germany, where capitalism had a much later start. Only in so far is a relationship shown to exist as modern capitalism requires a legal system which guarantees predictability and, in particular, freedom from arbitrary, unpredictable government interference. This guarantee is to a high degree given where legal thought is of the kind of logically formal rationality, but, as the example of England proves, it can also exist where that type of legal thought has not become dominant.[6]

In other words, were the historical process of the late sixteenth and early seventeenth centuries to have conformed precisely to Weber's ideal categories, we should be able to observe the smooth emergence of a formally rational legal system alongside a consistently rational capitalistic society. But as Weber himself perceived, this was by no means the case. Not only was it not true that the common law system became suddenly and pervasively formal and rational in Weber's sense; it was not true that the entire society became subjected to the norms and values of rational capitalism. Indeed, as we shall see, both legal system and society were only very ambiguously related to the rise of legal-rationality. Traditional forms of order continued to exert impressive influence upon English institutions until well beyond the period under discussion.

The most striking thing about the battle between the courts and the crown, in which the king's expanding sphere of patrimonial discretion

---

6. Max Rheinstein, Introduction to *Max Weber on Law in Economy and Society*, lviii.

was severely constricted, was that the lawyers substantiated their position, not by appeals to formal rationality, but on the contrary by appeals to the ancient realm. In this respect, the procedure of the lawyers is a manifestation of what Weber meant by traditional authority. In words that summarize with amazing precision the *modus operandi* of the English common lawyers, Weber produces the following example of opposition to patrimonialism on purely traditional grounds:

> When resistance occurs, it is directed against the person of the chief [or king] or of a member of his staff. The accusation is that he has failed to observe the traditional limits of his authority. Opposition is not directed against the system as such. It is impossible in the pure type of traditional authority for law or administrative rules to be deliberately created by legislation. What is actually new is thus claimed to have always been in force but only recently to have become known through the wisdom of the promulgator. The only documents which can play a part in the orientation of legal administration are the documents of tradition, namely, precedents.[7]

The prerogative power of the crown, both in broad government and social matters and in the more limited sphere of economic interference, was accordingly curtailed by the courts. The argument over and again, as we shall see, was exactly that Elizabeth, in her later years, and then James and Charles "failed to observe the traditional limits of [their] authority." They did not really conform to the old order of English society.

In certain ways, therefore, the legal system did not help to move English institutions in a clearly legal-rational direction. Rather, it served to glorify dependence upon ancient custom and convention, and in part to perpetuate a set of economic and social controls that from Weber's point of view were certainly "irrational" or "inefficient." To permit selected aspects of "immemorial custom" to dictate patterns of work, production, and exchange hardly fostered the kind of open market or voluntary labor that Weber adjudged essential for modern capitalistic society.

We are confronted, then, with a very complicated institutional picture, though one that is illumined, in a general way, by Weber's typology of order. There is clear evidence of tension between the more or less pure traditionalism of the lawyers and the patrimonial traditionalism of the Tudors and Stuarts. At the same time, the "pure tradi-

7. Weber, *Theory*, 342.

tionalism" of the lawyers turns out to be a strange, incoherent mixture of ancient precedent and original innovation. As Weber said, "what is actually new is . . . claimed to have always been in force." Although the lawyers assumed they were but reinstituting the old order, as a matter of fact they helped to introduce a set of economic and social patterns that undermined the ancient realm and paved the way for rational capitalism. Thus, in the name of the old order a distinctly new order was being prepared, an order that conformed as little with the designs of the Tudors and Stuarts as with the prescriptions of medieval England.

In short, we are confronted with an involved conflict in law and order. As we examine this in greater detail, the main contention will be that to see the English society of the late sixteenth and early seventeenth centuries in terms of the kind of conflict already sketched helps us to understand better not only the institutional struggles of the period, but also the relation of these struggles to the theological antagonism that has occupied our attention to this point.

On the surface, an "unpleasant, grasping, arrogant" and very much down-to-earth lawyer would appear to have little in common with the pious and lofty concerns of a Calvin, a Perkins, or a Hooker. Edward Coke's thoughts from first to last moved exclusively in the grooves of the common law, of seisin, tenure, rent, debt, and the whole range of minutiae that made up the legal system of his day. He had little time for theological or philosophical speculation.[8] Yet, with all that, he was an Elizabethan, and the tensions and strains of Elizabethan society disturbed his soul profoundly. In fact, from the point of view of social analysis, Coke is an intriguing character just because he embodied intricately and subtly the conflicts of his time, conflicts, as we have seen, that had an unavoidable theological dimension to them. His unconscious attempt both to do justice to these contradictions and to harmonize them in categories most remarkably congruent with the

8. Personally, Coke remained an Anglican his whole life, although he states that he regarded the Presbyterian Puritans as the "least dangerous" of the other religious groups in England. Several of Perkins's pamphlets were dedicated to Coke, indicating that the great jurist was not without esteem in Calvinist circles. Coke, and other common lawyers, sided with the Puritans on *ex officio* cases, though not too much can be made of that, it seems to me. This was one critical point where the lawyers could resist the "encroachments" of the prerogative courts (see Marchant, *op. cit.*).

theological motifs we have described, calls to mind Professor Hill's dictum: "it is time," he says, "to take legal history out of the hands of lawyers, as religious history has been taken away from the theologians, and to relate them both to social development."[9]

In the present study, Coke is a natural focus for attention. He was by no means simply a lawyer among lawyers, nor was he but another important jurist in the history of English law. "When I consider all the judges England has had," says S. E. Thorne, "I can think of no other whose absence would have had more serious effects on the course of English law than that of Edward Coke."[10] What is more, anyone familiar with the development of common law will know that the name Coke bespoke a well-nigh absolute authority for future generations. For good or ill, he struck the path along which the law would move for some time to come. Even in his own day, his name was beginning to be considered synonymous with the law.

Coke was born in 1552. He was educated at Trinity College, Cambridge, during the time when Cambridge was becoming a center of Puritan-Anglican collisions, and then at the Inner Temple. Ever since their probable origin in the fourteenth century, the Inns of Court had fostered a narrow, one-track legal education, an education that was greatly responsible at once for the insulation of the common law from the reception of the Roman system,[11] and for producing a profession which Erasmus called "the most unlearned sort of learned men."[12] The Honourable Society of the Inner Temple could well be proud of Edward Coke, for as a single-minded lawyer with a "fanatical reverence for the common law," he had no equal.[13] In 1578 he was called to the Bar, and very soon thereafter he had a thriving legal practice, thriving enough to attract Lord Burghley's coveted attention. He subsequently became Solicitor-General in 1592, Attorney-General in 1594, Chief Justice of the Common Pleas in 1606 and, finally, in 1613, Chief Justice of the King's Bench. He retained this exalted position until his

9. In "Recent Interpretations of the Civil War," *Puritanism and Revolution*, 28.
10. S. E. Thorne, *Sir Edward Coke, 1552-1952* (London, 1957), 17-18.
11. This is a favorite point of F. W. Maitland's. See, for example, his "English Law and the Renaissance," in H. M. Cam (ed.), *Historical Essays* (Cambridge, 1957), 145.
12. Ogilvie, *King's Government and the Common Law*, 14.
13. W. S. Holdsworth, "Elizabethan Age in English Legal History and Its Results" *Iowa Law Review*, XII, 4 (1927), 321-335 (at 332).

abrupt dismissal in 1616 at the hands of his arch antagonist, King James I.

His dismissal, however, by no means ended his career. In 1621 he carried on his defense of the common law in Parliament, and his activity on behalf of the Petition of Right of 1628 has rightly won him the reputation of defender of the "liberty of the subject."[14] It was through the influence of that activity, claims Holdsworth, that the supremacy of Parliament and the common law became basic principles of the English constitution, and the "old standing alliance" between them was cemented. Certainly, through his identity with the triumphant parliamentarians, Coke established his own significance in the history of English law.[15]

Perhaps it is because Coke's writing is so unsystematic and his interests, at least ostensibly, so fastened on the specificities of the law, that there has been surprisingly little attempt to pull his central frame of thought together and relate it to the intellectual currents of the time. Coke is usually treated as he wrote: disjointedly. Occasionally, brief references are made to the importance of the affinity between, say, Coke and Hooker, but they are either undeveloped,[16] or simply misunderstand the nature of the affinity.[17] There would appear to be an especially urgent need, in the case of so significant a figure as Coke, to wrench the law out of the hands of lawyers and set it in its wider context.

14. As Professor Hill has rightly pointed out in his brilliant essay "The Norman Yoke," *op. cit.*, "liberty of the subject" meant for Coke the rights of the propertied. In this, of course, Coke was at one with the Independents. It may be questioned, however, whether Coke was always quite so static at this point as Hill implies. Despite Coke's conscious inclinations, the *logic* of much of what he says pushes beyond an exclusive identification of rights and property.

15. Holdsworth, "Elizabethan Age," 331, 334.

16. For example, J. S. Marshall, "Richard Hooker and the Origins of American Constitutionalism," 55-58.

17. For example, Sabine, *op. cit.*, 383-386. Sabine incorrectly sees Coke as holding a notion of supremacy of common law above Parliament and, in this, as agreeing generally with Hooker. Precisely because of the complexity and subtlety of the pattern of order which Coke shares with Hooker, he has no very consistent or clear-cut attitude toward Parliament, as we shall see. Eusden's analysis (*op. cit.*, 142-144) of the relation between Hooker and the lawyers is still more curious. Without offering any documentation, he finds the lawyers opposed to Hooker because his monarchist tendencies were too strong. I find no grounds for such an argument. In many passages Coke, like other lawyers, speaks like a strong monarchist. In others he calls the king's authority radically into question. In the ambiguity of his position, he stands squarely with Hooker.

The conclusions we have reached about Hooker's thought suggest a useful means for crystallizing Coke's "theory of law," and for relating it to the divergent patterns of order considered so far. When these conclusions are the starting point, it becomes clear how accurate are Professor Sabine's words: Coke's "fundamental beliefs were extraordinarily like those of . . . Hooker."[18]

COKE'S LEGAL THEORY

For Coke, as for Hooker, the law, or more precisely, the common law, is the expression of the ultimate order of things: its total self-consistence and inner harmony bespeak the coherence and continuity of social life itself. The commands or imperative of the law arise harmoniously from the past and refer back to it again in a system of perfect, circular unity. In words that call Hooker to mind in a striking way, Coke describes this perfect unity and the divine source from which it comes:

> To the end that all the Judges and Justices in all the several parts of the realm, might, as it were, with one mouth in all men's cases pronounce *one and the same sentence;* whose learned works are extant, and digested into nine volumes, wherein if you observe *the unity and consent of so many several judges and courts in so many successions of ages, and the coherence and concordance of such infinite, several, and diverse cases,* (one, as it were with sweet consent and amity, proving and approving another) it may be questioned whether the matter be worthy of greater admiration or commendation: for as in nature we see the infinite distinction of things proceed from some unity, as many flowers from one root, many rivers from one fountain, many arteries in the body of man from one heart . . . so without question *Lex orta cum [ex] mente divina, and this admirable unity and consent in such diversity of things, proceeds only from God the fountain and founder of all good laws and constitutions.*[19]

According to Coke, "this admirable unity and consent" are founded in what he variously calls "fundamental law," "rule of common law," or "common right," that is, in the sum and substance of the ancient law of the realm.

18. Sabine, *op. cit.*, 384-385.
19. *The Reports of Sir Edward Coke in English in Thirteen Parts Compleat* . . . (7 vols., London, 1738), referred to henceforth as *CR;* Preface to 2, ii-iii; my italics. Cf. 3 *CR*, Preface.

For any fundamental point of the ancient common law and custome of the realm, it is a maxim in policy, and a trial by experience, that the alteration of any of them is most dangerous; for that which hath been refined and perfected by all the wisest men in former succession of ages, and proved and approved by continual experience to be good and profitable for the commonwealth, cannot without great hazard and danger be altered or changed.[20]

It is now almost credible to foresee, when any maxime, or fundamentall law of this realm is altered . . . what dangerouse inconveniences doe follow . . . [21]

Above all else, the common law is a given or predetermined legal system. What was decided in the past sets the mold for the law of today. *What was adjudged reasonable determines what is reasonable.*[22] It is in antiquity that the key to the present lies, and it is those who have immersed themselves in the old order who are reliable "judges" of contemporary action.

Any basic inconsistencies or contradictions in the law are ruled out by Coke:

If you observe any diversities of opinions amongst the professors of the laws, content you (as it behooveth) to be learned in your profession, and you shall find, that it is *hominis vitium non professionis.* And to say the truth, the greatest questions arise not upon any of the rules of the Common Law but sometimes upon conveyances and instruments made by men unlearned. . . . In all my time, I have not known two questions made of the right of discents, of escheats by the common law, etc. so certain and sure the rules thereof be: happy were arts, if their professors would contend, and have a conscience to be learned in them, and if none but the learned would take upon them to give judgment of them.[23]

The objective system is trustworthy, as is the judge who is properly trained or who knows the law. Interpretation is a matter only for "the wiser and more judicious sort," as Hooker said. They alone possess the

20. 4 *CR*, Preface, v, vi.
21. IV *Institutes*, 41; Coke's *Institutes of the Lawes of England* are divided into four parts: I (*Coke on Littleton*), London, 1629; II, London, 1662; III and IV, London, 1648.
22. It will be observed how close this is to Hooker's thought.
23. 2 *CR*, Preface, x-xiii.

requisite "judicial" or "legal reason," because they alone have been carefully brought up in the traditions and customs established "time out of mind" before the occupations of the "Romans, Saxons, Danes, or Normans."[24] He alone is reasonable who is thoroughly grounded in the "absolute perfection of reason." The unlearned and therefore irrational man is responsible for incoherences:

> And by reasoning and debating of grave learned men the darkness of ignorance is expelled, and by the light of legall Reason the Right is discerned, and thereupon Judgment given according to Law, which is the perfection of Reason. This is of Littleton here called *legitima ratio*, whereunto no man can attaine but by long studie, often conference, long experience, and continuall observation.
>
> Certaine it is, That in matters of difficultie the more seriously they are debated and argued, the more truly they are resolved, and *thereby new inventions justly avoyded.*[25]

Indeed, the law for Coke is more than the measure of reason. It is, it would seem, the measure and source of virtue as well. As Gooch has reminded us, "the law of England was a religion" and the lawyers of the realm the high priests.[26] The law had a numinous quality, just as it had for Hooker. Coke's advice to young lawyers sounds decidedly sacerdotal:

> For thy comfort and encouragement, cast thine eye upon the sages of the law, that have been before thee, and never shalt thou find any that hath excelled in the knowledge of these laws, but hath sucked from the breast of that divine knowledge, honesty, gravity, and integrity, and by the goodness of God hath obtained a greater blessing and ornament than any other profession to their family and posterity ... for it is an undoubted truth, that the "just shall flourish like the palm-tree; and spread abroad as the cedars of Libanus."
>
> Their example and thy profession do require thy imitation: for hitherto I never saw any man of a loose and lawless life, attain to any sound and perfect knowledge of the said laws: and on the other side, I never saw any man of excellent judgment in these laws, but was withall (being taught by such a master) honest, faithful, and virtuous.[27]

24. 2 *CR*, Preface, x-xiii.
25. *Coke on Littleton* (I *Institutes*), 232b; my italics.
26. G. P. Gooch, *Political Thought from Bacon to Halifax* (London, 1914), 62-63.
27. 2 *CR*, Preface, x-xiii.

It is the orientation to the old order that makes the use of precedent so important in Coke's system. His nine volumes of systematic case reports, which attempt to verify court decisions by reference to an infinite number of previous (often antiquated) decisions and statutes, are certainly the leading example of the introduction of "precedent" as a central and binding legal category.[28] Although the term was used in England as early as the twelfth century in the *Dialogus de Scaccario,* it meant there the application of rational principles to the law.[29] At no time until the sixteenth century did precedent signify that a previous judicial decision should have authority for deciding a later case. During the thirteenth century, Bracton assiduously recorded digests of hundreds of cases but, as Professor Berman points out, these cases "were not binding authorities but merely illustrations of legal principles."[30] From the fourteenth to the sixteenth centuries, the famous Yearbooks were compiled, but still the legal arguments they set down "were not treated as authorities in any sense." Thus, the breakthrough of precedent as a leading principle of legal interpretation, due in large measure to the influence of Coke, betokens in the strictly judicial sphere what was characterized in Chapter 5 as a discovery of the old order in post-Reformation England.

There is unquestionably in Coke an intensification of what we have called a pattern of conformation; his thought from first to last exudes a prejudice against the new: "And the wisdome of the Judges and Sages of the Law have always suppressed new and subtile inventions in derogation of the Common Law . . . *it is better to be turned to a default, than the Law should be changed, or any innovation made.*"[31] In utilizing the "old lawes," the lawyer must possess three capacities: the thorough knowledge of them, the "art to dispose them," and "the diligence to omit none of them."[32] All the ancient legal customs and traditions are to be used in unearthing helpful precedents. And the unearthing of precedents is nothing else than Coke's attempt to squeeze the present into what he thinks is the past.

---

28. Ogilvie, *op. cit.,* 17. Cf. Harold J. Berman, *Nature and Functions of Law* (Brooklyn, N.Y., 1958), 372-373.
29. Ogilvie, *op. cit.,* 17.
30. Berman, *op. cit.,* 372.
31. *Coke on Littleton,* 282; my italics.
32. 4 *CR,* Preface, v, vi.

The creative role played by Coke in appealing to precedent is incontestable. It was no mean achievement to make the historical judgments he did about the nature of the ancient realm. "Despite his intense concern with history, this most unhistorically-minded of men was no scholar . . . "[33] He accepted the legends about the pre-Conquest golden age with naïve credulity, being satisfied, for example, that the *Modus Tenendi Parliamentum* dated from the Conquest and reliably described the method of holding Parliament in Saxon times.[34] Actually, of course, it was an extremely fanciful document written in the fourteenth century.[35] He also believed that the highly imaginative *Mirror of Justices* was an accurate account of Anglo-Saxon law and institutions. But, as Holdsworth states, the *Mirror* was written by a lawyer in the thirteenth century as an attempt to construct an "ideal system of law, out of the shifting legal panorama of his day, by going back to Biblical first principles, and letting his fancy play upon the mixture of the archaic, the feudal, the Romanist, and the constitutional tendencies" of his time.[36] Furthermore, it is quite clear that many of the innumerable Latin maxims Coke used to lend antiquity and authenticity to his decisions "attained their classical form in [his] writings."[37] As Hobbes polemically remarked, with justification:

> He endeavours by inserting Latin sentences, both in his text and in the margin, as if they were principles of the law of reason, without any authority of ancient lawyers, or any certainty of reason in themselves, to make men believe that they are the very grounds of the law of England.[38]

While the point is not that Coke cut his views out of whole cloth,[39]

33. Thorne, *op. cit.*, 13.
34. 9 *CR*, Preface, iv.
35. See Hill, *op. cit.*, 58-59.
36. W. S. Holdsworth, *Some Makers of English Law* (Cambridge, 1938). Cf. Ogilvie, *op. cit.*, 162. Coke mentions the *Mirror* at 9 *CR*, Preface, iv, and at II *Institutes*, 230.
37. W. S. Holdsworth, *History of English Law* (9 vols., London, 1922-1926), V, fn. 3, 458.
38. Quoted by Holdsworth, *History of English Law*, from Hobbes's *Dialogue of Common Law. Works*, VI, 62.
39. Certainly Coke did not invent devotion to the past. The concern for legal tradition is to be noted in Fortescue and to some extent even earlier. See Holdsworth, *Makers of English Law*, 46 ff. and M. A. Shepard, "Political and Constitutional Theory of Sir John Fortescue," *Essays in History and Political Theory* (Cambridge, 1936), 290.

or that he was alone responsible for the backward trend,[40] he reflects an intensity of devotion and deference to the past that clearly marks a new period in the development of the common law. By referring to Coke as the leading exponent of a return to the old order, and by emphasizing the patent innovation and self-deception inherent in such a program, we seek to call attention to a pattern of order whose persuasiveness and influence cannot be explained by its accordance with the facts. Nor can its "pattern" be explained with reference to the structure of the way things are (or were), as Coke and Hooker firmly believed. The pattern of order at work here is a system of interpretation that derives its coherence not from "reality," but from the intrinsic connections of its own assumed categories.

Here we come to the central question of the specific relation of the common law to the other agencies of English government: Parliament, the Church, and the crown. The intricate problem of the relation between the fundamental law and Parliament has, of course, been extensively and learnedly debated. Does Coke have a notion of "judicial review" or of uncontrolled "parliamentary sovereignty"? Is he the father of the American or the English conception of law and government?[41] These questions, and the debate in general, now appear—on the basis of work done by S. E. Thorne and J. W. Gough—to have been misguided. The very phrasing of the questions in this way, says Gough, "implies a distinction between and a separation of the functions of legislation and jurisdiction which was not clearly drawn till later."[42] Our analysis of Coke brings us to precisely the same conclusion, even though Coke himself was never able completely to resolve the tension between the legislature and the judiciary.

So far as Coke's view of Parliament is concerned, three things bear remembering: it was, for him, as for Tudor and medieval people generally, a court of law; it was "very ancient" and it was representative of the "consent of the whole realm." "Parliament," says Coke, "is the highest, and most honorable and absolute Court of Justice of England, consisting of the King, the Lords of Parliament, and the

---

40. See Margaret A. Judson, *Crisis of the Constitution* (New Brunswick, N.J., 1949), 153-154, for a description of the breadth of this allegiance to the past—among parliamentarians and royalists alike.

41. J. W. Gough, *Fundamental Law in English Constitutional History* (Oxford, 1955). See 32 for a summary of the literature on the subject.

42. *Ibid.,* 46.

Commons . . . "[43] or, as he remarks elsewhere," . . . every member of the parliament hath a judiciall place . . . "[44] In fact, it was called Parliament because there every member may speak "judicially his mind."[45] "Of the power and jurisdiction of the parliament, for making of laws in proceeding by bill, it is so transcendent and absolute, as it cannot be confined either for causes or persons within any bounds. Of this court it is truly said: Si antiquitatem spectes, est vertustissima, si dignitatem, est honoratissima, si jurisdictionem, est capacissima."[46] The things Coke instances as legislation are definitely not what we have come, in modern times, to think of under that heading. For Coke legislation deals with questions of inheritance, ancestry, whether infants or minors are of "full age," and so on.[47] A parliamentary act is a judicial act.[48]

Secondly, Parliament existed as the highest court of the realm "long before and untill the time of the Conqueror . . . "[49] As Coke put it above, "Si antiquitatem spectes, est vertustissima . . . " It was unquestionably part of the legal structure of the old order, and it derived its authority from that fact. Thirdly, a statute is "no Act of Parliament" unless it is the result of consent among the king, the Lords, and the Commons,[50] who in turn embody the ancient sentiment and consensus of the realm. By this consensus was the English monarchical system and the very common law itself determined:

> . . . this your graces realm recognizing no superior under God but only your grace, hath been and is free from subjection to any mans laws, *but only to such as have been devised, made and ordained within this realm for the wealth of the same, or to such other, as . . . the people of this your realm have taken at their free liberty by their own consent to be used amongst them, and have bound themselves by long use and custome to the observance of the same,* not as to the observance of the laws of any forain prince, potentate, or prelate, *but as to the customed and ancient laws of this realm originally established as laws of the same, by the said sufferance, consents and custome, and none otherwise.*[51]

43. *Coke on Littleton*, 109a-110.
44. 9 *CR*, Preface, xxvi.
45. IV *Institutes*. 15.
46. IV *Institutes*, 36.
47. See Gough, *op. cit.*, 42.
48. G. W. Prothero, *Constitutional Documents of the Reigns of Elizabeth and James I* (Oxford, 1894), 288, 290.
49. *Coke on Littleton*, 110.
50. II *Institutes*, 158; IV *Institutes*, 25.
51. IV *Institutes*, 342, 43; my italics.

It will be observed how readily the terms "consent," "custome," and "ancient laws of this realm" are interchanged and virtually identified with one another. The people bind themselves, according to Coke, both by consent and by custom, or "long use," to the laws. In other words, what is customary must have been consented to, and what is consented to must become customary. Such, as with Hooker, is the inseparability of the consent of the realm and the law of the realm. In the circular, unitary way we have come to recognize as the hallmark of Anglican pattern of order, consent emerges from and re-enacts or reproduces the old order.

On this basis Coke significantly remarks: "The surest construction of a statute is by the rule and reason of the common law."[52] And, by extension, his reaffirmation of St. Germain's dictum is of the utmost importance: "It cannot be thought that a statute that is made by the authority of the whole realm as well as of the king, and of the lords spirituall and temporall, as of all the commons, will recite a thing against the truth."[53] Theoretically, at least, such a thing "cannot be thought." Parliament and the courts are, accordingly, complementary and fully harmonious aspects of the same "ancient" legal system. As Gough astutely comments, "to Coke parliament had the last word not because of its legislative sovereignty, whether acknowledged or unacknowledged, but because as the highest court there was no appeal against its supreme authority."[54]

It is true, of course, that the implicit tensions between judicial and legislative activity caused some inchoate difficulties for Coke's unitary system.[55] He was perfectly ready to recognize that Parliament has the power to make a "new law" in order to "redresse the State of the Church and of the Realme in those things that need amendment."[56] After all, the past must be related to the present, or in his more graphic words, "out of the old fields must come the new corne."[57] But this was at best a precarious undertaking because very often, as he said, acts of Parliament were "overladen with provisoes and additions, and many times . . . penned or corrected by men of none or very little judgment in law."[58] The common law judges must ever be vigilant to analyze

---

52. *Coke on Littleton*, 272b.
53. IV *Institutes*, 343.
54. Gough, *op. cit.*, 42-43.
55. See McIlwain, *High Court of Parliament*, 194 ff.
56. II *Institutes*, 158.
57. IV *Institutes*, 109.
58. 2 *CR*, Preface, xii.

statutes in the light of the rule and reason of the law. "If there is repugnancy in statute and unreasonableness in custom, the common law disallows and rejects it . . . "[59] Despite his sublime confidence in the unity of law and consent, Coke is forced, if reluctantly, to admit that Parliament can go astray by passing unreasonably constructed statutes. Such is the background for the famous and oft-quoted passage from *Dr. Bonham's Case:*

> It appears in our books, that in many cases, the common law will control acts of Parliament, and sometimes adjudge them to be utterly void: for when an act of Parliament is against common right and reason, or repugnant, or impossible to be performed, the common law will controul it, and adjudge such act to be void.[60]

Nonetheless, the arguments of Thorne and Gough are completely convincing. They show that Coke had no clear conception of an absolute body of "fundamental law" which stood over against the acts of Parliament (and the consent of the realm that they embody) and which possessed the last word on their validity. Thorne shrewdly demonstrates that in *Bonham's Case* Coke operates on a notion of strict statutory construction. When contradictions are seen to exist within the statute itself, or when elements in a statute conflict with previous statutory precedents, then, and only then, will the common law "adjudge such act to be void." Furthermore, there was nothing, in the last analysis, to prevent Parliament from enacting such contradictions if it so desired. As he made quite clear in his *Institutes:* "The Common Law hath no controller in any part of it but the High Court of Parliament, and if it be not abrogated or altered by Parliament it remains still."[61] It was devoutly to be hoped that Parliament would not make irrational changes, but when it did, Coke could only weakly and bewilderedly suggest that "those alterations have been found by experience to be . . . inconvenient for the Commonwealth . . . "[62] or, in another connection, that acts made against the basic guarantees of the common law "never live long."[63]

The point is that Coke, on the logic of his system, has no real answer to any such conflict between the judiciary and the legislature.[64] On the

59. Quoted by Thorne, "Dr. Bonham's Case," 550.
60. 8 *CR*, 118a.
61. IV *Institutes*, 42, 3.
62. Quoted by Gough, *op. cit.*, 41.
63. IV *Institutes*, 31.
64. Holdsworth, *History of English Law,* V, 475, underlines this conflict and Coke's inability to deal with it.

one hand, he stands firmly behind the ultimacy of consent in Parliament. On the other, he dogmatically asserts the supremacy of "judicial reason," at least as the measure of the true interest or "convenience" of the realm.[65] For him, as for Hooker, the old order was ever characterized by a sweet mutuality between consent and reason of law. To contemplate a fundamental estrangement between them was to cast doubt on the unity of order; such a notion was far too perplexing to be entertained. Consequently, Coke's response to the burgeoning conflict resembled his reponse to comparable conflicts set loose in other areas of Elizabethan and Stuart society. He simply reasserted—though perhaps with less assurance in this field than in the others—the ultimate impossibility of a breakdown in his legal universe. The balanced coherence and continuity embodied in the common law was a reflection of the same coherence and continuity in "so many successions of ages" of English society. Surely it was plain: anything that contradicted that, even though it be a judgment of the High Court of Parliament, could never live long!

The relations of common law to the Church and its ecclesiastical courts, and to the crown, present related aspects of the same problem. Coke's understanding of the social place and function of the Church concurs completely with the offical Anglicanism of Whitgift and Hooker. "In Gods name then," says Coke, "Let us joyne in our prayers, and Sacraments, and performe a due obedience to God, and to our King, as wee are all of one Nation, so let us be all of one Church, and Christ beeing onely our head, let us all desire as in one sheep folde, to be the sanctified members of his glorious bodie."[66] Church and realm are smoothly co-terminous spheres. For this reason, he stands strongly against the "treasonous" activities of the Catholic recusants in England. He speaks of "Pope Impius" as "his Hellishness" and as "his Horribleness," so antagonistic is he to the insinuation of any "forain precedent" or authority.

Although he barely mentions the Puritans, considering them by far the "least dangerous" among the religious groups outside the Church of England, he roundly attacks the Separatists as "a Sect not to be tolerated in any Monarchyall government."[67]

65. In 12 *CR*, 84, Coke says: "it was good for the weal public, that the Judges of the Common Law should interpret the statutes and Acts of Parliament within this realm: and that [,] if such interpretation ought to be made . . . "
66. *The Lord Coke His Speech and Charge*. Given at the Norwich Assizes, 1607, no pagination; referred to henceforth as *Charge*.
67. *Charge*.

And though their ignorance understands not what they doe, yet doe their endeavours strive to shake in sunder the whole frame of our Emperiall government, for if (as they desire) the forme of our Civill Lawes were abrogated, then should our Common Law, and it of necessity fall together. For they are so woven and incorporated in each other, as that without the one, the other cannot stand . . .

. . . Without the grave assembly of our reverend Bishops, his Majesties high court of Parliament, should be unfurnished, no law being there enacted, but that which is by the King, his Lord spirituall and temporall confirmed. These therefore that would have no Bishops among us, do in their desires strive, from his highnes, and the dignity of his State, to pluck the right hand of government, and as much as in them lyeth to break in sunder, the golden frame of just Authority for if no Bishops, then no Lawes, if no Lawes, no King; and to this height doth their presumption clime, although their ideot blindnes seems as if they did not understand so much, the mischiefe of their schisme is most unsufferable: For never was their a nation knowne to flourish having a Monarchie in the Kingdome, and a Mallachie in the Church.[68]

There is no suggestion in Coke's writings that he ever wished to do away with the ecclesiastical courts or with the civil law that had jurisdiction therein. They clearly have their traditional place and possess a legitimate claim as part of the law of England.[69] In fact, any attempt to reorganize the structure of the Church, including its courts, would be disastrous to the unity and harmony of the realm.

The only problem from Coke's point of view, arose from the fact that the Church courts did not always seem to realize that they were part of the wider common law and by no means independent of it. The boundaries of jurisdiction between the ecclesiastical and common law courts were historically extremely complicated, but it began to occur to Coke that the Church courts were overstepping their bounds. They started to claim for themselves, he thought, cases that could only be handled by the common law.[70] Anyway, it was not for them to decide the spheres of jurisdiction. In the famous *Fuller's Case*,[71] he thundered: "When there is any question concerning what power or jurisdiction belongs to ecclesiastical Judges, in any particular case, the determination of such belongs to the Judges of the common law." The point

68. *Ibid.*
69. II *Institutes,*, 608.
70. See Ogilvie, *op. cit., 129.*
71. *12 CR*, 41-42.

could not be made much more sharply: the Church and its courts were subordinated to the all-encompassing, omnicompetent laws of the realm. It was these laws and none other that defined the structure of relations for the whole society, and therefore its rightful interpreters, the judges, had the final say when those relations needed legal adjustment.[72]

It so happened that in the growing tensions between the Church courts and the common law, Archbishop Bancroft had been able to elicit the support of King James, convincing him that the crown, as supreme governor of ecclesiastical affairs, and not the common law courts, had the final power to decide jurisdiction. Consequently, the conflict was broadened to include the question of the king's power and prerogative. Alongside the problem of the relation of the courts and Parliament, the question of the boundaries between judiciary and executive became the most ambiguous political problem of the period under consideration.[73] Although it had long since been held that the king ruled *sub Deo et lege,* or within the accepted legal structure as the King-in-Parliament, the particular powers that "are rooted in and spring from [his] political person"[74] had undergone a decided expansion between the reigns of Edward I and Elizabeth. For most of the Middle Ages the king was regarded as little more than "a feudal lord writ large."[75] He was, as Maitland said, "every inch a man," and his prerogative powers were but slightly exaggerated feudal privileges and duties. Basic to these was an inherent respect for and defense of the inalienable property rights of the freemen of the realm. They constituted the "liberties of subjects" that were considered absolutely incapable of infringement by the crown.[76] They were, as McIlwain has said, "a barrier against absolutism."[77]

Nonetheless, already by the last quarter of the thirteenth century the king was beginning to enhance his power, a fact corresponding to the general collapse of feudalism as a system of government organization.[78] Under Edward I Parliament, the political position of which was

---

72. See Eusden, *op. cit.,* 92.
73. Judson, *op. cit.,* 23 ff.
74. Holdsworth, *History of English Law,* III, 458.
75. *Ibid.,* 460.
76. Paul Birdsall, "Non Obstante, a Study of the Dispensing Power of English Kings," *Essays in History and Political Theory,* 37-76.
77. Cited in Judson, *op. cit.,* 47.
78. Haskins, *Growth of English Representative Government,* 71-74, 45.

at that time a long way from being carefully defined, was strictly a court of law, consisting essentially of a permanent inner council. The judges and other members of the council were the legal servants, not the advisers, of the crown. They were, as Haskins remarks, " 'lions under the throne,' and what they did was done chiefly with the authority of the king's prerogative. 'No peer has the king in the realm,' writes Bracton, and it is literally true." In fact, Haskins continues, "Parliament was simply the efficient vehicle of the king's prerogative."[79]

The slow but generally consistent process of centralizing and "patrimonializing" royal power after the thirteenth century had the effect of extending the prerogative to meet the new and hitherto unknown aspects of post-medieval social, economic, and political life, until in the Tudor Age its use was "almost unlimited."[80] It was in the sixteenth century, according to Holdsworth, that "transcendent qualities" began to attend the king. His powers increased in foreign and domestic affairs, and he enjoyed the exercise of incidental prerogatives, such as making ordinances, awarding letters patent, granting charters, and dispensing statutes *pro bono publico,* to a degree undreamed of before the sixteenth century.[81]

Coke's own attitude toward the royal prerogative was by no means unambiguous. He was perfectly aware of the king's importance in English governemnt, and his allegiance to the crown throughout his life is unquestionable. As his biographer remarks: for him Elizabeth had been a "true sovereign, fearless, wise; while she lived, her Attorney General remained the open and vigorous champion of majesty and the prerogative."[82] Nor was his reverence restricted to Elizabeth. James and Charles received their encomiums as well.[83] In fact, as the *Journals*

79. *Ibid.,* 71, 73.
80. Maitland, *Constitutional History of England,* 237.
81. Says Holdsworth, *op. cit.,*III, 459: "By virtue of these prerogatives he is personally sovereign, and has the preeminence over all within his realm; he can do no wrong; he can never die; he is the representative of the state in its dealings with foreign nations; he is part of the legislature, the head of the army; the fountain of justice, always present in his courts; the fountain of honour; the arbiter of commerce; the head of the church."
82. Bowen, *The Lion and the Throne: The Life and Times of Sir Edward Coke* (Boston, 1956), 178.
83. James, said Coke, "is over us all the Lord's anointed, and in these Realms and Dominions, in all causes, and over all Persons, as well Ecclesiasticall as Civile, next under Jesus Christ our supreame Governour" (*Charge*). Of Charles: to "trust in him is all the confidence we have under god. He is gods leiuetenant" (quoted in Judson, *op. cit.,* 17).

of the House of Lords report,[84] "it was a wonder for [Coke] to hear
that the liberty of the Subject should be thought incompatible with the
Regality of the King." Such was the balance and harmony of English
tradition. Within that tradition, the king's legitimate place was not to
be questioned, nor his rights doubted.

Still, given Coke's high view of common law and his assertion that it
and nothing else can define the structure of social relations, a conflict
with the absolutist tendencies of James was almost inevitable. Particularly since the prerogative or chancery courts were actively challenging
the authority of the common law to determine jurisdiction and to issue
injunctions and prohibitions.[85] With or without historical foundation,[86] that was the kind of threat Coke simply could not abide. So
strong was his confidence in the supreme validity of the common law,
that he obstinately held his ground against James. The latter was convinced that, as king, he was both highest judge in the land and possessed
of reason every bit as reliable as the common lawyers, and that therefore he was capable of deciding the law. To these claims Coke
responded:

> God had allowed His Majesty excellent science and great endow-
> ments of nature; but His Majesty was not learned in the laws of his
> realm of England and causes which concern the life or inheritance or
> goods or fortunes of his subjects; they are not to be decided by
> natural reason and judgment of law, which law is an act which
> requires long study and experience before that a man can attain
> to the cognizance of it. . . . With which the king was greatly of-
> fended, and said that then he should be under the law, which was
> treason to affirm, as he said. To which I said that Bracton saith *quo
> Rex non debet esse sub homine sed sub deo et lege.*[87]

Not long after this exchange, James summarily dismissed Coke and the
battle lines were clearly drawn, certainly more clearly than they had
ever been before.

Coke's position was unequivocal and unflinching: he laid it down
that "the King hath no prerogative but that which the law of the land

84. Quoted in Judson, *op. cit.,* 64.
85. See Ogilvie's treatment of the conflict of the courts; *op. cit.,* 118 ff.
86. From an impartial point of view, says T. F. T. Plucknett, *A Concise History of
the Common Law* (London, 1956), 54, such a conflict "only revealed the disconcerting fact that the Crown had everything to gain by an appeal to antiquity, and that it was the common law itself, of which the prerogative was a part,
which was the source of offense."
87. 12 *CR,* 65.

[the common law] allows him,"[88] and that the king was limited by Parliament and by "ancient custom."[89] Further, Coke declared that the "laws of England consist of three parts, the common law, customs, and acts of Parliament . . . "[90] The prerogative or proclamatory power of the king was conspicuously missing. For Coke the crown was, at bottom, "an hieroglyphic of the law."[91]

Coke's language here illustrates in bold terms one aspect of the tension emphasized at the beginning of this chapter. The "pure traditionalism" of the lawyers is asserted with a vengeance against the patrimonial inclinations of the crown. This particular conflict underlies many of the legal decisions on corporations that were set down around the turn of the seventeenth century. However, as we would expect, the whole matter is complicated by the interjection of attitudes and sentiments toward economic behavior that reflect a quite novel outlook. In the decisions on corporations, the old order of the lawyers manifests some vitally new dimensions side by side with the more traditional emphases. At no point did all the dilemmas of order converge more strikingly than in this next area of corporation law.

COKE AND THE LAW OF CORPORATIONS

The organization of associations of people, their goals and purposes, the functions they fulfill and the way they fulfill them, the rights, privileges, and duties they possess, are but the articulation and specification of social life itself. The nature and province of associations, or corporations, in any given society, is one reliable indication of the structure and dynamics of that society. Certainly, nothing focuses more effectively the revolutionary conflicts within the entire English social order around the turn of the seventeenth century than the process of determining the legal status of corporate life. We should not be surprised to discover that amid the other conflicts of the time, the conflict of order traced so far in religious categories is manifested in social and legal terms as well. It merely reflects the intimate interweaving of religion and society.

No aspect of the growth of prerogative power was more important than its gradual extension into the economic and corporate realms of

88. Quoted by Ogilvie, *op. cit.,* 139.
89. II *Institutes,* 60-61.
90. 4 *CR,* Preface, iv.
91. 7 *CR,* 7b; cf. 9 *CR,* 123a: "The king cannot by his charter alter the law."

English life.[92] The absorption of previously sovereign, self-determining municipal and guild corporations by the crown, as well as the subordination of all aspects of economic activity to its power, was in itself a dramatic symbol of the changing character of England between the thirteenth and sixteenth centuries. The history of that period is a story of nationalizing, centralizing, and unifying, by means of a liberal use of letters patent and royal charters. It is, as Laski says, "a steady tale of oppression that we read," until by the time of Elizabeth corporations, and especially business corporations, were virtually "organs of the state."[93]

It was this direct control and regulation of corporate life that offended Coke. For him the ever growing assertion of prerogative power in this field spelled the most dangerous kind of innovation and departure from the past. After all, it was the common law that ultimately determined social relations, not the crown. His attempt to subordinate the prerogative to common law is sharply reflected in many of his decisions in the law of corporations, decisions that in the profoundest way "set the mold"[94] for legal interpretation for many generations to come.

As P. T. Carden has shown,[95] the two definitive decisions that Coke reports, *Prince's Case* and the famous *Sutton's Hospital Case*, reveal in a complementary way Coke's essential view. The former boldly affirms that "A Charter alone cannot cross and change the Common Law."[96] No matter what the royal charter says in founding a corporation, there

92. While economic and business activity was controlled and regulated by various types of corporate life, e.g., guilds and mysteries, corporations as such included far more than simply economic life. For instance, Davis, *op. cit.*, I, VI, classifies guilds in four categories: frith guilds (associations to stabilize private ownership of land); social-religious guilds; ecclesiastical guilds; and merchant or craft guilds. Even the merchant guilds were not exclusively oriented toward economic life. Beyond these different forms, municipalities, educational and eleemosynary institutions, poor houses and hospitals were understood to be, and were organized as, corporations. As we shall see, one of the important confusions in the law was over the relation of these wider, noneconomic corporations to the "business corporation."

93. Harold J. Laski, "Early History of the Corporation in England," *Harvard Law Review*, XXX (1916-17), 560-88, 569, and Davis, *op. cit.*, I, 128-129, 202.

94. Julius Goebel, Jr., Introduction to A. B. Dubois's *English Business Company 1720-1800* (New York, 1938), fn. 3, viii-xi.

95. Percy T. Carden, "Limitations on the Powers of Common Law Corporations," *Law Quarterly Review*, XXVI (1910), 320-330.

96. 4 *CR*, 186.

are transcendent common law rules and principles that finally determine its validity and the scope of its operations. In *Sutton's Hospital*, it was determined (among other things) that there are certain inalienable "incidents of corporation" defined by the common law and attendant on incorporation, whether the charter lists them or not. The particular question at issue was whether corporate property could be alienated even though all the stipulations of the charter were not yet executed. As long as the charter had been granted, declared Coke, the corporation exists "in abstracto," even though it may not yet exist "in concreto." Therefore, all the "incidents" automatically accrue to it. These incidents include the ability to purchase and alienate property, to sue and be sued, to constitute survivors who shall continue the corporation, and so on.

Coke proceeds to report that even the king's wishes expressed in the charter are of no ultimate avail against these incidents at common law: "to restrain them from aliening or demising but in certain form; that is an ordinance testifying the King's desire, but it is a precept, *and doth not bind in law.*" Though Coke says that "none but the King alone can create or make a corporation, . . . " the statement is somewhat unclear since later he remarks that a corporation may be lawfully brought into being "*by the Common Law, as the King himself,*" by Parliament, by king's charter, or by "prescription." He repeats the same authorities in *Coke on Littleton*, 250. The point is that even the exclusive prerogative of the king to create a corporation through charter or letters patent is brought abruptly into doubt by introducing these other authorities and by tacitly identifying the incorporating activity of the common law with the "king himself."

Coke's assertion on the authenticity of corporations founded by "prescription" is of still further interest in this connection. Blackstone later defined such associations in a way quite consistent with Coke's interpretations: they are "those which have existed beyond the memory of man, and therefore are looked upon in law to be well created, such as the City of London and many other."[97] Contrary to the widespread opinion that Coke held a simple, unambiguous notion of *persona ficta*, based on a concessionist conception of corporations, there is the hint here of a "realist" view. Such a view would, of course, grant at least limited reality and independent existence to a corporation on the basis of custom, quite apart from the fiat of the crown.

97. William Blackstone, *Commentaries on the Laws of England* (New York, 1830), Bk. I, ch. 18, sec. 473.

In any case, when the king charters a corporation, it is done, says Coke, "in the same manner as if all [the "incidents" determined by common law] had been comprehended in the letters patent themselves." Or, to quote the most famous dictum in *Sutton's Hospital* (one that he recites twice on the same page): "a corporate aggregate of many is invisible, immortal, and *rests only in the intendment* (or process) *and consideration of the law* ... " In other words, reading *Prince's Case* and *Sutton's Hospital* together, we infer that a charter may acceptably define the purposes for which a corporation is founded, but that the ultimate arbiter of the validity and scope of the charter is the common law; Carden states: "the common law supplies corporations created by the crown with certain necessary and incidental powers without words in the charter to confer them."[98] Furthermore, the words of the charter are good so long as they "do not conflict with common law rules; words that do conflict with the common law are but an ordinance, and not binding in law ... "[99]

The supremacy of statute, custom, and precedent over royal prerogative in Coke's understanding is further illustrated by other cases he reports as corporation law. In the *Dean and Chapter of Norwich Case*,[100] which concerned the legality of a change or a surrendering of corporate existence, he lays it down that "a corporation created by the King's charter, may be altered by accepting a new charter; *but the constitution of a corporation depending on a statute, cannot be changed by their acceptance of a charter from the crown.*" In the *Case of Corporations*,[101] Coke staunchly supports the right of municipal common councils (and not the wider citizenry) to elect city officials, " ... because divers attempts were of late in divers corporations, contrary to the ancient usage [,] to make popular elections ... " These ancient elections, which could not, says Coke, have come into being "without common consent," can be assumed to be in force *even though no specific charter can be shown.* "According to this resolution the ancient and continual usages have been in London, Norwich, and other ancient cities and corporations: and God forbid that they should be now innovated or altered; for many and great inconveniences will thereupon arise ... "

Coke is in the habit of relating the right to special corporate privi-

98. Carden, *op. cit.*, 325.
99. *Ibid.*, 326.
100. 3 *CR*, 73a ff.
101. 4 *CR*, 77b.

lege—such as local economic or political control—not to the royal charter, but to custom or parliamentary enactment. Accordingly, in the *City of London Case*,[102] Coke concedes the "ancient" right of London to impose monopolistic controls upon its commercial life:

> ... No person whatsoever, not being free of the city of London, shall by any colour, way, or mean whatsoever, directly or indirectly, by himself or any other, keep any shop or any other place whatsoever, inward or outward, for shew or putting to sale of any wares or merchandizes whatsoever by way of retail, or use of any trade, occupation, mystery of handicraft, for hire, gain, or sale, within the city of London ... [103]

Very significantly, he adds that *"no corporation made within time of memory can have such a privilege, unless it be by act of parliament."* That obviously means that a corporation not resting upon custom or rights of prescription, as those do that were made time out of memory, gains its basic privileges by statute. At the same time, he allows that "the King may erect *guildam mercatoriam,* i.e. a fraternity of society or corporation of merchants, to the end that good order and rule should be by them observed for the increase and advancement of trade and merchandise, and not for the hindrance or diminution of it." However, measured in the light of the rest of this case and of his other opinions and presuppositions, it is clear that such a grant by the king would be subject to the regulation of the common law, statute, and custom.

In the *Chamberlain of London's Case*[104] Coke again supports town ordinances made in the restraint of trade, and he sustains an action of debt in favor of the Chamberlain against the defendants who broke the ordinances. In justification of these monopolistic controls, precedents existing "time out of mind" and acts of Parliament receive the greatest weight:

> It appears by many precedents, that it hath been used within the City of London time out of time, for those of London to make ordinances and constitutions for the good order and government of the citizens, etc., *consonant to law and reason,* which they call Acts of Common Council. Also all their customes are confirmed by divers Acts of Parliament, and all such ordinances, constitutions, or by-laws are allowed by the law, which are made for the true and due exception of the laws or statutes of the realm, or for the well government

102. 8 *CR*, 121b-131b.
103. 8 *CR*, 124b.
104. 5 *CR*, 62b ff.

and order of the body incorporate. *And all others which are con-trary or repugnant to the laws or statutes of the realm are void and of no effect:* and as to such ordinances and by-laws, these difficulties were observed; inhabitants of a town without any custom may make ordinances or by-laws for the repair of the church, or a highway, or of any such thing which is for the general good of the public; and in such case the greater part shall bind the whole without any custom. But if it be for their own private profit, as for the well ordering of their common pasture, or the like, there, without a custom they cannot make by-laws, and if there be a custom, then the greater part shall not bind the less, if it be not warranted by custom. *For as the custom creates them, so they ought to be warranted* [directed] *by the custom.*[105]

This is obviously a striking formulation, one that goes to the heart of Coke's attitude on the law of corporations. The basis upon which "common profit" as opposed to "private profit" is determined is cer-tainly unclear, for the "well ordering of their common pasture" would appear to be in the interests of the community. Nonetheless, the fact that private profit may, to Coke's mind, be laid down *by custom* is a point worth emphasizing. The central exception to the making of by-laws "for the general good of the public" is a custom. In other words, if the making of a law neglects the "general good" of the public, there ought to be an "ancient" (customary) reason for it. Coke does conclude this passage with a reference to the king's charter, and the fact that it may grant the right to make ordinances. But this reference, as usual, is not elaborated nor is it fitted into the center of the main argument.

The general control and specification of corporate life by the laws, statutes, and customs of the realm—to the conspicuous subordination, if not neglect, of royal prerogative—could hardly be more consistently emphasized. Coke underlines his attitude in the *Institutes:* the special rights and privileges of "Towns corporate" are to be respected, but only because they are allowed by Parliament; "*such privileges could not be granted by Letters Patent.*"[106]

However, this method, by which Coke opposes his legal tradition-alism to the patrimonialism of the crown, is by no means all there is to his view of corporations. There remain some loose ends that do not quite fit into this neat pattern. Indeed, certain elements raise doubt about the coherence and stability of the view expounded so far. One or

105. 5 *CR*, 63a; my italics.
106. III *Institutes*, 184-185; my italics.

two new dimensions in Coke's thought reveal deep conflict, if not confusion, within his understanding of the nature and function of corporate life in England. Such a dimension is hinted at in what is, on the face of it, a baffling conclusion to the *City of London Case*. Coke discusses the "reasonableness" of customary monopoly rights extended to a baker in the county of Northampton, in order to lend weight to his decision in favor of London's monopoly. However, he then injects a comment that seems to call into question the ultimate desirability of special corporate privileges: "There are divers customs which are against common right, and the rule of common law, and yet they are allowed on our books, and *eo potius,* because they have not only the force of a custom, but are also supported and fortified by authority of parliament."

We encounter here the same kind of reasoning that was observed in the treatment of the relation of common law to Parliament—a conflict that, by all rights, ought not to be present is perceived. If statute, custom, and "common right" all form a grand unity of order, how is it that contradictions appear? Yet, quite plainly, here is an instance of custom and Parliament extending special privileges that apparently contradict the "rule of common law." What, then, is this "rule," this "common right" that Coke talks about; and what does it mean for the law of corporations?

In *Davenant* v. *Hurdis*[107]—perhaps the first case in which the monopoly privileges of corporations were seriously challenged by the courts—Coke begins to formulate a notion of "common right." The question at issue in this case was whether the Company of Merchant Tailors of London, by appealing to an ancient custom that was confirmed both by statute and letters patent and that enabled them to make ordinances for the supervision and control of trade, had the right to require members to employ only company clothworkers. The object, claimed the company, was "for the better maintenance and relief of the poor [members]." Davenant, who was a member, refused to conform to the ordinance and refused to pay the fine, and he brought suit against the company. The case was argued by then Attorney-General Coke for the plaintiff and by Francis Moore for the defendant.

107. 41 and 42 Eliz. I am indebted here to D. O. Wagner's essay, "Common Law and Free Enterprise: An Early Case of Monopoly," *Economic History Review,* VII, 1 (November 1936). See Bibliographical Essay B, esp. pp. 243-246. For a review of the literature on the question of economic regulation and the law.

Coke's preliminary arguments are rather trivial, but his central contention, and the one most determinative of the decision, was that the ordinance created a monopoly and thereby limited trade. By it, he argued, the tailors would be subordinated to the interests of the company clothworkers and compelled to exist on relief. Such, he said, is "against common right and the nature of a by-law, for a by-law must be made in furtherance of the public good and the better execution of the laws, and not to the prejudice of subjects or for private gain." By-laws that establish monopolies, states Coke, "are against common right and void."

Moore agreed that if the ordinance created a monopoly it would be void, but said that it could not be so construed. After all, he claimed, it involved only company members and, at that, only half their cloth. Moore said that if this was a monopoly, then all exclusive privileges given to corporations should be void—an implication that was not far from Coke's point of view. However, the judges decided in favor of Davenant "because the by-law is to make monopoly: and prescription of such nature to induce sole trade or traffic to a company or a person, and to exclude all others is against the law." In other words, *Davenant* v. *Hurdis* suggested it was the sum and substance of the traditional law of England that *all* monopolies were against "common right" and the common good.

To justify his position Coke cites three precedents, including one from the civil law, that prove simply that ordinances made against the common good are void. However, he by no means shows that monopolies are necessarily against the public good, as it was traditionally understood, because they regulate employment. It is hard to conceive of the medieval guild as anything other than monopolistic, that is, as having the right, by definition, to control employment, as well as wages, prices, and quality of work.[108] Though it has been suggested that "regulation" of economic activity was not the same as "restriction" in medieval and Tudor England,[109] the distinction is difficult to establish. The widespread and thoroughly accepted practice of "regulating" the number of guild members undoubtedly looked like "restriction" from the point of view of those excluded from the guild, or those

108. See Lipson, *op cit.*, I, 329.
109. Barbara Malament, "The 'Economic Liberalism' of Sir Edward Coke," *Yale Law Review*, LXXVI (1967), fn. 114, 1321, 1341. This is an important contention in her article. Unfortunately, she does not substantiate it. See Bibliographical Essay B, pp. 244-246.

compelled to join.[110] The public good, including such venerable values as full employment,[111] was understood within a context of pervasive control.[112]

In the light of the history and function of the guilds, it is therefore odd to argue, as Coke does, that guild by-laws are void because they establish monopolies. That is what guilds were for! One might contend, as the few precedents Coke cites do, that *certain* guilds are against the public good for specific reasons.[113] To proceed in that way, it would be necessary to show not that restrictions were being placed on craftsmen, but that particular by-laws were needlessly burdensome. Moore tried to argue just this way for the defense, but Coke did not respond in kind. He, and the judges, simply concluded that the tailors had a monopoly, and that was that.[114]

A new mentality is at work in *Davenant* v. *Hurdis*, one that can hardly be explained by referring to the regnant legal tradition of the realm. To be sure, the judges, together with Coke, strove manfully to make the new motifs conform to the old order and to the logic of their system. But the motifs do not fit; they drive in a new direction and involve new presuppositions, different from anything hitherto found either in the legal tradition itself or in the pattern of order claiming to represent that tradition. Indeed, they call both the tradition and the system of thought into question.

Toward the end of the sixteenth century, there was much parliamentary agitation against monopolies and the letters patent of the crown. By 1597, in a move with unquestionably revolutionary implications for politics and economics as well as for law, Elizabeth conceded that all letters patent could be tested in the common law courts. This was a significant surrender of royal prerogative and one, quite obviously, that harmonized with the objective of Sir Edward Coke. There was some delay in bringing the cases to common law, and *Davenant* v. *Hurdis* was not tried until 1599-1600.

The most famous case in this connection would not be heard until 1603. It was the so-called Case of Monopolies, or *Darcy* v. *Allen*, probably rightly singled out "for the momentous effect which it pro-

110. See Lipson, *op. cit.,* I, 319, 349, 389.
111. Malament makes much of this, *op cit.,* 1342.
112. Wagner, *op. cit.,* 218-219.
113. Lipson, *op. cit.,* I, 293.
114. Heckscher points out: "The attitude taken by the courts could certainly undermine essential aspects of medieval economic ideas" (*op. cit.,* I, 284).

duced on modern jurisprudence."[115] "In the whole of legal history,"
says Gordon, exaggerating considerably, "there is no other deliverance
in any tongue which has proved to be so fruitful of results, nor any
which has contributed more to the advancement of society in modern
times."[116] One need not include all of legal history to indicate the
significance of this case. It is quite enough to indicate the radically new
understanding of social order which it expresses, one that certainly did
have great importance for the development of modern society. The new
understanding is an extension and elaboration of the motifs already
sketched in *Davenant* v. *Hurdis*.

The fact that Elizabeth promiscuously granted letters of patent to
favorite industrialists is common knowledge. The monopolies that these
grants created caused strong reaction, mainly because of the open
abuses that attended the system. It is the ability of the crown to dispense these royal grants of monopoly that is challenged in *Darcy* v.
Allen. Accordingly, the conflict between the common law and the prerogative is focused in the sharpest possible way. Edward Darcy, a groom
in the privy chamber, had received from Elizabeth complete authority
over the manufacturing, importing, and selling of playing cards within
England for twenty-one years. Allen, who was apparently a London
merchant, infringed the patent, and suit was brought against him. The
plaintiff claimed that the queen had the right to dispense patents with
respect to "things of vanity," like playing cards, for they "were not any
merchandize, or thing concerning trade of any necessary use." Allen, on
the other hand, pleaded not guilty. He argued that the City of London
was an ancient city that had from time immemorial recognized and
given special place to the Society of Haberdashers. For this reason he
claimed he was *civis et liber homo de civitate et societate illa . . .*

It is interesting to observe that a potential conflict exists in this case
between the monopoly privileges of a municipal corporation and those
of a business company. The conflict is an intriguing one, and there is
evidence that the City of London was behind Allen in this suit, testing
its own rights through him.

The sequel to *Darcy* v. *Allen*, *Allen* v. *Garrard* (1605), shows that
"Allen was not an independent, unsupported protagonist on behalf of
the liberty of the subject to pursue lawful and established trades, but
rather a freeman of the City actively instigated to resistance to the
monopolist by the most influential authorities of the City of
London."[117] There was widespread resistance among the city officials

115. J. W. Gordon, *Monopolies by Patents* (London, 1897), 193.
116. *Ibid.*, 193.
117. D. Seaborne Davies, "Further Light on the Case of Monopolies," *Law
    Quarterly Review*, 48 (1932), 395.

to the monopolies granted by Elizabeth, resistance undoubtedly based, like Allen's, upon their ancient, customary rights. The defense, namely, the supremacy of antiquity over the crown's prerogative, was ready made.

A decision on such a problem would have been interesting for the historian of corporation law. However, one of the most important aspects of *Darcy* v. *Allen* is that neither the defense nor the opinion of the court displayed the slightest interest in the customary privileges of London. This is remarkable, particularly in the case of Coke, who could easily and consistently have argued that tradition outweighs prerogative and, accordingly, have delivered the desired blow against royal prerogative. Such an argument would have coincided completely with his opinions as discussed above.

Despite this fact, counsel for the defense Fuller and the judges now take an entirely different direction. They have their minds on what they consider profounder issues. Fuller begins his defense with a familiar appeal to the sovereignty of common law over the king, "All Patents," he says, "concerning King and his subjects are to receive exposition and allowance how far they are lawfull and how far not by the Judges of the Law."[118] Furthermore, the judges are not to be guided by the specific letters and words of patent, but "by the Laws of the Realm, the Laws of God, and according to the antient allowance thereof." Fuller then goes on to argue that Darcy's patent is contrary to all three authorities, mainly because, as he says, restraint of labor is against the law of God and man. "The Ordinance of God is, that every man should live by labour, and that he that will not labour, let him not eat." He develops this line of thought into the central point of his defense:

> Now therefore it is as unlawful to prohibit a man not to live by the labour of his own trade, wherein he was brought up as an apprentice, and was lawfully used, as to prohibite him not to live by labour, which, if it were by act of Parliament it were a void act: for an act of Parliament against the law of God, directly is void, as is expressed in the book of Doctor and Student, much more Letters of Patent against the laws of God are void.... But Mr. Darcy will take from men against their wills, their living and lawful trade, and force them to seek other trades, directly contrary to the law of God.[119]

118. Gordon, *op. cit.,* 174.
119. This, of course, is Fuller, not Coke, speaking. His remark that an Act of Parliament is void if against the law of God is probably more extreme than Coke would make. Yet the religious tone is very close to what one generally finds in Coke and other judges of the time. Freedom of economic activity is no secondary question—it is primary.

This biblical justification of voluntray labor sets the background for the ultimate decision of the court in favor of Allen. The judges, including Coke, declared Darcy's patent to be "utterly void," in the first place because it was "a monopoly, and against the common law" and because "all trades . . . which prevent idleness . . . are profitable for the commonwealth and therefore the grant . . . is against the common law, and the benefit and liberty of the subject." In the second place it was declared void because it was "against divers acts of parliament." Coke concedes the general *non obstante* power to the king, but he remarks that "when the wisdom of Parliament has made an act to restrain pro bono publico importation," the king may not dispense with it.[120] Such dispensation, says Coke, is "utterly against law."

Coke further argues that there are three "inseparable incidents" connected with monopolies which contribute to their general "mischief or wickedness." They inevitably raise prices, impair the quality of merchandise, and tend to impoverish artisans formerly engaged in the trades concerned.[121] He also claims that Darcy's patent was a "dangerous innovation," because it extended monopoly privileges to an untrained and unskilled person, while excluding the trained artisans. Above all, from Coke's point of view, the patent—"against freedom of trade and traffic"—is void because it contradicts statute and Magna Carta.

> So . . . if grant be made to any man to have the sole dealing with any other trade, that grant is against the freedom and liberty of the subject, that before did or might have used that trade, and consequently against this Charter. Generally, *all monopolies* are against this great Charter because they are against the freedom and liberty of the subject, and against the law of the land. [Italics added.]

From the perspective of the history of English law, *Darcy* v. *Allen,* following *Davenant* v. *Hurdis,* establishes as the law of the land the remarkable innovation that *all* monopolies are void. That Coke himself made certain exceptions to this principle did not alter the fact that the

---

120. See Birdsall, *op. cit.:* "This interpretation advances the boundaries of the subject's interest beyond all limits set by the earlier law books" (61). The fact that Coke later recanted this interpretation of *non obstante* simply demonstrates the great instability of the lines of thought at work here (62).

121. Wagner, "Coke and the Rise of Economic Liberalism," *Economic History Review,* VI, 35 (1935), 37.

lawyers were developing a mentality against economic control,[122] and one that was to raise serious questions about the nature of corporations in general.

The inadequacy of the precedents used by Coke in the attempt to tie this new principle to the old order is as manifest as it is in *Davenant* v. *Hurdis*. Thorne has shown how anomalous the whole undertaking was:

> Much is brought forward, including a chapter in Fortescue's *De Laudibus Legum Angliae*, a writ out of the Register, cases in the reigns of Edward III and Henry IV, a passage in the Old Testament, and one from Justinian's Institutes, but they are hardly convincing precedents. They form a disappointing collection, not at all characteristic of Coke's remarkable ability to find the answers to present discontents in the past. We may take them to show how little persuasion Coke and his colleagues needed and also how new the problem was, for what is being enunciated is Elizabethan law, disguised, as legal innovations usually are, in the clothes of the past.[123]

One of the important precedents Coke employs is none other than *Davenant* v. *Hurdis!* A case whose historical foundation was dubious is now being pressed into service to justify *Darcy* v. *Allen*. The "old law" has become strangely recent. To prove that monopolies as such are invariably mischievous, all Coke can muster is Fitzherbert and a decision from Henry IV's reign, citations proving merely that grants are void if they burden the subject. "That they invariably did so," says Wagner, "still rested on Coke's bare assertions, which testified to his

---

122. See Lipson, *op. cit.*, III, 360. During the seventeenth century, says Lipson, it became increasingly clear that the common law judges were "tending to look with disfavor upon restraints of trade" and that they regarded the common law as "incompatible with the exercise of the royal prerogative in economic affairs." Heckscher remarks in the same vein: "In spite of their willingness to uphold age-honored rights, and in particular the position of the local corporations, the common-law courts therefore proved a great hindrance to the further development of industrial regulation," *op cit.*, I, 285. Or, as he puts it elsewhere, "The courts . . . provided more powerful resistance to industrial regulation than would have been otherwise reconcilable with the doctrines which they represented. They sometimes took decided pleasure in repudiating the ties of industrial freedom and in denying the claims connected therewith, even if they were based on recognized legal rulings or written law," I, 289.

123. Thorne, *Sir Edward Coke*, 10.

own economic views rather than to the illegality of monopolies in general."[124]

Coke's use of statutory analogy would appear to be highly questionable,[125] and his use of Magna Carta as ground for invalidating all monopolies is simply fanciful. Coke's general use of Magna Carta to justify whatever it is he happens to want to justify has been aptly exposed by W. S. McKechnie:

> Although this commentary [in II *Institutes*], like everything else written by Coke, was long accepted as a work of great value, its method is in reality uncritical and unhistorical. The great lawyer reads into Magna Carta the entire body of the common law of the 17th century, of which he was admittedly a master. He seems almost unconscious of the changes wrought by the experience and vicissitudes of four centuries. The clauses of Magna Carta are merely occasions for expounding the law as it stood, not at the beginning of the 13th century, but in Coke's own day. In the skilful hands of Sir Edward, the great charter is made to attack the abuses of James and Charles, rather than those of John or Henry. . . . In the clause of Henry's Charter which secures an open door to foreign merchants in England "unless publicly prohibited," he discovers a declaration that Parliament shall have the sole power to issue such prohibitions, forgetful that "Parliament" did not exist in 1215, and that *regulation of trade was then an exclusive prerogative of the Crown.*[126]

Or, as Thorne comments, "I need hardly point out that 'liberties' in Magna Carta is the equivalent of 'immunities and franchises' and that ideas about free trade were Elizabethan ideas, not those of the barons petitioning King John."[127] On the basis of precedent, then, the case is certainly not proved.

Attention should be drawn here to the subtle but important shift

---

124. Wagner, *op cit.*, 37-38. Ogilvie, *op. cit.*, comments: "[*Darcy* v. *Allen*] is a good example of the way in which unscrupulous interpretation of the 'incognoscible' Common Law could be used—in this instance to counter a dishonest use of the prerogative, and curtail a manifest abuse. The attempt was not successful, but it helped to make the Common Lawyers appear in the light of protectors or at least would-be protectors of trade . . . " (140-141).

125. Wagner, *op. cit.*, 39.

126. *Magna Carta. A Commentary on the Great Charter of King John* (Glasgow, 1914); my italics. Heckscher also remarks: "It was probably only because the Magna Charta was generally believed to be the foundation of every liberty and right, that it was considered a precedent against monopoly; for in actual fact the great Charter provided no such assistance," I, 276.

127. Thorne, *op. cit.*, 10.

that has taken place in the general discussion of law of corporations. No longer is the only issue prerogative *versus* common law control, or patrimonialism *versus* legal traditionalism, as has been argued.[128] It is not simply that Coke and the lawyers wished to exert the authority of the courts over the prerogative power of the crown and so to pass judgment on particular excesses of that power. That was, of course, one dimension of the struggle, and the clear sovereignty finally achieved by the courts was in itself a startling innovation.[129] But, as we have seen, Coke said more. He virtually undermined the right of the crown to grant patents altogether[130] by invalidating, as he said many times, "all monopolies." Ogilvie sees the matter aright:

> The debate of 1601 [over monopolies] should have been a sufficient indication that the way to remedy the evil was to attack individual grants, and show that they had resulted in extortion and oppression, and constituted a public grievance. Coke, however, was determined to prove that monopolies, at least of the kind usually granted, were illegal, and made a valiant attempt to extract yet another type of "new corn from old fields."[131]

Actually, there was very little interest in asserting the power of the courts over particular abuses. "King James was probably right that calling in a patent would lead to its condemnation and therefore became in itself a brand of condemnation of it."[132]

During the last years of the sixteenth century and the opening years of the seventeenth, the outlines of a legal understanding of economic

128. Malament, "The 'Economic Liberalism' of Sir Edward Coke," 1350-1351.

129. See E. Wyndam Hulme, "History of the Patent System under the Prerogative and at Common Law," *Law Quarterly Review*, XVI (1900) [see also *LQR*, XII (April 1898)]. It is odd that Miss Malament (*op. cit.*, fn. 200, 1355) does not comment on Hulme's conclusions. He argues that by 1601, "the whole case for the Crown was ignominiously surrendered. . . . The Commons secured under the color of a redress of grievances a substantial addition to their common law rights . . . " (54). Cf. Ogilvie: "The law had nothing to say about monopolies. During its formative period the regulation of trade, domestic as well as foreign, had been exclusively a royal prerogative, and the right of the King to advance local industries or encourage inventions by the grant of monopoly was difficult to counter by purely legal argument," *op. cit.*, 139; see also 140.

130. Even Malament admits nearly as much, *op. cit.*, 1350.

131. Ogilvie, *op. cit.*, 140.

132. Elizabeth Reed Foster, "Procedure of the House of Commons against Patents and Monopolies, 1621-24," in W. A. Aiken and B. D. Henning (eds.), *Conflict in Stuart England*, (New York, 1960), fn. 61, 82.

relationships that is decisively new begin to emerge. This is exceedingly important for the whole development of the common law. The question, Who is to control economic life broadens and deepens to include the question, What kind of control? The minute and direct restrictions which had been imposed and sanctioned by the law of the land were now at various points dismissed. Individuals acting economically possess, it was thought, the capacity for a high degree of self-regulation and self-determination. The place and function of the law was to provide the broad framework within which men would be both encouraged and enabled to develop economic self-control.

The emergence of this new understanding of control is marked in the field of contract law by what Professor Plucknett refers to as the "momentous" decision of *Slade's Case* (1602).[133] "No decision in the books," writes Simpson, "is ... more important in the history of ... contracts."[134] It was this case, with its emphasis upon the "mutual executory agreement of both parties," which focused the new place being made for the legal recognition of simple voluntary business arrangements, in contrast to direct legal controls of "high technique and inflexible rigidity."[135] By means of the changes in contract law, the individual was in effect set free to regulate his business relationships voluntarily or consensually within certain broad limits,[136] a develop-

133. Plucknett, *A Concise History of the Common Law*, 647-648. In Plucknett's words, *Slade's Case* "obliterates the distinction between debt and deceit, between contract and tort." Moreover, "the deceit element has been eliminated, and the contractual element, long latent ... became the sole basis of the action, which now rested on the 'mutual executory agreement of both parties.' " Seen against a historical background, *Slade's Case* marked no small revision in the law. As J. W. Salmond in "History of Contract," *Law Quarterly Review*, III (1887), 166-179, remarks: " ... the early law [of debt] did not include a promise or agreement. The idea of the obligatory nature of a mere executory agreement seems to have been unknown, and part performance was a condition precedent to the existence of an obligation" (169). Of course, *Norwood* v. *Reed* (1558) and *Strangborough and Warner's Case* (1589) began to lay emphasis upon a promise in itself as the basis for legal action rather than a sealed agreement. Thus they served as forerunners to *Slade's Case*. *Slade's Case* is reported by Coke in 4 *CR*, 94a.

134. A. W. B. Simpson, "The Place of Slade's Case in the History of Contract," *Law Quarterly Review*, LXXIV (1958), 38. Simpson continues: "the results of this new look at the antecedents of the case seem to suggest that its status as a leading decision is greater than has been supposed" (396).

135. Berman, *op. cit.*, 376. The law of contract, according to Berman, is "the 'pure type' of voluntary legal arrangements," or "voluntarism within limits" (Professor Berman's words in private conversation).

136. Ogilvie, *op. cit.*, 38-39.

ment that shows striking congruence with aspects of the Calvinist Puritan system of thought.[137]

It is true, specific references to and developments of contract law in Coke are simply too limited to permit the kind of analysis we have made of the law of corporations. There are not the same extensive ideological justifications, even though, as Simpson points out, elements in *Slade's Case* "can only be viewed as an astonishing act of judicial legislation."[138] But if the elaboration of the idea of contract is slight in the legal activity around Coke's time, the congruence of thought with the Elizabethan Puritans is extremely important. As it turns out, what Perkins called "thoughts and inward motions"—the source of true relationships with God and man—were coming to play a more significant role in the "courts of men" than even he (Perkins) perceived. The emphasis which the Puritan gave to "inward motions" as the primary basis for proper social order was becoming implemented in the law itself toward the turn of the seventeenth century, with the most important consequences. Like the Calvinist Puritan frame of reference, and precisely because of the same emphasis upon internal or self-determination of relationships, the idea of contract introduced a high degree of flexibility and innovation into economic action. This flexibility, says Berman, under which promises are "fungible . . . corresponds to the great flexibility of the free market and of the money economy, in which the great variety of different goods and other concrete economic values are rendered commensurable and hence exchangeable as abstract 'commodities.' So the legal personality—the right-and-duty-bearing unit—became the legal counterpart of economic man."[139] In other words, the new legal evaluation of economic relationships which comes to life during this period regards direct government or juridical interference as in principle highly undesirable. The "new order" of proper economic relationship is, as much as possible, an independent order characterized by self-initiative and individual responsibility. This mentality explains the general antipathy to the existing

137. The controls implicit in the new notions of contract may best be described as indirect: they allow much more room for freedom of action than did the old forms of legal regulation. Of course, throughout the discussion of "control" it is well to remember that taxation was never abolished, nor were the minimal standards of what was and was not considered to be "lawful" activity (for example, standards for business practice as defined by tort law).

138. Simpson, *op. cit.*, 392.

139. Berman, *op. cit.*, 390.

kinds of political and legal regulation over economic activity discovered previously in *Davenant* v. *Hurdis* and *Darcy* v. *Allen*.

The antipathy to direct intervention becomes particularly clear in the *Tailors of Ipswich Case*.[140] In accordance with their charter, ratified by the justices of assize in keeping with an Act of 19 Hen. VIII c. 7, the Tailors Company sought to enforce an ordinance prohibiting tailors from practicing their craft until they had been licensed by the company. The judges rejected the company's ordinance. Coke reports the basis for the decision:

> ... The law abhors idleness, the mother of all evil, *otium omnium vitiorum mater*, and especially in young men, who ought in their youth, (which is their seed time) to learn lawful sciences and trades, which are profitable to the commonwealth, and whereof they might reap the fruit in their old age, for idle in youth, poor in age; and *therefore* the common law abhors all monopolies, which prohibit any from working in any lawful trade. ... [The ordinances of the Tailors Company] are against the liberty of the subject, and a means of extortion in drawing money from them ... or of oppression of young tradesmen, by the old and rich of the same trade, not permitting them to work in their trade freely; and all this is against the common law and the commonwealth ... [141]

Coke does concede that "ordinances for the good order and government of men of trades and mysteries are good, but not to restrain anyone in his lawful mystery." He does not give (either here or anywhere else) any criterion by which to decide between "order" and "hindrance." But such a problem does not trouble Coke or the court, because his heart is. not in refinements of this kind. He is concerned to set men free for work and generally, it appears to him, corporate controls militate against that objective.

The Tailors Company had been established in Ipswich for two hundred years, and it had been incorporated by the king. If the defendant had infringed the charter during the reigns of Henry VII or VIII, the case, as Thorne points out, "would have been quickly and easily decided in the plaintiff's favour. The defendant would have gotten little sympathy from the courts."[142] Yet Coke confidently asserts that the spirit of the *Ipswich Case* "is and always has been the common law."

140. 11 *CR*, 53a. ff.
141. 11 *CR*, 54a; my italics.
142. Thorne, *op. cit.*, 11. Miss Malament's essay (*op. cit.*, 1336-1337) suffers by not taking seriously these judgments of Thorne's.

"In this outrageously unhistorical statement," continues Thorne, "several centuries of gild life are brushed aside as though they had never existed."

> Clearly we have left the fifteenth century behind, broken completely with the past, yet out of isolated remarks in fourteenth-century cases, and by ignoring others, Coke somehow managed to give this seventeenth-century view a semblance of historical support. So in his next point. In the middle ages the gild had supervised production, and seen to it that goods were well produced and that a man practising an art was skilful at it. It is not the past but the future that is implicit in Coke's remark that *anyone may practise an art*, for he who takes work upon himself is unskilful, his ignorance is a sufficient punishment for him. He will get no clients.[143]

In his *Institutes*, Coke elaborates and reinforces his reaction to economic control in keeping with his ideology of voluntary labor. "Monopolies in times past," he says, summarizing his entire position, "were ever without law, but never without friends."[144] Coke gives the term "monopoly" an extremely broad definition; it is, he argues,

> . . . an Institution, or allowance by the King by his Grant, Commission, or otherwise to any person or persons, bodies politique, or corporate, of or for the sole buying, selling, making, working, or using of anything whereby any person or persons, bodies politique, or corporate, are sought to be restrained of any freedome, or liberty that they had before, or hindered in their lawfull trade.

> And the law of the Realm, in this point is grounded upon the law of God, which saith, "No man shall take a mill or an upper millstone in pledge, for he would be taking a life in pledge:" Whereby it appeareth that a mans trade is accounted his life, because it maintaineth his life; therefore the Monopolist that taketh away a mans trade, taketh away his life, and, therefore is so much more odious because he is *vir sanguinis*. Against these Inventors and Propounders of evill things, the holy ghost hath spoken, *Inventores malorum*, etc. *digni sunt morte*.[145]

"That Monopolies are against the ancient and Fundamentall laws of the

---

143. Thorne, *op. cit.*, 12; my italics. See the discussion of *Davenant* v. *Hurdis* above.
144. III *Institutes*, 182. From the point of view of the law, this is an incredible statement.
145. III *Institutes*, 181. Special attention should be called to the biblical justification for this ideology. The use of the Bible tells us much more about Coke's point of view than it does about the text.

Realm . . . and that the Monopolist was in times past, and is much more
now punishable, for obtaining and procuring of them, we will demonstrate it by reason, and prove it by authority."[146] Or, as he says in
another connection, "this conclusion is necessarily gathered, that all
monopolies concerning trade and traffique, are against the liberty and
freedom declared and graunted by this great Charter, and against divers
other Acts of Parliament, which are good commentaries upon
[it] . . ."[147]

Perhaps Coke's bias against economic control becomes strongest in a
passage from II *Institutes*. It is, he says, "most commonly hurtfull to
the Commonwealth" to create *"New Corporations trading into foreign
parts, or at home, which under the fair pretence of order and government, in conclusion tend to the hindrance of trade and traffique, and in
the end produce Monopolies."*[148] The logical relation he draws between the formation of corporations and the development of monopolies is a clear example of the new mentality regarding corporations in
general to which we have referred. There is an important hint that the
very organization of economic life into corporate forms whose status
and function are limited and controlled by the common law is in itself
repressive and detrimental. Quite unconsciously, and in complete contradiction to themes discovered earlier, we see emerging in Coke's
theory of corporations not only the obvious deprecation of patrimonial
control over economic activity, but also (implicitly, at least) *the rejection of many of the established forms of political-legal regulation of
economic life*. There is an inclination in Coke's writing in favor of the
autonomy of business and industry, of general freedom from restraint,
so that individuals may become, in Coke's own word, "voluntaries."

Because Coke and his colleagues were only beginning to establish in
the most halting and incomplete way some of the institutional patterns
that would become regnant in the age of laissez faire, it is all the more
remarkable to note the similarities of language between Coke and Adam
Smith, particularly in the fields of monopolies and guild regulations.
Like Coke, Smith argues: "The exclusive privilege of an incorporated
trade necessarily restrains the competition, in the town where it is
established, to those who are free of the trade."[149] Again, as Coke
claimed in *Darcy* v. *Allen*, "It is to prevent [the] reduction of price,

146. III *Institutes*, 181.
147. II *Institutes*, 63.
148. *Ibid.*, 540; my italics.
149. *Wealth of Nations* (London, 1893), 93.

and consequently of wages and profit, by restraining that free competition which would most certainly occasion it, that all corporations, and the greater part of corporation laws, have been established."[150] As to the matter of guild regulations, Smith speaks in language that might have been found in *Davenant* v. *Hurdis* or *Tailors of Ipswich:* "The pretence that corporations are necessary for the better government of the trade, is without any foundation. The real and effectual discipline which is exercised over a workman, is not that of his corporation, but that of his customers. . . . If you would have your work tolerably executed, it must be done in the suburbs, where the workmen, *having no exclusive privilege,* have nothing but their character to depend upon . . . "[151]

Although it would be fanciful to claim that Coke, or anyone else in the early seventeenth century, was a thoroughgoing exponent of free enterprise, it is notable that there is a profound resistance to the legal task of defining and regulating economic corporations. As in the statement quoted above on new corporations, Coke at important points apparently feels that the very process of incorporation carries with it the kind of direct legal interference in economic life which he opposes. Because Coke stands so close to the medieval conception of corporation, in which "monoply" and "direct control" are the conditions *sine qua non,* it is perhaps not surprising that he takes such a negative view. To talk of corporations is, for Coke, to talk of undue restraint. It does not occur to him that new forms of legal association might be worked out in accord with his "voluntaristic" objectives. At least, he shows no concern whatsoever in constructing a corporate theory to meet the demands of the times.

There is, in other words, a selective devaluation of traditional corporate structures. It begins to appear that this dimension of "free enterprise" (quite restricted, to be sure) is what Coke means by the "rule of the common law." For him, here is the true measure of what the law has always really been, although he regretfully tolerates certain special corporate privileges because they have the "force of custom" as well as the "authority of parliament."

As we have glimpsed already, Coke's position is by no means only negative. He is not simply opposed to monopoly restraints. From his

---

150. *Ibid,* 97.
151. *Ibid.,* 102; my italics. Lipson also connects the widespread bias among the lawyers with the roots of laissez-faire theory, which he sees emerging around the turn of the seventeenth century. Lipson, *op. cit.,* II, cxxxv ff.

points of view, the "old law" has free-willing industriousness for its goal. While, on the one hand, the law must emancipate economic life from direct restraints and special privileges, it must, on the other, throw its whole weight behind the encouragement and nourishment of voluntary labor. The positive functions of the law in this respect are spelled out more fully in Coke's attitude toward the poor laws than in his decisions and pronouncements on corporations. Indeed, an examination of his treatment of the poor laws fills in important dimensions of the mentality at work in the cases on corporation.

The intense preoccupation with "the execution of good laws" to "set the young and idle people as voluntaries on worke"[152] is summarized in Coke's *Charge* given at Norwich in 1607:

> And the tranquilitie of our Publicke weale preserved: which so great happinesse, that it may the better be accomplished, I would request, that all imployed in any place of authoritie, would have an speciall care to suppresse that root of evill, from whence all mischiefs do proceed, and that is idlenesse.... For were the Justice of the Lawe rightly executed uppon such offendors ... [they] would be inforced to betake themselves unto a better course of life, and live as becometh good Subjects in the list of a more commended obedience.

The attitude toward poor laws expressed in this sentence must, of course, be seen against a background of growing concern in England over the impoverished and the idle. Already in the thirteenth century public sentiment for the poor and vagrants had been awakened. However, due to the enclosures, the dissolution of the monasteries, and so on, it was not until the sixteenth century that beggars and vagrants became "a chronic plague."[153] Legislative relief became imperative, and many experiments were developed, none of which was particularly effective in itself, but each contributing to the shaping of a general Elizabethan policy. Among these experiments was the creation of Bridewell, an almshouse which was to serve as the model for the later Houses of Correction. Bridewell was an attempt to meet the increasing demand that something be done with the army of "sturdy beggars" that roamed the countryside. Its punitive character marked the rising antagonism against vagrants, voiced in the latter part of the sixteenth century and throughout the seventeenth. Coke reflected that growing antagonism.

But Coke was not at all satisfied with the various pieces of major

152. II *Institutes*, 734.
153. Leonard, *Early History of English Poor Relief*, 11.

legislation which had been passed toward the beginning of the seventeenth century. Despite the extremely harsh bills against the vagrants in
1572 and 1597,[154] Coke could still remark in his *Institutes:* "True it is
that there be good lawes already to punish idlenesse, but none of sufficient force or effect to set youth, or the idle on work."[155] Coke is
concerned to root out all forms of idleness with unrelenting zeal. He is
as opposed to the "sort of seeming Gentlemen" as he is to the sturdy
beggar. The law must find out such fellows and teach them "that the
wisdome of a Kingdome's state, in the framing of a statute Law, could
not be deluded by a vaine and shallow braind idlenesse of their ridicu-
lous Foolery."[156]

Consequently, he praises 7 Jac. Regis, 4 (1609-10) as being far superior to 39 Eliz. c. 4 (1597) for the instruments of enforcement it
provides, and for its profounder grasp of the problem of idleness. The
main intention of the bill is to intensify the activity of the justices of
peace in the job of ferreting out idle persons and making sure they are
sent to Houses of Correction. According to Leonard, this bill is completely unconcerned with the "deserving poor" and focuses its attention exclusively upon transforming the indolent. It probably marks the
time, she says, "when Houses of Correction ceased to be half-work
houses and became much more like gaols."[157] Coke points out in his
commentary on the statute, that 39 Eliz. resolved that able-bodied
persons who refused to work should be sent to a House of Correction.
Nonetheless, the distinction between 39 Eliz. and 7 Jac. at just this
point was, for Coke, crucial:

But [said 39 Eliz.] if they have any lawfull meanes to live by,

---

154. It was 39 Eliz. that Perkins spoke so highly of. According to Black, *op. cit.*,
     223-224, the Act of 1572 made the treatment of the sturdy beggar much
     harsher than previous measures: "He was to be whipped and bored through
     the gristle of the right ear, and if he continued in his roguery he was to
     suffer, in the last resort, death for felony." By an amendment in 1576,
     rogues "were to be sent to 'houses of correction,' two of which were to be
     erected in each county, and there disciplined to labour." The Act of 1597,
     says Black, modified the brutality somewhat, although only relatively: "Bor-
     ing of the ear was dropped, but the sturdy beggar, after being whipped 'until
     his or her body be bloody,' was to be sent back to his birthplace, or, if that
     was unknown, to the place where he last dwelt, and there to be thrown into
     a house of correction or the common jail until he could be placed in
     service."
155. III *Institutes*, Epilogue.
156. *Charge.*
157. Leonard, *op. cit.*, 137.

though they be of able bodies, and refuse to worke, yet are they not
to be sent to the House of Correction.

But by this Statute of 7 Jac ... *though they have lawfull meanes
to live by,* yet if they be idle or disorderly persons, the Justices of
Peace have power to committ them to the House of Correction, a
generall and large power given to them, *without exception of any
person.* And their Mittimus to the House of Correction may be more
safely upon this Statute, *Quia otiosa et inordinata persona:* for that
he is an idle person, or that he is a disorderly person, according to
the words of this Act, [than] upon the statute of 39 Eliz.[158]

This passage is crucial to the general concerns of our analysis. It
designates unavoidably the significance of *work as an end in itself.* Even
though individuals possess "Lawfull meanes to live by," if they are idle,
they must be set on work! It is not so much poverty and mendicancy
that is of primary importance here, but the disinclination to work.
That, above all, is what must be rooted out; that is what the law must
change. For this reason, Coke hopes for "the better and more Speedy
execution of these excellent Statutes ... " "For that few or none are
committed to the common Gaole amongst so many malefactors but
they come out worse than they went in. And few are committed to the
House of Correction, or Working House, but they come out better."[159]

It cannot, of course, be argued that the strong emphasis upon work
and the strictures against idleness among the lawyers are as such completely new. During the Tudor period, and especially in the reign of
Elizabeth, there was widespread aversion to "that lothsome monster
Idelnesse (the mother and breeder of Vacabounds) ... that pestilent
Canker ... which is the root of all mischief."[160] But there is a crucial
difference between the use to which Coke puts this kind of language
and the use to which it is put by Elizabeth and Colbert. Coke's appeals
to the virtues of voluntary labor have the effect of undermining the
patrimonial forms of economic control (i.e., monopolies, special privileges, etc.) that are characteristic of the "autarky" of Elizabeth and
Colbert. (As we have shown, it also had the effect of undermining

158. II *Institutes,* 730-731; my italics.
159. II *Institutes,* 734.
160. Stone, *op. cit.,* 115; cf. R. H. Tawney and E. Power (eds.), *Tudor Economic
     Documents* (London, 1924), II, 240, 389. This sort of language is found, for
     example, in the Elizabethan poor laws. Furthermore, there was an equally
     strong campaign against idleness in Colbert's France, Heckscher, *op. cit.,* II,
     154-155; cf. Kurt Samuelsson, *Religion and Economic Action* (London,
     1961).

long-standing customary forms of control.) It is inconceivable that proponents of the autarkic state would have so employed the rhetoric of work. For them labor was a tool for the enrichment of the State, clearly subordinate to the discretionary economic intervention of the crown. For Coke (as for the Puritans), work was coming to have an importance that was quite distinct from traditional assumptions about the political domination of industry; it was coming to be set in a relatively autonomous context.

So if we take the emphasis upon voluntary labor that is found in Coke's treatment of the poor laws together with the sentiments expressed in *Davenant* v. *Hurdis, Darcy* v. *Allen*, the *Tailors of Ipswich Case*, and in sections of the *Institutes*, it becomes obvious that there are dimensions of thought which conflict drastically with Coke's broader "theory" of law, as well as with many of the ideas we discovered in such decisions as the *City of London Case* and the *Chamberlain of London's Case*. The concept of an omnicompetent, all-encompassing common law—able directly to control, define, and reflect the unity and harmony of the entire social order in accord with existing or established patterns—has now been sharply altered. The idea that the common law sanctions and regulates the special economic privileges of "ancient" corporations as, for example, in the *City of London Case*, is now replaced by a notion of law which *sets a considerable portion of the social order free to act by its own laws and to develop its own order*. Coke's passion for an economic society in which men become unrestrained "voluntaries" is every bit as intense as Perkins's; indeed, important similarities can be found between the Calvinist Puritan pattern of order and this set of new dimensions in Coke's thought. There is here a quite different understanding of social action and relations, one that introduces tension into Coke's thought compellingly analagous to the kind of tension we have seen between Puritanism and Anglicanism.

For Whitgift and Hooker, the kind of emphasis upon self-initiative in economic relations which is found in the Calvinist Puritan pattern of order, and which here finds such a striking parallel in Coke, threatens to "overturn the world and make every man his own commander." Hooker writes: "Those things which the law of God leaveth arbitrary and at liberty are all subject unto positive laws of men, which laws for the common benefit abridge particular men's liberty in such things as far as the rules of equity will suffer."[161] Yet with respect to existing

161. Hooker, *Laws*, II, 363.

corporation law, at least, we find Coke brushing aside several centuries of positive laws on the assumption that direct intervention in economic activity is deleterious. Not only does he make room for "free enterprise," he also turns the law to the service of what Weber called "inner-worldy asceticism," i.e., to the encouragement of self-initiated and self-determined activism. To use the law in this way would have horrified Hooker and Whitgift. For them, the law does not drive toward or point to any independent source of order beyond itself.

The general point here is simply that the sentiment for direct common law control of corporate association discovered in the earlier analysis, and the sentiment for freedom of economic action discussed in this section, are congruent with a similar theological conflict.

So far as the impact of voluntarism on the law of corporations is concerned, one cannot help recalling part of Hooker's statement on the social effects of Puritanism. Among its other destructive consequences, he says, it "shaketh universally the fabric of government . . . dissipateth . . . corporations . . . and whatsoever is now through the providence of God by authority and power upheld."[162] The dimensions of Coke's thought just analyzed, which correspond so remarkably to the implications of the Puritan system, had an exceedingly "dissipating" effect upon his attitude toward corporations. Corporations tended, after all, to produce monopolies! On the other hand, Coke was not ready to do away with all corporations, or with all their special privileges. Under certain circumstances, exclusive corporate control is acceptable, though it must of course be subjected to the common law.

The problem is that these two different approaches to corporations do not get on well together. Francis Bacon saw the deep confusion very perceptively in a speech made in the House of Commons in 1601. After eloquently defending the queen's right to the full use of her prerogative, he remarked with not a little sarcasm: "If her Majesty makes a patent, or a monopoly, to any of her servants; that we must go and cry out against: But if she grants it to a number of burgesses, or corporation, that must stand; and that, forsooth, is no monopoly."[163] The process of reasoning by which an industrial or craft monopoly was rejected and a municipal monopoly (e.g., London) accepted was, of course, just the issue. If the "rule of common law" or "common right" stood consistently against *all* monopolies (as Coke said more than once), and if it sponsored freedom from restraint and control, how was

162. Hooker, *Laws* II, 362; see above.
163. Reprinted in Price, *op. cit.,* 154-155; referred to in Neale, *op. cit.,* II, 378.

it that the "ancient law" could also justify the most rigorous kind of
corporate monopoly privilege? And if liberty of economic action was
such an obvious "rule" of the old law, enacted by so many "divers acts
of parliament," how was it that so many other acts of Parliament and
so many customs had so often endorsed and extended these monopoly
privileges? Coke's mind boggled at these questions. He had no answer.
He could only utter the solemn refrain: "It is to be observed that acts
of parliament that are made against the freedom of trade . . . never live
long."[164]

Some sort of uneasy co-existence had to be struck between these
contending views, and that was soon accomplished in the Statute
of Monopolies (21 Jac. I, c. 3, 1623), the drafting of which was inspired by Coke himself. The statute is the fruit of over thirty years'
agitation against monopolies, which had first come to a head in the
Parliament of 1601. Elizabeth had assuaged Parliament's ire by conceding common law jurisdiction over letters patent and by promising
that the most obnoxious monopolies would be promptly eliminated.
Parliament and the country were temporarily satisfied, especially so
since the beginning of James's reign was punctuated with pious statements against the issuing of exclusive patents. Such statements appeared, for example, in the *Book of Bounty* (1610). This treatise
announced the king's opposition to "all grants of monopolies," but
soon after it appeared James commenced a wild policy of patent-
granting to exceed anything seen up to his time. The Statute of Monopolies held against him his early remarks in the *Book of Bounty:*

> For as much as your most excellent Majesty . . . did in [1610] . . .
> publish in print to the whole realm and to all posterity, that all
> grants of monopolies and of the benefit of any penal laws, or
> of power to dispense with the law, or to compound for the for-
> feiture, are contrary to your Majesty's laws, which your Majesty's
> declaration is truly consonant and agreeable to the ancient and
> fundamental laws of this your realm . . .

In broad and inclusive language, the statute proceeds to lay it down
that

> *all monopolies and all commissions, grants, licenses, charters, and
> letters patents heretofore made or granted, or heretofore to be made
> or granted to any person or persons, bodies politic or corporate
> whatsoever,* of or for the sole buying, selling, making, working or
> using of anything within this realm or the dominion of Wales, or of

164. IV *Institutes,* 31.

any other monopolies or of power, liberty, or faculty to dispense with any others, or to give license or toleration to do, use, or exercise anything against the tenor or purport of any law or statute . . . *are altogether contrary to the laws of this realm, and so are and shall be utterly void and none effect,* and in no wise put in use or execution [italics added] :

However, at Section V a long discussion on exceptions to this pronouncement begins. Permission is given for the special protection of infant industries, new inventions, and the like. Then, at Section IX, appears a set of provisions of the greatest interest to us:

Provided also, and it is hereby further intended, declared, and enacted that this act or anything therein contained shall not in any wise extend or be prejudicial unto the city of London, or to any city, borough, or town corporate within this realm, for or concerning any grants, charters, or letters patents to them or any of them made or granted, or for or concerning any custom or customs used within them or any of them or unto any corporations, companies, or fellowships of any art, trade, occupation, or mistery, or to any companies or societies of merchants within this realm, erected for the maintenance, enlargement, or ordering of any trade of merchandise, but that the same charters, customs, corporations, companies, fellowships, and societies, and their liberties, privileges, powers, and immunities, shall be and continue of such force and effect as they were before the making of this act, and of none other . . .

These contrasting passages are full of confusions. In Section I the statement that "all monopolies . . . granted to any person or persons, bodies politic or corporate whatsoever . . . are altogether contrary to the laws of this realm" is, as should by now be obvious, patently absurd. Historically, the creation of "companies or societies of merchants . . . for the maintenance, enlargement, or ordering of any trade of merchandise" (IX) involved by definition "the sole buying, selling, making, working or using" (I) of a given trade, craft, or range of goods. It would, for example, be hard to show that the Company of the Ipswich Tailors, established for some two centuries, was not "erected for the maintenance, enlargement, or ordering" of a trade. Yet it was rather arbitrarily adjudged under the strictures of Section I and rendered illegal. The point is these definitions are so broad and so overlapping that there is no specific criterion by which to make a decision. Consequently, common law decisions as to what was and was not a "monoply" were as in the *Tailors of Ipswich Case,* simply arbitrary, depending on ideological assumptions of the judges.

The means of jamming contradictory tendencies together in the statute of monopolies is hardly satisfactory. That there is no explicit or implicit attempt to relate or harmonize Sections I and IX may be taken as evidence of the same sublime confidence we have discovered in Coke. Somehow, apparent contradictions and unclarities within the law simply do reconcile themselves eventually. Such is the unity and harmony of the "ancient and fundamental laws of this your realm." It is an article of faith.

PART IV.
CONCLUSION

Max Weber was fascinated by the problem of order. That problem stimulated him to investigate the various ways in which societies structured their institutions and designed centers of authority, and to examine the process by which a pattern of social order became "significant" or "legitimate" in the hearts and minds of "whole groups of men." Accordingly, Weber was unwilling to dissociate normative patterns of belief and action from the actual elaboration of institutional arrangements. For him, the problem of order was at once a matter of religious-moral commitment and a matter of organizing political, familial, and economic relations.

More particularly, Weber wished to understand the process by which modern capitalism developed into a way of life, into a pattern of order that commanded loyalty. Assuming, as he did, that institutional developments are never self-authenticating, but always rely on "higher" justifications, Weber set out to show that the leading characteristics of rational capitalism found religious warrant in English Puritanism. Correspondingly, he claimed that "traditionalistic" social patterns (whether patrimonial or otherwise) were deeply opposed to rational capitalism and thus rested on religious-moral foundations quite contrary to those of Puritanism. Weber, of course, thought of Anglicanism and its aristocratic social bias in just these terms.

In other words, Weber's argument in *The Protestant Ethic and the Spirit of Capitalism* depends upon the truth of three propositions:

(1) that "rational capitalism" constitutes a recognizable way of life, with its own inherent institutional and normative characteristics, a

way of life that conflicts with the equally recognizable patterns of traditionalism;

(2) that England in the seventeenth century was the setting for at least the beginnings of a struggle between these two types of social order; and

(3) that Puritanism and Anglicanism can be shown to polarize meaningfully along the lines of this conflict, and to have rendered the two types of order respectively legitimate on the basis of distinctive religious presuppositions.

So far as the first two propositions are concerned, we have argued that part of the radical social tension of late-sixteenth- and early-seventeenth-century England involved a conflict between rudimentary rational capitalism and traditionalistic economic organization. Throughout, the category of "differentiation" has been considered central. According to Weber, rational capitalism is distinguished, above all, by modes of calculation and behavior that are specifically and systematically "oriented, by deliberate planning, to economic ends." This means that the market becomes relatively free of outside control. Rational economic activity, in becoming more autonomous, encourages private or voluntary enterprise on the universalistic basis of "saleable services" or functional capabilities. Preferential treatment, whether as the result of political favoritism or customary privilege, is minimized. In fact, severe limitations are placed upon the opportunities for economic interference permitted the political-legal agencies. In Rheinstein's words, "modern capitalism requires a legal system which guarantees ... freedom from arbitrary, unpredictable government interference."

Naturally it has here and there been emphasized, as Weber knew very well, that rational capitalism did not come into its own in any unmistakable way until the nineteenth century. However, the analysis of certain early-seventeenth-century decisions in corporation law—decisions like *Davenant* v. *Hurdis, Darcy* v. *Allen,* and *Tailors of Ipswich*—reveals a remarkable foreshadowing of the characteristics of rational capitalism. Not only did Coke and his colleagues greatly circumscribe the economic power of the crown (*Prince's Case* and *Darcy* v. *Allen*); even more significantly, they overturned such longstanding forms of industrial regulation as the guild monopolies (*Davenant* v. *Hurdis* and *Tailors of Ipswich*). Indeed, the Statute of Monopolies of 1623 boldly instituted Coke's unhistorical judgment that "monopolies in times past were ever without law, but never without friends."

All of this innovation contributed to the emancipation of industrial activity from the fetters of tradition and to the development of a few rational legal categories as general ground rules for business practice. The law of contract, the law of patents (contained within the Statute of Monopolies),[1] as well, of course, as the law against all monopolies not specially provided for, are examples of these general ground rules. Of most interest to us is the set of appeals made: to "free voluntarism" in trade, to the opportunity for anyone to practice a trade, and so on.

Against the background of the Middle Ages and the age of the Tudors, Coke's determinations in the field of industrial activity amounted to a pronounced departure from tradition. As we saw, the foundations were laid here—however incomplete they might be—for the emergence of a free market economy some two centuries later.

There are grounds, then, for identifying the late sixteenth and early seventeenth century as the setting for an important breakthrough in the elaboration of economic institutions, a breakthrough of the kind sought by Weber. There are also grounds for contrasting these inclinations toward rational capitalism with the configuration of patterns appropriately called "traditionalism."

Whether we are considering the pure traditionalism of the lawyers or the patrimonial traditionalism of the Tudors and Stuarts, it should be clear that neither represents a type of order conducive to economic differentiation. The kind of general position Coke developed on corporations *only in spite of itself* encouraged independent business action. The judgments of the *City of London Case* and the *Chamberlain of London's Case,* both of which tolerated customary town monopolies, do not harmonize with the antimonopoly decisions. A similar discrepancy was noted in the Statute of Monopolies.

As a matter of fact, legal traditionalism in itself could never be relied upon to provide anything more than arbitrary and sporadic restrictions against market interference. To take the patterns of the ancient realm as the final standard was to open the door for all kinds of irrational controls such as were allowed in decisions like the *City of London Case.* It does not take much wit to appreciate that the ancient realm consisted of a system of very extensive town, guild, and patent monopolies. Even Coke would have had a hard time ignoring them completely. Certainly, without the introduction of some new ideas, ideas that substantially undercut the patterns of the old order, the antimonopoly

1. See *General Economic History*, 231.

decisions could never have been determined in the way they were. Thorne is right: "It is not the past but the future" that is implied in many of Coke's legal judgments.

Patrimonialism, like unaided legal traditionalism, does not possess the requisites for economic differentiation. The tendency of the Tudors and Early Stuarts to encourage "court-bound capitalism" in direct opposition to a free market is abundantly obvious. Political absolutism is no more suited to rational capitalism than are the patterns of medieval industrial life.

What is especially interesting about the struggle between the lawyers and the crown in this period is that it amounts to more than a simple conflict between customary law and royal prerogative. Indeed, this is one of the major conclusions of our study of the cases on corporation. Had the lawyers been concerned only to assert traditional rights and privileges against the crown, a decision like *Darcy* v. *Allen* would have turned out quite differently. As we saw, a persuasive case could have been made for the "ancient rights" of London as opposed to the "arbitrary" and "recent" patent which Elizabeth had dispensed. Were that argument adopted by the courts, it would merely have represented one form of market regulation against another. That kind of contest would have been understandable in terms of the ancient law.

But the conclusion of *Darcy* v. *Allen*—that all monopolies are void— is a decision not only against the crown, but also (unconsciously) against established law. It places the discussion of industrial activity in a new context, revealing that the tensions of pre-Revolutionary England do not by any means exhaust themselves in the conflict between legal and patrimonial traditionalism. At least at the point of *Darcy* v. *Allen*, *Tailors of Ipswich*, *Davenant* v. *Hurdis*, etc., the struggle is between the two types of traditionalism on the one side, and the beginnings of rational capitalism on the other.

The general relevance of Weber's typology of order to late sixteenth- and early seventeenth-century England has, hopefully, been established. The tensions of society, as reflected in the legal decisions, constitute the social institutional setting within which we examined the third of Weber's propositions: that Puritanism and Anglicanism can be shown to be wrestling in religious terms with this very conflict of order.

In dealing with Weber's conclusions—both on the independence of a religious-moral system and on the connection between religious-moral commitment and a conception of social life—a new method has been suggested. We have claimed that it is fruitful to analyze religious language in terms of the ingredients of "order." Different religious systems will have a different symbolic understanding of the source and nature of order (the command and structural dimensions), as well as of the demands of obedience and the character of disobedience and disorder. Religious systems will respond in some coherent way to all the essential implications of "order," and the kind of response given will lead to a particular concept of social order. Indeed, the fact that religious language handles the problem of order provides a theoretical basis for pursuing connections between theological assertions and social institutional arrangements, just as Weber did.

We have taken issue with all the critics of Weber who declare that a positive association between Puritanism and the spirit of rational capitalism is impossible. The heart and soul of Calvinism and late sixteenth-century Puritanism is the idea of a differentiated new order. As we argued at the end of Chapter 4, the ethical implications of the new order correspond strkingly with Weber's characteristics of rational capitalism. Above all, the principle of the new order sanctioned an independent sphere of behavior, one that devalues political authority and established social patterns. It emphasizes instead voluntary, consensual participation on the basis of universalistic criteria, and it gives special place to self-initiated economic behavior as an aspect of one's religious calling.

Through the investigation of Calvin, Cartwright, and Perkins, we have demonstrated the fundamentally common theological-moral pattern of order they all share. In other words, we have made clear the degree to which theological continuities existed between Calvin and the Elizabethan Puritans, despite their discontinuities and differences. Given the understanding Weber had of the spirit of rational capitalism, it is indeed possible that for good theological reasons the Calvinist Puritan system could be associated with it.

It may be, however, that Weber's own conclusion about the association between Puritanism and rational capitalism as stated in *The Protestant Ethic* is, finally, oversimple. As we have tried to make clear, Calvinist Puritanism has its own inner dynamics; just as it does not lead automatically to a "free Church," neither does it lead automatically to a "free economy." While Calvinism is noticeably distinct from either Anglicanism or Lutheranism in elaborating a theological basis for differentiated order, it possesses countervailing tendencies as well. It has on its hands what I called the dilemma of earthy power, and under certain circumstances it inclines to *de*-differentiate the new order from the old.

Geneva, Colonial New England, Scotland, even Cromwellian England, are all examples of this important aspect of Calvinist Puritanism. In these instances, it could hardly be argued that either the Church or the economy institutionalized in any very radical way the characteristics of independence, voluntarism, etc.

Yet the characteristics of ascetic Protestantism are never eliminated entirely, for the good reason that they are inherent in the fundamental theological and ecclesiological affirmations of Calvinism. They are, so to speak, carried with Calvinism wherever it goes. Calvin's own thought was analyzed in detail precisely to demonstrate how the ingredients of ascetic Protestantism could emerge from the theological position of one who is not in any obvious sense a free churchman or a free enterpriser.

At various points, the historical picture is more complex than some of Weber's judgments imply. It is possible to gain the impression from *The Protestant Ethic* that ascetic Protestantism more or less inevitably "homes" toward the characteristics of a differentiated, rational capitalist economy and that once Puritanism appears, an ever-expanding open market cannot be far behind. Of course, this was not the case in the early American colonies or, for that matter, in Puritan England. As we have argued, the study of Calvinist Puritanism must do full justice to the tensions within the system; we must be able to show how the inclinations toward social, religious, and economic regimentation (so obvious in colonial New England, for example) can and did live side by side with inclinations in the opposite direction—toward vigorous, voluntary action in Church and world to the glory of God.

Given the sort of method developed here, *the association between Calvinist Puritanism and the modern capitalist spirit remains always a live possibility, but never a necessity.* It remains a possibility for critically important theological, ecclesiological, and ethical reasons within its pattern of order. We can agree with Weber's conclusions in *The Protestant Ethic* up to a point: when Puritanism appears, there will be special pressure toward voluntary, self-initiated economic behavior.

At the same time, the association is never a necessary or inevitable one—both because of historical contingencies and of the countervailing tendencies within Calvinist Puritanism. The notion of the new order very readily generates a religious elite which seeks, to a degree at least, to subordinate the old order to its perceptions of righteousness. When that happens, a fully rational economy is not exactly around the corner.

Nevertheless, while I have seen fit to introduce a number of qualifications into Weber's understanding of Puritanism, I would certainly not agree with Kolko so far as the English experience is concerned. Kolko asserts that Weber misunderstood the nature of Puritanism and sharply exaggerated "its differences with Anglicanism as a means of social control and economic stimulus."[2] If our investigations have established anything, it is that there is nothing in the official Anglican position even to begin to sanction a differentiated pattern of order, or any of Weber's marks of a rational society. Our judgment here can be quite categorical. If Anglicans ever did come to favor a free market, independent of political and traditional regulation, if they ever came to side with voluntarism in ecclesiastical and social affairs, they did not derive this attitude from sixteenth-century Anglicanism (just as Coke did not derive his attitude toward monopolies from Anglicanism or from the ancient realm). So far as these things are concerned, there simply is no ambiguity in Whitgift and Hooker. Their views on social control and economic stimulus are almost diametrically opposed to the views of Cartwright and Perkins.

There is, of course, one notable point of ambiguity within the Anglican position, a point of utmost relevance to our examination of the tensions between legal and patrimonial traditionalism. Both Whitgift and Hooker straddle the fence on the question of royal authority *versus* the authority of the old order. Both make room for the discretion of the crown in Church and society; yet both come very close to a kind of Cokian theory of fundamental law. Both affirmed with Bracton that the king rules *sub Deo et lege*. What is important is that before the turn of the seventeenth century a serious conflict between crown and law was not anticipated. The old order was seen to be a harmonious, integrated whole, with all the parts complementing one another. The discretion of the crown was understood to be part of the ancient pattern—as it assuredly was.

My own impression is that the early seventeenth-century struggle between the two types of traditionalism did pose questions of social order for which no ready answers could be found in the ancient realm or the Anglican tradition. Obviously, the crown and the courts could not work together indefinitely so long as each was making the kind of claims to authority it was. A solution had to be found, but it would have to come from sources other than the old English order. In one

2. Gabriel Kolko, "Max Weber on America: Theory and Evidence," in George H. Nadel (ed.), *Studies in the Philosophy of History* (New York, 1965), 196. See Bibliographical Essay A for a further discussion of Kolko's essay.

sense it was a struggle that should not have been taking place at all. The deep-seated tensions of early seventeenth-century English society had to be solved by some rather novel rearrangements of political and legal institutions. However, such rearrangements never were the strong suit of the Anglican Establishment.

At the beginning of this book it was questioned whether, in roughly sixty years, Max Weber has been dispensed with, or whether there are suggestions in his method that can be helpful to the study of religion and society. There should be no mistaking the answer. Weber made an abiding contribution not only to the systematic study of society, but to the investigation of religious phenomena as well. The key concept of order elaborated here provides an important link in relating religious-moral language to the issues of social organization. It is hoped that this book has helped to emphasize Weber's true significance and to supplement and revise his work fruitfully.

Bibliographical Essays

A. Representative Literature Critical of The Protestant Ethic

The literature critical of Weber's conclusions on mainly historical grounds is immense; to list all the relevant material would be too tedious. I shall simply identify authors who advance one or more of the criticisms mentioned in Chapter 1, and briefly evaluate some of their arguments. (For an excellent summary of literature on the Weber thesis up to 1944, see Ephraim Fischoff, "The Protestant Ethic and the Spirit of Capitalism," *Social Research* [February 1944]. Also, for a good anthology of the debate, see R. W. Green, *Protestantism and Capitalism* [Boston, 1959]).

H. R. Trevor-Roper, in "Religion, the Reformation and Social Change," in G. A. Hayes-McCoy (ed.), *Historical Studies, IV: Papers Read Before the Fifth Irish Conference of Historians* (London, 1963), 18-44, attempts to undercut Weber's argument by contending that there was nothing original or distinctive about the spirit of capitalism in post-Reformation England, or about Calvinism as compared with other intellectual movements of the time. This is an impressive and scholarly essay; one can learn from it. However, apart from a number of minor questions, I have two criticisms: (1) Trevor-Roper makes the mistake of confusing kinds of capitalism: "The idea that large-scale industrial capitalism was ideologically impossible before the Reformation is exploded by the simple fact that it existed. Until the invention of the steam engine, its scope may have been limited, but within that scope it probably reached its highest peak in the age of the Fugger" (29). Weber was aware that large-scale industrial capitalism existed outside seventeenth-century England. It existed in Tudor and Stuart England, in the France of Colbert, as well as in the age of the Fuggers. But all these forms of capitalism were politically oriented. It is not the matter of size that tells the tale, but the degree of differentiation (i.e.,

226

rationalization). (See *The Protestant Ethic,* 65.) If this is the case, then we still must deal—as Trevor-Roper does not—with the emergence of a quite distinctive kind of capitalism. (2) The other criticism is much more relevant to the matter of Calvinism itself. At Trevor-Roper's hand, Calvin turns out quite wondrously to be little more than an "Erasmian," a child of the Renaissance. "For Calvin, far more than is generally admitted, was the heir of Erasmus" (31). Whatever ideas Calvin had that were relevant to the world (such as "calling"), he got from Erasmus (30). While conceding the undeniable connections between Erasmus and Calvin, I think Trevor-Roper has exaggerated them beyond the bounds of reason, as I try to show in Chapter 3. Thus at two central points Trevor-Roper's essay is anything but adequate.

Reformation scholars such as André Biéler, *La pensée économique et sociale de Calvin* (Geneva, 1959), 493 ff., Josef Bohatec, *Calvins Lehre von Staat und Kirche* (Breslau, 1937), and to some extent Karl Holl, *Cultural Significance of the Reformation* (New York, 1959) have asserted a fundamental divergence between primitive Calvinism and English Puritanism. Calvin was not, say they, an advocate of atomistic or unrestrained economic individualism, nor were the doctrines of calling and predestination so central in his thought as Weber emphasized. The Puritans were only very distantly Calvinists.

Along more or less the same lines, E. Beins, "Die Wirtschaftsethik der calvinistichen Kirche der Niederlande, 1565-1650," *Nederlandsch Archief voor Kerkgeschiednis* (1931) tried to demonstrate that in post-Reformation Holland, the Calvinist churches repressed rather than encouraged independent economic activity. Such authors as J. M. Yinger, *Religion and the Struggle for Power* (Durham, N.C., 1946), Leo Strauss, *Natural Right and History* (Chicago, 1953), cf. his "Comment" in *Church History*, XXX, 1 (March 1961), 100-102, Kurt Samuelsson, *Religion and Economic Action* (London, 1961), H. M. Robertson, *Aspects of the Rise of Economic Individualism* (Cambridge, 1933), Felix Rachfahl, "Calvinismus und Kapitalismus," *Internationale Wochenschrift*, III, 1909; IV, 1910 (see Ernst Troeltsch's extensive review and criticism, "Die Kulturbedeutung des Calvinismus," *Gesammelte Schriften* [Tübingen, 1925], IV, 783-801), and C. H. and K. George, *The Protestant Mind of the English Reformation* (Princeton, N.J., 1955), all hold that Calvinism was basically opposed to capitalism in any form and that Puritanism was simply an accommodation or a corruption of the original theological system. They are of the opinion that such factors as the Renaissance, the rise of the nation-state, scientific and banking discoveries, and the growth of religious tolerance were much more the causes of the capitalist spirit. In roughly the same camp, Winthrop Hudson, "Weber Thesis Reexamined," *Church History*, XXX, 1 (March 1961), 88-98, contends that the association between Calvinism and the spirit of capitalism in England was a "historical accident," to be understood as a manifestation of the general decline of religion and its social controls.

In various ways, one of the objectives of all these studies is to prove the theological incoherence between original Calvinism and "accommodated" seventeenth-century Puritanism. If, as alleged, there is no coherence between them, then it must be conceded that Puritanism does not represent an independent tradition of theologically grounded meaning and value. Such a conclusion would lead one to look in some other direction for the legitimacy of the capitalist spirit. However, we must be most careful in coming to this kind of judgment. It is significant that none of the aforementioned scholars and, indeed, very few of the other critics of Weber have made a painstaking comparative study of Calvin and the Puritans on the basis of primary sources read afresh. Studies are normally made of one or the other. In dealing with the problem of connections, the most arduous and systematic kind of theological analysis is demanded, for which facile generalizations are no substitute. It may be that Weber's particular conclusions about these connections have to be revised, but if connections are found, such revisions need not alter the basic validity of much of his work.

Because the studies of Samuelsson and the Georges are fairly recent and have attracted a good deal of attention, they call for special comment. Samuelsson's book demands attention not because of its contribution to the general literature (which is negligible), but because it is the most recent expression of so many of the typical and wildly inadequate rejections of Weber's thesis. In the first place, the criticism of lack of arduous and systematic comparative theological analysis applies directly to Samuelsson. There is one vague reference to Calvin's *Institutes* (30) and an extremely random and superficial treatment of the Puritans. I have attempted to refute his conclusion that "the economic views of the Puritans neither encouraged nor obstructed the spirit of capitalism" (42).

In the second place, there is an amazing lack of appreciation of the important differences between types of capitalism and of the obvious distinctions between mercantilism and modern capitalism. The unsophisticated way in which "Colbertism" is compared with the spirit of capitalism in England simply overlooks the unavoidable contrasts between them. While political control over industry was being extended in France during the late sixteenth and early seventeenth centuries, it was being diminished in England. The point at issue is the question of differentiation between politics and economics, of the development of an autonomous sphere of "free," individually initiated economic action. Such a spirit could hardly have prospered in seventeenth-century France under Colbert.

The Georges' book, among many other deficiencies, is filled with self-confident assertions on questions of sociology of religion which demonstrate the most appalling lack of scholarly competence, not to say naiveté. For example, they speak constantly of the Christian religion as a recrudescence of "kinship religion," not far from tribalism. To anyone acquainted with the literature of sociology of religion, that is obviously absurd: what characterizes primitive Christianity is its emphasis upon the differentiation of religion from kinship ties, of religious association from political and national affiliation, and so on. Moreover, the Georges' treatment of Puritanism and Anglicanism leaves much to be desired. As I have tried to show, the distinctions between these two movements are much more important than the Georges understand.

The recent arguments of Michael Walzer, "Puritanism as a Revolutionary Ideology," *History and Theory*, III, 1 (1963), 59-90, and *Revolution of the Saints: A Study in the Origins of Radical Politics* (Cambridge, Mass., 1965), are another form of the criticism that Calvinist Puritanism had very little to do with the rise of liberalism of any kind, including economic liberalism. The Puritans, according to Walzer, were exclusively a repressive lot, concerned to impose their discipline on everyone by political means. "Such men, narrow, fanatical, enthusiastic, committed to their 'work,' have little to contribute to the development of either liberalism or capitalism. To expect freedom from their hands is to invite disappointment. Their great achievement is what is known in the sociology of revolution as the *terror*, the effort to create a holy commonwealth and to force men to be godly" (88). They are alienated men who fundamentally seek political power, rather on the pattern of the Jacobins and Bolsheviks. Walzer is undoubtedly right in emphasizing the repressive aspects of Puritan discipline as well as the attempt on the part of the Puritans to impose it politically. He is also partially right that Puritanism is "a response to disorder and fear, a way of organizing men to overcome the acute sense of chaos" (77). As I have tried to show, the problem of order *is* at the heart of Puritan thought and action. Still, an adequate analysis of Puritanism cannot stop here, as Walzer does. Puritanism is not just repressive discipline without content and without direction, it is not just a random obsessive response to social chaos. Though Walzer emphasizes the importance of discipline in the Puritan experience, he does not adequately analyze the substantive nature of that discipline. Consequently, there is no means for explaining the different shades of emphasis in the wider phenomenon of Puritanism, some of which is highly repressive, some much less so. In short, Walzer does not understand what we have called the tension between differentiation and subordination in Calvinism. It is particularly striking that Walzer ignores the left-wing Puritans (viii). The importance of Puritan ecclesiology for the rise of liberal democracy has been noted by A. D. Lindsay in his classic *Modern Democratic State* (New York, 1962):

> Perhaps the most significant thing about Puritan democratic theory is that the Puritans began the experience of working a small and thoroughly democratic society, the Puritan congregation. Their idea of a church is that it is a fellowship of active believers. The Puritans of the Left, with whom democratic theories mostly originated, were all congregationalists—to use the later term. The self-governing congregation was for them the church. In such a society all are equal, in the sense . . . that they were all equally called of God. That fundamental fact outweighed their differences of ability, capacity, character, and wealth so completely that these differences could be freely recognized and made use of. The Puritan congregation is a fellowship of equals who are recognized to be different. They are all alike called by God and guided by him, and therefore all equally called on to contribute to the common discussion about the purpose and actions of their small society. Their genuine experienced democracy was not political, but the democracy of a voluntary society—a society which did not use force in the putting into practice of its decisions, but was a fellowship of discussion . . . Because the Puritan tradition started with the experience of a society which rested on consent and abjured the use of force, it tended to conceive the state on the analogy of such a society (117-118).

Furthermore, Walzer overlooks what may be called the latent consequences of Puritanism for liberalizing English society. Haller's treatment of the failure of Presbyterianism in the 1640's, and the consequent flowering of diversified patterns of Puritanism which the Presbyterians often unconsciously encouraged, is brilliant. Haller understands the matter of latency in the Puritan system far better than most. In

Liberty and Reformation in the Puritan Revolution (New York, 1955), he writes:

> By the end of 1644 the divines of the [Westminster] assembly had failed to silence opposition in the press as completely as they had failed to secure agreement among the members of their own order. The Independent minority in the assembly still held out against centralized control over individual preachers and congregations. . . . The truth was that there was no effective action parliament could take to enforce its own regulations, and its members were unwilling to do the entire bidding of the Westminster divines in this or any other matter. The preachers had done their pulpit-work well, but with practical results that few of them had looked for and many of them deplored. They had sown the Word without foreseeing the harvest they had had now to reap. They had preached the doctrines of calling and covenant, evinced by faith, manifested in action, to be crowned by success here or hereafter, and they had thus planted in many minds dreams of new heaven and new earth. *But it is one thing to launch men on a quest for the New Jerusalem, quite another to stop them when they have gone far enough* . . . Hence all attempts in 1644 to impose a presbyterian frame upon revolutionary Puritanism served simply to evoke the many-headed hydra of English dissent (141-142; my italics).

See also a critical essay in which I attempt to detail some of the difficulties with Walzer's approach, "Max Weber Revisited: The 'Protestant Ethic' and the Puritan Experience of Order," *Harvard Theological Review*, LIX (1966), 415-428, reprinted in *Yearbook for Sociology of Religion* (Cologne and Opladen, 1967).

As to the argument that Puritanism is basically a religious movement with no distinctive social and economic outlook, three recent studies require comment. I am inclined to think my method does greater justice to the conflict between the Puritans and official Anglicans than do the categories employed by John F. H. New in his book, *Anglican and Puritan, 1558-1640* (Stanford, Calif., 1964). New does understand the theological character of the conflict. He is rightly opposed to reducing the conflict to nontheological matters, whether "administrative or temperamental, or economic in origin, rather than doctrinal" (17). Without question, New's book is a useful antidote to the Georges' *Protestant Mind* (see New's explicit criticism at 104 ff.). Also, New's approach is interesting and sometimes revealing. However, on balance, the grace-nature typology, at least as New uses it, does not grasp the dynamics of Puritan and Anglican thought. There is something rather wooden and flat about this typology, though it is not entirely wrong. The main problem is that in New's hands it leads to some very doubtful judgments about Puritanism.

In his essay, "The Non-Existent Controversy: Puritan and Anglican Attitudes on Work and Wealth, 1600-1640," *Church History*, XXXV, 3 (September 1966), 273-287, Timothy Breen shows that in the early seventeenth century there was no sharp difference between Puritans and Anglicans in their attitudes on idleness and the irresponsible use of wealth. Though Breen says he is not speaking to the "Weber thesis" one way or the other (287), he does wish to question whether there is anything distinctive about Puritanism so far as economic attitudes go. While Breen demonstrates the need for care in contrasting Anglicanism and Puritanism so far as economic views go, his study does not, unfortunately, shed much light on our area of concern. As far as I can tell, a specific and very fundamental point of difference between late-sixteenth-century Puritans and Anglicans in socio-economic matters centered in the attitude toward holy days—see Hill, *Puritanism and Society* (New York, 1967), 153-159, a section to which Breen curiously does not refer. That is, both groups might urge industriousness in a lawful calling (though prominent sixteenth-century Anglicans like Whitgift and Hooker did not show much enthusiasm for doing so), but how did each group construe such a concern in the light of the well-established Anglican custom of maintaining holy days when work was prohibited? Puritans like Cartwright wished to overthrow Church custom in favor of "the liberty of working six days in the week" (The Puritan Admonition to Parliament of 1572 made a good deal of that); Anglicans certainly did not. This was a critical issue between Whitgift and Cartwright and, if Hill is right, an abiding issue into the seventeenth century. In other words, what is interesting is how the exhortation to industriousness is applied *institutionally*, particularly when an aspect of Church and political authority is at stake.

Furthermore, Breen's study does not shed light upon the relation of Puritanism and Anglicanism to the broader characteristics of the spirit of capitalism outlined in Chapter 2. Things may have changed during the seventeenth century (though I doubt it), but there is little question of basic differences between the two groups on the five characteristics used here.

Gabriel Kolko, "Max Weber on America: Theory and Evidence," in George H. Nadel (ed.), *Studies in the Philosophy of History* (New York, 1965), 180-197, is very critical of Weber's judgments about rational capitalism in the early American colonies. He, like many others before him (Thomas Jefferson Wertenbaker, *The Puritan Oligarchy*, and E. A. J. Johnson, *American Economic Thought in the Seventeenth Century*), emphasizes the theocratic and interventionist practices of the Puritans, practices that do not lead to a differentiated, market-oriented society. The historical evidence he cites should of course be taken seriously as a basis for revising some of Weber's incautious statements about the uniquely rationalistic character of the Puritan economy. Anyone who has read American Puritan sources knows that divines like John Cotton were hardly "free enterprisers."

However, while I am not competent to make a sophisticated judgment about colonial America, I have read some of the same books Kolko relies on, and I should have thought a rather different interpretation, at least of the Protestant ethic in early America, was possible Certainly, the weakest and least persuasive section of Kolko's essay is the one on the Puritans (182-184). In the first place, the section is ambiguous in its conclusions: "In its total context . . . Puritanism in America was *both a help and a hindrance* to systematic economic behavior . . . " (182; my italics). That is fair enough, but Kolko spends all his time talking about Puritanism the hindrance. He never says how it helped. This is particularly strange since he depends on Perry Miller's chapter, "The Protestant Ethic" in *The New England Mind: From Colony to Province* (Boston, 1961). As I understand it, Miller's main conclusion in that chapter deals with the "two-sidedness" of Puritan attitudes toward vigorous economic activity. The divines both urged the people in the direction of self-initiated work and were troubled by the consequences. " . . . The sermons [of the ministers] were more than ministerial nagging of worldlings, more than hypocritical show, more than rhetoric. They were releases from a grief and a sickness of soul which otherwise found no surcease. They were professions of a society that knew it was doing wrong [by its diligent industry], but it could not help itself, because *the wrong thing was also the right thing"* (51; my italics). For a catalogue of quotations revealing the further emphasis upon the Protestant ethic among the Puritan divines, see Karl H. Hertz, "Max Weber and American Puritanism," *Journal for the Scientific Study of Religion* I, 2 (Spring 1962), 189-197. This same ambiguity within the theological-moral beliefs of the Puritans is revealed in Bernard Bailyn's *The New England Merchants in the Seventeenth Century* (New York, 1964), a book that Kolko also relies on. The early merchants were clearly Puritans. Bailyn concludes: *"From the same texts* the Puritan magistrates and the merchants read different lessons . . . " (43; my italics). We have also emphasized the inner strains within Calvinist Puritanism.

Secondly, Kolko misunderstands what Weber was saying about Puritanism. Labor as "an absolute end in itself" is not the same thing as showing "excessive concern with wealth." Weber could hardly make that clearer. In other words, the divines could advocate the religious duty of voluntary labor (which they did) without condoning the accumulation of unlimited wealth. That one tended to lead to the other was part of the ambiguity of Puritanism: the wrong thing was the right thing!

Two scholars in particular represent the contention that Puritanism harbored a negative view of social relations and served more than anything else to dissolve the ties of social order. The first is R. H. Tawney, *Religion and the Rise of Capitalism* (New York, 1958). His analysis of the relation of religion to social order is certainly one of the most scholarly and careful in a field where scholarship and care are not usually very apparent. Furthermore, he represents a point of view often taken as complementary to Weber's own: one still hears of the Tawney-Weber Theory. Unlike many fellow critics of the Weber thesis, Tawney makes a sincere effort to compare the teachings of the Reformers, and especially of Calvin, with the later attitudes of the Puritans. He concludes that, while there was some relationship, something in the spirit of Calvinist Puritanism that made a unique and independent contribution to the growth of the capitalist mentality in seventeenth-century England, Puritanism represents a process of development, so that its similarities to original Calvinism are all but destroyed. The Geneva of John Calvin was "the very soul of authoritarian regimentation," of extreme discipline and control. There existed in Geneva what Tawney refers to as the "dictatorship of the ministry," under which the kernels of individualism contained in Calvin's theology were rigorously suppressed, not to say eliminated. Tawney describes the work of Calvin and Beza as an attempt to perpetuate "with new intensity the mediaeval idea of a Church-civilization . . . to make Geneva a pattern, not only of doctrinal purity, but of social morality and commercial morality" (179). It is the element of discipline and social control that gets lost in the development of Puritanism. Not that Puritanism was opposed in principle to discipline in social relations; in fact, says Tawney, it advocated a still more stringent self-control. But it rejected the idea that the Church and the State should any longer be the agents of regulation; the emphasis now was upon the will of the individual (167) and its solitary communion with God (189). Although Puritanism was not without its collectivist, centralist tendencies (represented by the right-wing Presbyterians and Independents), these "naturally" became separated from the emphasis laid upon the individual and his will, and in the process the Puritan's sense of social solidarity was corroded (191). Society increasingly became pictured as a group of atomistic individuals claiming their rights but ignoring their obligations—a picture, according to Tawney, which coincided congenially with the developing economic and social patterns:

> The distinctive note of Puritan teaching was . . . individual responsibility, not social obligation. Training its pupils to the mastery of others through the mastery of self, it prized as a crown of glory the qualities which arm the spiritual athlete for his solitary contest with a hostile world, and dismissed concern with the social order as the prop of weaklings and the Capua of the soul (226).

The story of Puritanism is a story of the devaluation of social responsibility and of the rejection of the Church as an independent source of moral control. It is, in effect, the story of the *withdrawal* of religion from any positive relationship with the social order. It tells of the moral abandonment of society to a system of "snatching to hoard, and hoarding to snatch," a system that is "absolutely irreligious, without internal control" (235).

It is difficult to understand how Tawney's name ever became linked to Weber's. They are saying very different things. For Tawney, Puritanism aided in *dissolving* the ties between society and religion, in permitting irreligious values to take over. For Weber, Puritanism contributed positively to the re-evaluation of the social order in new categories of meaning and understanding. Tawney sees in Puritanism the decline of moral authority and control; Weber sees in it the redirection and the reinterpretation of the place of moral authority in the social order. He perceives not a one-sided emphasis on rights to the exclusion of obligations, but a redefinition of both rights and obligations in accord with a new system of meaning and values. See O. H. Taylor, "Tawney's *Religion and Capitalism,* and Eighteenth Century Liberalism," *Economics and Liberalism* (Cambridge, 1955), 24-36, for a criticism of Tawney at this point.

Second, an essay that attempts to extend Tawney's analysis is Christopher Hill's "Protestantism and the Rise of Capitalism" in F. J. Fisher (ed.), *Essays in the Economic and Social History of Tudor and*

Stuart England (Cambridge, 1961), 15-39. The essay is written with
Hill's usual, stimulating insight. Insofar as he seeks to take the independent contribution of theology to social life seriously, he introduces an
interesting perspective. As he says, he is concerned with what "flowed
from the logic of [Luther's] theological position" (24). However, the
essay also brings to light some of the doubtful assumptions that lurk in
Hill's other works. He claims that the Reformation in no way supplies a
new ethic, but that it simply intensifies the individual's inward,
"spiritual" relation to God: "For the reformers, the direct relationship
of the soul to God was what mattered: the priest, the Church as an
institution, were quite secondary" (19). (For the Calvinist Puritans, at
least, this statement about the Church as an institution, being of secondary importance is simply not true.) This new theological emphasis on
the internal condition of the heart "helped to dissolve the hard crust of
custom, tradition and authority" (35). It was, thus, that the social
order sanctioned by traditional scholastic theology could be radically
questioned. The end result of Reformation theology was, according to
Hill, a removal of religious restraint from a burgeoning capitalist mentality, and a "rationalization" of the Protestant's adjustment to it. Protestantism allowed "social pressures" to "influence individual conduct
more freely" (34). "There is nothing," says Hill, "in protestantism
which leads automatically to capitalism: its importance was rather that
it undermined obstacles which the more rigid institutions and ceremonies of catholicism imposed" (36). Protestantism's "most obvious
effects were negative" (36). "In a society already becoming capitalist,
protestantism facilitated the triumph of the new values. There was no
inherent theological reason for the protestant emphasis on frugality,
hard work, accumulation; but that emphasis was a natural consequence
of the religion of the heart in a society where capitalist industry was
developing. It was, if we like a rationalization; but it flowed naturally
from protestant theology, whose main significance, for our present purposes, is that in any given society *it enabled religion to be moulded by
those who dominated society*" (my italics).

The similarity of this view with Tawney's is notable, and I would
level the same criticism against it that I level against Tawney. There is
here no genuine appreciation of the central emphasis of Calvinist theology (the examination of Luther is curious, because for Puritanism and
the rise of capitalism it is largely beside the point). One is forced to
conclude that with Hill's essay, as with most recent historical treat-
ments of the Weber thesis, there is no grasp of the patterns of a theolo-

gical-ethical system of thought.

I have dealt only with representative criticisms of the Weber thesis because they seem to characterize the most recent and widespread historical evaluations of the specific relationships between Calvinism, Puritanism, and the spirit of capitalism. Apart from the older "defenses" of Weber (see Fischoff, *op. cit.*, for a treatment of the "adherents"), there are, of course, important efforts on Weber's behalf by such authors as Talcott Parsons, B. N. Nelson, R. K. Merton, and Robert Bellah. But in the case of Merton—"Science, Technology and Society in 17th-Century England," *Osiris,* IV, 2 (1938)—and Nelson— *Idea of Usury* (Princeton, N.J., 1949)—Weber's thesis is simply extended and broadened, and neither author attempts a systematic re-examination of the particular affinities between Calvinism, Puritanism, and the spirit of capitalism. Parsons defends Weber (e.g., in "H. M. Robertson on Max Weber and His School" in *Journal of Political Economy*, XLIII [1935], 688-696), but more on theoretical than historical grounds. In *Structure of Social Action* (Glencoe, Ill., 1949), Parsons argues that Weber's "method of difference" (i.e., of comparing and contrasting the presence of rational capitalism in the West with its absence in other civilizations) "is a perfectly valid scientific method *provided, of course, that Weber's allegations of* fact are correct" (513, my italics). Historically speaking, Weber's "allegations" about Calvinism and Puritanism are precisely what is at issue. It is their validity that is so often attacked. Therefore, a systematic re-examination of the material from which Weber drew his conclusions may not be out of place in supplementing social-theoretical concerns.

B. The Question of Economic Regulation in Pre-Revolutionary England

As with the criticisms of *The Protestant Ethic*, the literature on the connection of law with the emergence of modern capitalism in pre-Revolutionary England is extensive. I shall simply list here some of the major books and articles on the subject, sort out the arguments, and indicate the outlines of my own response.

While my initial interest in law as it relates to the rise of capitalism and to religion was stimulated by Weber, the writings of Roscoe Pound carried that interest farther. Even though most of his conclusions must be rejected, Pound posed some suggestive theses. He argued that what he calls the classical common law period (the end of the sixteenth and the beginning of seventeenth century) was the nurturing ground for the development of "ultra-individualism," or "an uncompromising insistence upon individual rights and individual property as the central point of jurisprudence," ("Puritanism and the Common Law," *The American Law Review*, XLV [1911], 811-829, 816, see also *History of Legal Interpretation*). Before this period, according to Pound, the common law tradition held as central the legal regulation of the individual in favor of social interests (*The Spirit of the Common Law* [Francestown, N. H., 1947], 69). Perhaps, says Pound, the "controlling factor" in the radical reinterpretation of the function of law was the influence of Puritanism (*ibid.*, 36-37), with its "conception of a maximum of abstract individual self-assertion exempt from social control" (*ibid.*, 49). The core of Puritanism is contained in its "principle of consociation," which held that "we are to be with one another but not over one another." "The whole is to have no right of control over the individual beyond the minimum necessary to keep peace" (*ibid.*, incidentally, Pound is sometimes given to characterizing the development of "individualism" from the seventeenth to the twentieth century as the Puritan element). It was these notions that led to a preoccupation with the

238

freedom of the individual will (see "The Role of the Will in Law," *Harvard Law Review,* LXVIII [1954] , 4) in all legal and social matters, making social legislation such a difficult affair in the seventeenth and eighteenth centuries. As a result of Puritanism, the power of the magistrate and the legislator was minimized, and the Englishman came to view his property not as something to be used in the service of the commonwealth but as a sphere over which his private interests were totally sovereign.

While suggestive, Pound's conclusions are a bit impressionistic and oversimple. As he himself implies in other contexts (see his *Introduction to the Philosophy of Law* [New Haven, Conn., 1959] , 15, 16, 21; also *Spirit of Common Law,* IV, "Rights of Englishmen and Rights of Man," 85 ff.), there were many factors involved in the shaping of legal individualism, so that he certainly does not prove that Puritanism was the controlling factor in the process. Such proof would require far more documentation than Pound supplies. In fact, there is a question whether "individualism," in the sense Pound uses it, accurately describes the legal tenor of the seventeenth century in England and, even if it does, whether Puritanism itself can be so simply equated with it. But surely the most disconcerting aspect of Pound's study is his failure to indicate the concrete ways in which religious sentiment influenced the common law at the turn of the seventeenth century. There is no analysis of the legal decisions of the time in order to establish the revolutionary changes Pound claims were taking place. Pound's examples of individualism in law are drawn rather indiscriminately from the eighteenth and nineteenth centuries, from English and American judges.

This deficiency is particularly acute in the light of the conclusions of Charles Niehaus in his unpublished Harvard Ph.D. thesis, *The Issue of Law Reform in the Puritan Revolution* (1954). In a careful way, Niehaus analyzes the attempts by various Puritan groups to reform the common law during the Revolution. He concludes that their impact was extremely minor, and though some degree of law reform was enacted under Cromwell at the behest of the Puritans, it was mostly swept away at the Restoration. Even the great law reforms of the nineteenth century "owed nothing either in principles or inspiration, to the efforts of their 17th-century predecessors" (iii). In other words, explicit Puritan influence on the particulars of the common law was nil.

Niehaus's study is valuable in that it renders unnecessary any further examination of the explicit, intentional connections between Puritanism and the common law. However, such an investigation is not our concern, nor, one has the feeling, is it really Pound's concern. In a rather unsystematic and impressionistic way, Pound is attempting to understand how a system of law comes to embody and perpetuate a general way of looking at social life—a special system of values or a conception of order, I have called it. It is my contention that the concurrence of important tensions and changes in legal and religious outlook toward the end of the sixteenth and at the beginning of the seventeenth centuries is more than coincidence. In this I believe I am not far from Pound's interest, however far I may be from his method of analysis and from many of his conclusions. These fundamental changes and tensions have not been analyzed by Niehaus, or by any other scholar to my knowledge. (For an exceedingly tedious account of more or less the same period, see F. A. Inderwick, *The Interregnum* [London, 1891].)

For all these deficiencies, however, Pound has opened up a problem area well worth investigating. The years between 1570 and 1640—which Pound refers to as the classical common law period—were indeed a time of radical change in the conceptions of social authority and control. We have already pointed to the struggle for sovereignty between the courts, the crown, and Parliament. As the power of the king became increasingly limited, the position of the Anglican Church was also decisively altered. At the same time, economic transformations were taking place, whose relation to the redefinition of authority and control was important. According to the conclusions of the eminent economic historian John U. Nef, in his *Cultural Foundations of Industrial Civilization* (New York, 1960):

> There are grounds for speaking of an early industrial revolution in the north of Europe, and particularly in Great Britain . . . They rest on a novel movement during the late sixteenth and early seventeenth centuries, especially in Great Britain, towards a concentration of industrial enterprise upon the production of cheap commodities in large quantities. If . . . history is concerned with human beings, it is changes in the values which men and women attach to life, changes in the purposes to which they devote their minds and bodies in their daily work, that are of decisive importance in orienting economic endeavor in new directions. In these respects the decades from about 1580 to 1640 *were* a turning point. It was then that persons in the north of Europe, and particularly in Great Britain, began to lay an emphasis on utility as the goal of industrial life—on productivity as a self-justifying end. (59-60)

The first part of this book summarizes much of the earlier work of Nef in the field of economic history. For that reason it is very valuable. Nef seems to me to prove conclusively that the economic revolution in the latter part of the sixteenth century, most centrally in England but also in Scotland, Holland, and Sweden, produced patterns of industrial life qualitatively different from preceding Renaissance forms of capitalism. He shows that Renaissance economic life was oriented toward beauty, artistic objects, and fine buildings for the enjoyment of the aristocracy. "[It] was hardly a movement in the direction of the mass consumption which is characteristic of the recent industrialized age. The common citizen in the towns had much less direct stake in the new palaces than his ancestors had in the old churches and cathedrals" (42). Indeed, precisely when new forms of vigorous economic activity were appearing in England and northern Europe toward the end of the sixteenth century, the countries of greatest industrial supremacy during the Renaissance (central and southern Europe) experienced drastic economic decline.

Nef's work should silence Weber's critics on the point that capitalism, in the sense that he meant it, is to be found "well before" the sixteenth and seventeenth centuries in southern Europe. It will be recalled that Weber's interest was in the extension of economic rationality to "whole groups of men." That is Nef's interest too, and his careful examination should be marked as a complete confirmation of Weber on this point. Is it simply a historical accident that the rise of Puritanism concurs with the first industrial revolution in England, the country that was at the center of modern economic development?

In his celebrated volume, *Industry and Government in France and England, 1540-1640* (Ithaca, N.Y., 1962), Nef demonstrates that whereas in France monarchical authority and power over economic life was extended and intensified, in England the opposite occurred. There economic life was being set free from certain political and legal restrictions, it was beginning to gain its own autonomy, to set its own goals and to develop its own rationality (to use Weber's terms). Economic activity was becoming, in other words, a sphere in which individuals were set free from traditional patterns of regulation, a sphere in which they stood, to an important degree, above the State and the courts, possessing an authority independent of the time-honored centers of restriction and control. As Nef puts it:

After the accession of Henri IV in 1589 the authority of the French crown in matters of industrial regulation steadily increased. The authority of the English crown as steadily diminished. In spite of the extensive system of industrial legislation built up in England, the actual regulation of industry was very much less effective than in France between 1589 and 1640. This was particularly true in expanding industries like mining, metallurgy, salt-making, and new branches of the textile manufacture, in which large scale enterprise of various kinds was becoming common. (138)

The early English industrial revolution . . . weakened the doctrine that human affairs are best ordered when controlled from above. It strengthened another more novel doctrine, that progress depends upon allowing free scope for individual initiative. (157)

The idea of an early industrial revolution in England roughly between the years 1560 and 1660 is confirmed by Ephraim Lipson in his classic study, *Economic History of England* (London: I, 1956, new edition; II, 1948; III, 1948). See particularly his fascinating, if perhaps overstated, description of the vast transformations of pre-Revolutionary English society in the Introduction to Volume II: "The ideal of the old order was stability: that of the new order was progress. For a century (1558-1660) England was distracted by the conflict of these rival concepts. . . . . The 'Industrial Revolution' [of the eighteenth century] was not the cause of the trimph of the entrepreneur—on the contrary, it came first to England because the entrepreneur had already been liberated from the prison-house of tradition and authority" (II, cxvi). As I say, this is extravagant language—far too neat and tidy to depict the complexities of the period. Nevertheless, Lipson is pointing to an important change taking place in England, and the change does consist, in large part, of a revision—or at least the beginnings of a revision—of social authority and order. For similar conclusions, see W. J. Ashley, *Economic Organization of England* (London, 1932), especially chapter VII. Eli Heckscher's monumental study, *Mercantilism,* translated by M. Shapiro (London, 1935), also goes a long way toward supporting the idea of substantial economic and social change in seventeenth-century England. Heckscher's work is a broad comparative analysis of England and France from the sixteenth to the eighteenth centuries. On the matter of economic regulation, he states: "There is therefore no doubt that the regulation of industry even at the time of the later Stuarts, that is, at the same time as Colbert's great system of regulation in France, was considered obsolete in those English circles which were already influential at that time and were to become even more so after the

1688 revolution" (I, 321).

To turn now to the attitude of lawyers like Sir Edward Coke toward economic regulation, the essays of Donald O. Wagner ("Coke and the Rise of Economic Liberalism," *Economic History Review*, VI, 35 [1935] and "The Common Law and Free Enterprise," *Economic History Review*, VII, 217 [1937] have produced a very important discussion. Wagner would readily agree with the judgments of Nef, Lipson, and Heckscher regarding the beginnings of industrial capitalism and free enterprise in pre-Revolutionary England. Furthermore, Wagner contends that the common lawyers, and especially Coke, were doing everything in their power to loosen the bonds of economic regulation and thereby to liberate "a free scope for individual initiative," in Nef's words.

Wagner's point of view has been accepted and further substantiated by S. E. Thorne in his distinguished essay, *Sir Edward Coke, 1552-1952* (London, 1957). It is of the utmost significance that Thorne, an eminent legal historian and a leading Coke scholar, undertakes in an important general lecture on Coke's legal contribution, to examine the antinomies and tensions involved in Coke's decisions over corporations and free trade. The point is that these tensions are *not* incidental or of secondary or random interest. They are indispensable to understanding what was central in the legal activity and thought of the day, and they characterize Coke's creative, innovative function in the law.

Still more recently, Christopher Hill has given his unqualified support to Wagner's ideas. Hill mentions Wagner in *Puritanism and Revolution* (London, 1958), 24, but he has since expanded the thesis in *Intellectual Origins of the English Revolution* (Oxford, 1965), 225-265. As Hill puts it, "Coke's unspoken assumption that men have a right to do what they will with their own persons and skills represents the thread of continuity running through all his decisions. It explains his campaign for economic liberalism" (236). In his section on Coke, Hill also included a broad-ranging discussion of Coke's general legal activity. He comes to the conclusion that Coke was not only a great systematizer of the common law, but also a great "myth-maker," since he read into the law his own consistently liberal assumptions.

One of the best general studies of the relationship between the king and the common lawyers is Charles Ogilvie's *King's Government and the Common Law* (Oxford, 1958). Ogilvie persuasively puts Wagner's arguments on the law and economic control into a larger historical context (esp. 134-143).

The attack on the Wagner thesis has recently been led by Barbara Malament in her impressive essay, "The 'Economic Liberalism' of Sir Edward Coke," *Yale Law Journal*, LXXVI (1967), 1321 ff. The essay is tightly reasoned and well documented—as one would expect from a student of J. H. Hexter. As I argued in Chapter 6, I do not find Miss Malament's basic contention convincing, but she has succeeded in adding a dimension to the discussion which was overlooked by Wagner and even more by Hill. Both Wagner and Hill leave the impression that Coke was a self-conscious economic liberal, busily and consistently laying the legal foundations for industrial capitalism. In contrast, Miss Malament shows that much of Coke's thought worked in the opposite direction, that of defending the ancient realm as he understood it. This is particularly true of some of Coke's decisions in corporation cases. Miss Malament's arguments serve to undo Hill's hasty assertion about Coke's "campaign for economic liberalism." The matter is a good deal more complex than that.

By the same token, Miss Malament overdoes the unity and consistency of Coke's views on economic regulation the other way. My view is that the courts were operating in a maelstrom of ideological crosscurrents and, therefore, that their own ideology was ambiguous and even contradictory. There simply was not one consistent set of ideas at work in figures like Coke (and certainly by the time of the Puritan Revolution a firm "doctrine of economic liberalism" had not emerged in the courts or anywhere else). On the other hand, Wagner is right to the degree that at least some of Coke's legal decisions in the field of economic regulation do constitute a radical break with the past and do lay some legal foundations for what later amounts to modern rational capitalism. Whether Coke was conscious of the novelty of his decisions is impossible to say, given his mode of operation, which was to dress up innovations in the clothes of the past.

Because of its bearing on our argument, Miss Malament's essay requires extended comment in addition to those references made to it in Chapter 6. Aside from my specific disagreements over the interpretation of monopoly cases (see Chapter 6), I believe Miss Malament underrates seriously the recurrent emphasis in Coke to the effect that "all monopolies" are illegal. I do not consider the provisions he makes for corporate regulation to be so much qualifications on this conviction as contradictions to it. That is, there is much more ambiguity and downright confusion in Coke's thought than Miss Malament allows. I would have great difficulty in dividing Coke's career into less and more radical stages, as Miss Malament does (1351); the task amounts to attempting to resolve in chronological form the abiding (and essentially irreconcilable) tensions in his thought.

One important set of statements in her essay needs particular examination. At 1350-1351, Miss Malament contends that the problem of monopolies boils down to a conflict between the crown and the courts and Parliament. Hence Coke was mainly concerned, she says, with particular excesses of the prerogative power and, so she suggests, remained quite within the bounds of traditional common law understanding. But at this crucial point in her argument her claims are very confusing. She says:

> Neither Coke nor the King's Bench was prepared to deny the legitimacy of this prerogative. But on the basis of common law doctrine they (rightfully) voided all royal patents of monopoly and not just [one of them]. This came perilously close to denying the Crown's right to grant patents altogether, hence Coke's elaborate attempt to justify the court's decisions by demonstrating how frequently the Crown had misinterpreted the public interest and how frequently royal actions had aroused protest. The "free trade" argument was used first to fill a constitutional no-man's land and later to justify Parliament's invasion of the royal prerogative.

These sentences are not consistent with each other, nor is much of what they admit in line with the central themes of Miss Malament's essay. It is true that Coke did not consciously wish to deny the prerogative, but simply to limit it. It is also true that his decisions were made in a "constitutional no-man's land," which means that no clear precedent for relating letters patent to common law jurisdiction existed. Coke had to *invent* the relation, and he did so in such a way as "to justify Parliament's invasion of the royal prerogative," as Miss Malament rightly says. The relation between letters patent and Parliament was historically unclear, but the way Coke resolved it was unquestionably novel—it did constitute "an invasion" (see fn. 129, p. 203 above). Again, Miss Malament is right when she says the invasion has to do with the fact that Coke "came perilously close to denying the Crown's right to grant patents altogether," despite (she should have said) his "elaborate attempts" at justification for particular decisions. There is obviously no historical precedent for such a total denial.

All this is correct. Why, then, does she state: "But on the basis of common law doctrine they (rightfully) voided all royal patents of monopoly ... "? According to her other statements, and certainly according to tradition, that is precisely what the courts might not "rightfully" do. Moreover, how can she feel that what she admits above in any way confirms her central judgment that Coke "dealt fairly" with precedent (1339) and did not "challenge the fundamentals of the prevailing regulatory structure" (1321)? Finally, how does this corroborate the notion that Coke was concerned only to correct monopolies that were specifically abusive?

C. The Social Implications of Humanist Thought

In arguing that "the Renaissance, from a sociological point of view, was fully unproductive," Troeltsch seems to mean that, as a rule, humanists neither reflected on nor were involved in the creation of new institutional structures that in any way altered the existing state of social affairs. Troeltsch continues: "The Renaissance is anarchistic and aristocratic in its most intimate circles, but outside of these it adhered, with complete lack of independence, to the established ecclesiastical and political powers. Sociologically the Renaissance creates the aristocracy of culture and the salon, but beyond this it pays homage to power and violence" (276). Further on, he remarks: "Such an aristocracy of culture necessarily has something of a parasitic character sociologically. So far as anybody devised any ideas concerning sociological subjects, the ideas of the Renaissance were conservative. The Renaissance founded the theory of absolutism. . . . In this field the chain of thought runs from Machiavelli to Bodin and Hobbes" (287-288). Likewise, Weber writes in *Sociology of Religion*; "In keeping with their entire pattern of life, these humanist groups of the classically educated were altogether antipathetic to the masses and to the religious sects. They remained alien to the turmoil and particularly to the demagogy of priests and preachers, and they remained fairly thoroughly Erastian or irenic in temper, for which reasons they were condemned to suffer progressive loss of influence" (133-134). In the same vein, Lord Acton remarks that Renaissance men "were innovators but not reformers," *Lectures on Modern History* (New York, 1961), 85-86.

Whether this same lack of social influence applies also to specifically political thinkers like Machiavelli, I am not competent to say. Certainly, it would be easy to understand why Machiavelli's political influence has been greatly exaggerated (as, for example, J. W. Allen argues, *History of*

Political Thought in the 16th Century [London, 1957] , 492) if Herbert Butterfield's engaging interpretation in *Statecraft of Machiavelli* (London, 1960) is accepted as accurate. Butterfield claims that, in all, Machiavelli was irrelevant because he was so rigorous a humanist. His thought contains perhaps "the most typical features in Renaissance theory on the subject of the past" (28). For him, "the world throughout the centuries remains essentially the same" (30). His political thought consisted in attempting to re-create, in the present, "ideal" situations that occurred in classical antiquity. "He is simply a channel for classical influence" (81), hardly a modern political thinker. In general, Butterfield feels that Machiavelli's thought suffers from having no understanding of history, no appreciation of novelty. Still, there is ambiguity here, as Troeltsch's words cited above make clear. For if it is true that "the Renaissance founded the theory of absolutism," then it is not quite true that there is nothing novel or influential about Machiavelli, no matter how much he relied upon the past. Though Machiavelli's writings are filled with illusions and distortions—as a result, in part, of his wooden devotion to the past—he nevertheless spoke to certain significant sociological developments of his time, as Federico Chabod shows in his impressive book, *Machiavelli and the Renaissance* (Cambridge, 1960).

Be all this as it may, what interests us most is the sort of social theory Machiavelli develops on the basis of his humanist orientation. It will be recalled that we, like Weber, are concerned to understand the emergence of a differentiated society characterized by relatively autonomous spheres of action. We are suggesting that there is no foundation for a genuinely differentiated society in Stoicism or in its spiritual descendant, Renaissance humanism. Clearly, Machiavelli offers no such foundation either. On the contrary, "he aims in his thinking at the undisputed dominion of central power, which will crush every other social and political force" (*Machiavelli and the Renaissance*, fn. 1, 121). In Chabod's eloquent description, "we have here a first attempt to reform the individual man; and in the very fact that the call to political action drowns every other voice, human or divine, there is such a painful, tragic grandeur that the State may well demand the sacrifice of every passion and require the absolute renunciation of every other sentiment in those who wish to control it" (125). Or, as Garret Mattingly puts it in his essay, "Changing Attitudes Towards the State during the Renaissance" (*Facets of the Renaissance* [New York, 1963] , 19-40), "the conscious imitation of Greece and Rome in political feeling meant a long step in the direction of substituting the religion of patriotism for the religion of Christ" (31; cf. 36). See also C. J. Friedrich, *Constitutional Reason of State* (Providence, R. I., 1957), 23, where essentially the same point is made.

In Weber's terms, one finds in Machiavelli a justification for political patrimonialism and, therefore, for a type of politically oriented capitalism; but one in no sense finds a basis for differentiated or rational capitalism. This point must be made against all Weber's critics, such as H. M. Robertson, the Georges, and Leo Strauss, who erroneously argue that Machiavelli manifested the great Renaissance contribution to the "rise of economic individualism." Robertson, for example, cites two passages from *The Prince* which are supposed to demonstrate Machiavelli's emphasis upon "economic man." The first one, chapter 17, is totally inconclusive; but the other, chapter 22, illustrates our point precisely: the Prince "should encourage his citizens to go about their [economic affairs] in tranquility . . . ", he "should reward such citizens and any others who may in any way enrich his state or city." He should occasionally mingle with these citizens, though he should always preserve *"the majesty of his dignity, for this should never be allowed to suffer in any way"* (italics added). It would be hard to find a more fitting example of the spirit of patrimonialism!

In several passages that capture exactly the distinction Weber saw between Renaissance capitalism and modern rational capitalism, Chabod's discussion should (in my opinion) bring an end to the confusions that have clung to this whole aspect of the Weber thesis. "To Alberti's maxim 'art for art's sake,' to Machiavelli's theory of 'politics for politics' sake,' there is certainly no corresponding affirmation of principle that can be expressed in the phrase 'economic activity for economic activity's sake,' or that can be said to contain even the germ of that principle of 'production for production's sake' or 'making for making's sake' which is characteristic of modern capitalism . . . " (188). Chabod points out that though there was vigorous mercantile activity in the Renaissance it was uniformly conducted with a bad conscience. "In the historical and political sphere Machiavelli replaces the God and devil of Villani with man and man alone. But in the sphere of economic thought nothing happens—until the triumph of Calvinism—to change the old attitude . . . " (187; see 57-58 and 185-188).

D. Some Problems in the Interpretation of Puritanism

There are four specific problems raised in the vast literature of Puritanism that call for further comment here: (1) the relationship of Calvin to the Puritan movement, (2) and (3) the distinctiveness and the theological character of Puritanism, and (4) its economic implications.

(1) The flat denial of Calvin's influence upon the Puritans, such as one finds in the Georges' *Protestant Mind,* 190, or even the minimization of that influence by L. J. Triterud in his well-known essay, "The Origins of Puritanism," *Church History,* XX (1951), both strike me as puzzling judgments. Many scholars would rightly refrain from reducing the Puritans to Calvin. Haller loves to say that the Puritans were "Calvinists with a difference" (*Rise of Puritanism* [New York,1957], 84-85). And Perry Miller in *Seventeenth Century* (Boston, 1961) mentions a number of the diverse sources of Puritan thought: European Protestantism (including, certainly, Calvin); "peculiarly 17th-century preoccupations and interests"; Renaissance humanism; and medieval scholasticism (92). With respect to the first, one ought to follow Triterud, Haller, and others in including the Rhineland Protestants like Oecolampadius, Capito, Martyr, as well as Bucer and Bullinger. No doubt one also would want to take account of the Lollard tradition in England; see A. G. Dickens's fascinating discussion of the Lollards in *The English Reformation* (New York, 1964), 22-37, and cf. William A. Clebsch, *Early English Protestants* (New Haven, Conn., 1964).

Having said all this, surely there can be no question that "the major part of Puritan thought was taken bodily from 16th-century Protestantism," as Miller asserts *(op. cit.,* 92*).* Furthermore, there can be no doubt that so far as the Reformed tradition goes, the influence of men like Bullinger and Bucer was complementary to the impact of Calvin. I completely agree with John McNeill: "It is misleading ... to assume that the English response to Bucer and Bullinger can be sharply separated from Calvin's English influence. These men were not Calvin's rivals but his heralds" (*History and Character of Calvinism* [New York, 1954], 310); cf. C. D. Cremeans, *The Reception of Calvinistic Thought in England* (Urbana, Ill., 1942). For further evidence on the importance of Calvinism in the development of Puritanism, see Horton Davies, *The English Free Churches* (London, 1952), 13-19; Knappen, *Tudor Puritanism: A Chapter in the History of Idealism* (Chicago, 1939), 135; G. Yule, "Theological Developments in Elizabethan Puritanism," *Journal of Religious History*, I (June, 1960), 20-21. Given, then, the obvious fact of some connection (Cartwright lived and taught in Geneva for a time under Calvin's direction!), our problem is to trace the similarities between Calvin and sixteenth-century Puritans in handling the problem of order.

A very fruitful comparative examination could be made between Calvin's thought and that of Martin Bucer, not to mention other reformers. Bucer is particularly significant so far as the question of relating a Reformed pattern of order to later developments is concerned, because he actually taught at Cambridge toward the end of his life, and he wrote his *De Regno Christi* for King Edward VI. I am sure he had no little influence on the thought of sixteenth-century Puritans, and an analysis of his thought would prove, I am convinced, a great deal of similarity between him and Calvin. If that could be shown, it would mean some substantial revisions of the leading book on the relation between Bucer and English life, Wilhelm Pauck's *Das Reich Gottes auf Erden: Utopie und Wirklichkeit. Eine Untersuchung zu Butzers 'De Regno Christi' und zur Englischen Staatskirche des 16 Jahrhunderts* (Berlin, 1928). Pauck does not, I believe, sufficiently distinguish the dimensions of "new order" that are at work in the thought of Bucer. Therefore, he too easily equates Bucer's conception of a social welfare state with the Elizabethan *raison d'état*. Pauck even admits that Thomas Cartwright is really closer to Bucer than the more typical Elizabethan Anglican, John Whitgift (156). And in other places, Pauck does not seem content with the identity between Bucerism and Elizabethanism. But Pauck does not take his uncertainties seriously enough. For example, in my judgment he superficially identifies both Hooker and Bucer with the idea of a national Church (159), without seeing the fundamental difference of direction that the thought of each implies. If Bucer is close to Calvin (as I believe), then he is certainly not close to Hooker.

Though it is clear that Calvin favored the Puritans in England, his passion for ecumenicity no doubt explains his liberal attitude toward Anglican polity. As A. M. Hunter puts it in the *Teaching of Calvin* (London, 1950), Calvin "was mastered by the vision of a world-wide church one in Christ, and he regarded it as one of the great ends of his earthly mission to promote its realisation" (161). Over and over again he attempted to hold a mediating position, by which doctrinal extremes could be reconciled. "He was," says Hunter, "prepared to allow a large measure of liberty on other matters such as ceremonial usages . . . " (163). In 1552, he replied to Cranmer that some sort of ecumenical meeting was imperative in order "by a unanimous decision [to] hand down to posterity some certain rule of faith . . . " "As to myself, if I should be thought of any use, I would not, if need be, object to cross ten seas for such a purpose. If the assisting of England were alone concerned, that would be motive enough for me" (quoted by Hunter, 164).

(2) The problem of the distinctiveness of Puritanism as against Anglicanism is posed by works like the Georges' *Protestant Mind of the English Reformation* and A. L. Rowse's *England of Elizabeth*. Throughout their book, the Georges put the term "Puritan" in quotes, as though it were not legitimate. At best, "Puritan" means for them an incidental, lunatic fringe consisting of Cartwright, Travers, and Udall, and existing but a brief time. (They do not even deal with Separatism and the whole Massachusetts exodus!) They inform us that there is no evidence that "Puritanism" between 1580 and 1640 had any appreciable influence on the Puritan Revolution. Whatever connections there be are "devious." Rowse states in his characteristically cavalier way that "theologically, Whitgift was as much of an orthodox Calvinist as Cartwright" (469). Or, we are told, "like Whitgift, [Hooker] was nearer the Puritan point of view doctrinally than he was to the Roman" (485). These conclusions are not at all accurate. Nor is Rowse's interpretation of the Puritans very instructive. He believes that the theological disputes of the sixteenth century are so many "endless fooleries." Rowse informs us that the real point of conflict between the Anglicans and the Puritans was not theological or doctrinal; it was that the Anglican representatives, such as Richard Hooker, were reasonable and the Puritans were not. He thinks it historically obvious that "by the time [Hooker] had finished with the Puritans he had left them—in the gentlest, most reasonable manner—with hardly a foot to stand on" (486). But the Puritans "went on standing, since few people are ever persuaded by

rational argument." According to Rowse's objective analysis, the Puritans were simply a group of ambitious, egotistical individuals. "Power was—as usual—what they wanted; and therefore the issue of Church government was the important one." The motives of the Puritans are summarized with the remark: " . . . as we all know, human egoism is the greatest motive force in the world" (488). It is hardly necessary for Rowse to confide to us that he likes Puritanism so little (479).

The Georges and Rowse make much of the theological similarities between Puritans and Anglicans. Certainly by 1583 when Whitgift became archbishop, there is little justification for this view. One notable Marian exile who returned to an important post in the Anglican Church was Edmund Grindal, a rather strong Calvinist and (it could therefore be argued) an unsuccessful Archbishop of Canterbury (1575-83). His vacillation toward the Puritans no doubt accounted for Elizabeth's choice of Whitgift, a staunch anti-Puritan, as his successor. The Georges and others make much of these Calvinists among the Anglicans in order to prove that Calvinists were not necessarily Puritans. While it is true the lines were not, during this early period, sharply drawn, it by no means follows that the Elizabethan Church was Calvinist. There was undoubtedly some influence, but it was at best tenuous and temporary. As P. M. Dawley points out in *John Whitgift and the English Reformation* (New York, 1954; see chapter 5), Whitgift encouraged the anti-Calvinists within the Anglican Church. H. C. Porter, *Reformation and Reaction* (Cambridge, 1958), 413, confirms this. He discusses the strong Cambridge opposition of Overall, Baro, Barrett, and Lancelot Andrewes, all of whom contributed to the "eclipse of Calvinism" in the Anglican Church. "The Calvinist claim was more tenuous, and less overriding, in the Elizabethan Church of England than has sometimes been believed. It has been one of the aims of this study to demonstrate that John Whitgift, too, was aware that 'our church holds the middle path': *mediam viam tenens.*" Cf. also, D. J. McGinn, *Admonition Controversy* (New Brunswick, N.J., 1949), 30, for a confirmation of Whitgift's anti-Calvinism.

As stressed in Chapter 4, Haller's view of Puritanism as a distinctive phenomenon with theological as well as ecclesiastical significance, and a phenomenon with distinguishable but overlapping subgroups (right, center, and left), is most persuasive. Along with Haller's *Rise of Puritanism* (New York, 1957), see his *Liberty and Reformation in the Puritan Revolution* (New York, 1955). No less an authority than Edmund S. Morgan confirms this continuity in Puritanism when he writes in *Visible*

Saints: the History of a Puritan Idea (Ithaca, N. Y., 1965), "The fact is that before the disputes of the 1640's virtually all Puritans agreed on certain basic principles of church organization and on the basic nature of the church" (13).

As my study is confined to particular manifestations of Elizabethan Puritanism, I am not directly concerned with the rise of Separatism and Sectarianism within Puritanism. These aspects began to develop in the late sixteenth century, and flourished just prior to and during the Puritan Revolution (1640-60). It is important, in passing, to mention this continuity which points to a coherent center of thought and action in Puritanism as a whole. M. M. Knappen in his solid (though in places very disputable) work, *Tudor Puritanism: A Chapter in the History of Idealism* underlines the same point: "The term 'Puritan' is used in this book to designate the outlook of those English Protestants who actively favored a reformation beyond that which the crown was willing to countenance and yet stopped short of Anabaptism. It therefore includes both Presbyterians and Independents, Separatists and Non-Separatists" (1). Knappen, Haller, Perry Miller *(Orthodoxy in Massachusetts,* [Boston, 1959]), and Horton Davies *(The English Free Churches)* all show how deeply united were the Presbyterians and the Separatists, or Brownists. Pushing the emphasis upon continuity still further, Haller argues that the sects were very little influenced by continental Anabaptism and were, rather, simply the further extension of implicit dimensions of Puritanism itself (see esp. *Rise of Puritanism*, 174-176 and fn. 2 on 390). In agreement, J. Frank, in his *The Levellers* (Cambridge, 1959), refers to the strong Calvinist Puritan roots in that sect. He does not mention the continental Anabaptists. Certainly, one of the distinctive elements of the Puritan sects was their active endeavor to *extend* the patterns of the Church to the society, in one way or another. (In this connection, see A. S. P. Woodhouse, *Puritanism and Liberty* [London, 1938].) Such a spirit cannot be said to characterize continental Anabaptism, whatever its influence may have been upon such communities as the Scrooby and Gainsborough groups.

(3) As for the theological character of Puritanism, Knappen (*op. cit.,* 348) argues that Weber far and away exaggerated the importance of *certitudo salutis* in Calvinism and Puritanism. It is, he says, "only one small point in a maze of doctrines, and the facts of everyday Puritan existence suggest that in reality the average Reformed churchman, like Calvin himself, worried very little about securing this assurance" (*op. cit.,* 348). However, if there is an ambiguity, the concern with salvation

was certainly not a "small point." What Knappen misses and Weber saw is the strong relationship between the electing will of God and the electing will of the chosen man. That is, God's decision makes a *manifest or empirical difference* in the world of human action. Where there was old disobedience, there is new obedience; where there was old order, there is new order. Election means a new conscience and a new way of acting; it is, by definition, discernible. Therefore, the concern to draw up some kind of criterion between the old and new man was central in this pattern of order. As we see in Perkins, this concern was far from negligible.

There is in Cartwright the same ambiguity over the question of *certitudo salutis* that there is in Calvin. "Although we owght charytably to thinke," he says, "that he that hath given good tokens off repentance / hath trewlie repented / and there fore is off the electe church of God: yet that foundation alwaies remaineth / that when the question is of another man's election / God knoweth who are his," *SR*, 171. This ambiguity is not unimportant in evaluating Puritanism. There is always present in Cartwright's and Perkins's expressions a guard against a crude empiricism in matters of salvation. It is God who decides, not man, and the sovereign decision always rests with him. In terms of our scheme, such a reservation on the question of *certitudo salutis* is quite consistent with the emphasis on the sovereignty of God. It is, further, important to note that the nature of Church organization advocated by Calvin and the Elizabethan Presbyterians (at least) articulated this ambiguity, as against, say, strictly Anabaptist forms. For Cartwright, there are both sheep and goats within the Church. Presbyterians urged uniformity and a parish (not a gathered) system. That means that the lines of division between saved and unsaved always remain relatively open and fluid: one could not be sure simply on the basis of membership, or of any ready-made discipline. (This stituation altered somewhat with the Separatists, though they also advocated uniformity.) It will be recalled that Calvin vacillated a little on the question of discipline as a mark of the genuine Church (just because, I think, of this built-in equivocation). Also, the establishment of "pure" and "impure" members was never completely clear-cut. The same vacillation is certainly present in Cartwright and Perkins.

Incidentally, it is most interesting that Henry Robinson, a leftish Puritan, put his finger squarely on an abiding problem the Presbyterians faced, the question of Christian freedom and political coercion. As W. K. Jordan points out in *Men of Substance* (Chicago, 1942), "it must be granted by the Calvinists according to Robinson that those who have not been elected by God cannot possibly be saved despite the compulsion of the most violent persecution. Uniformity of profession, he caustically reminded the Presbyterians, cannot be confused with certainty of grace. Those who persecute, therefore, may be said to attack the validity of the doctrine of predestination" (131). So far as one of the implications of their position went, Robinson had the Presbyterians cold.

(4) Though his work often suffers from hasty generalizations, Christopher Hill always offers stimulating insights into the socio-economic implications of Puritanism. (See, esp., *Economic Problems of the Church* [Oxford, 1956], *Society and Puritanism* [New York, 1964], and *Intellectual Origins of the English Revolution* [Oxford, 1965]). On two points in particular Hill has made a telling case. First, there appears to be some substance to his suggestions that free trade in business life is interrelated with free exercise in religious life (*Economic Problems*, 185, and *Society and Puritanism*, 46).

It is very significant that a radical Puritan like John Lilburne connects his antipathy toward monopolistic domination of economic life with his hatred of monopolistic control of religious life. In business affairs he is sharply opposed to politically supported monopolies on cloth, bread, beer, etc., and similarly in religious affairs he opposes "forced Religion." Examples of the latter are for him Roman Catholicism, Anglicanism, and Presbyterianism. "Of all Monopolies or Patents, the monopolizing of ingrossing the Preaching of Gods Word into the Tything and gripeing clawes of the Clergy . . . is the most wicked and intollerable . . . " *Englands Birth-Right* (1645), reprinted in Haller's *Tracts on Liberty in the Puritan Revolution* (New York, 1934), 300. On this point see Frank's discussion of the Leveller opposition to all monopolies (*op. cit.,* 62, 114). On 207, Frank writes: "The chief new [economic] points in this final *Agreement* are those which go beyond the Levellers' *usual laissez-faire* attitude in politics and economics . . . " (my italics).

Haller makes the same point about Henry Robinson, who "though identified with no sect . . . quickly reached a position indistinguishable from that of extreme separatism," *Liberty and Reformation,* 160. "In spiritual as in civil affairs, every man understands his own business best and every man's business thrives best when he looks after it himself" (160). "Would not the encroachments [of the Church] in any other trade, be damned for a monopoly—the 'greatest infringing of the Subjects property?' Robinson grants that ministers must be maintained, but the laborer should be worth of his hire, and men should be free to buy truth where it suits them best" (161).

This matter of the free exercise of religion and free trade raises the crucial question of the understanding of "contract" in Calvinist theology. In his essay, "The Marrow of Puritan Divinity," Colonial Society of Massachusetts (Boston, 1936), Perry Miller has helpfully shown how "covenant" or "contract" became a central concept in the "Federal theology" of seventeenth-century Puritanism. He argues that the emphasis upon a contract between man and God served to modify the irrational, incomprehensible aspects of John Calvin's God, and make him more reliable (to use Miller's word), or more predictable. Miller sees this notion as, in general, an elaborate extension, if not a departure from, the theology of Calvin and of a late sixteenth-century Calvinist like Perkins. So far as Miller can tell, "the special quality of the Puritan emphasis upon the covenant does not . . . seem to derive from historic theology at all" (fn. 2, 258). He suggests that the background of the Puritan notion may be the "common-law conception of the covenant, the idea of a formal agreement of legal validity, a promise or contract under seal." Miller finds almost no mention of the covenantal idea in Calvin, and rather little emphasis in Perkins.

I am not completely happy with Miller's formulation, not so much because of what he does as what he does not say. It is certainly true that the idea of contract is developed and takes on dimensions in the seventeenth century in ways quite foreign to primitive Calvinism. But there are suggestions in Calvin and Perkins of a kind of contractualism that squares at a fairly deep level with the pattern of order they share. Certain references to contract in Calvin, for example, bear further investigation: "For the sacraments resemble covenants (contracts), or instruments of agreement, by which God conveys his mercy to us, and in it eternal life; and we, on the other hand, promise him obedience" (IV, 13, 6). "And since the Lord calls his promises *covenants,* and the sacraments *seals of covenants,* we may draw a similitude from the covenants of men" (IV, 14, 6). For Calvin a sacrament is a profession "by which we *testify our agreement with all Christians* in the worship of God . . . " (IV, 15, 13; my italics). As Miller himself points out, Perkins uses the term "Covenant of Grace," meaning God's "contract with man, concerning the obtaining of life eternall, upon a certaine condition" (I, 32). Perkins also uses the term in connection with his discussion of marriage. It is central to making a contract, he claims, that there be "the free and full consent of the parties, which is indeed the very soule and life of the contract" (III, 681). The emphasis upon free-willing or consensual agreement as the basis of a relationship between God and man or man and man is implicit in the system of thought we are treating. In fact, in Calvin, Cartwright, and Perkins there is no other basis for relationship than "contract" or "covenant," if these terms mean voluntary, uncoerced agreement.

It may well be, as Miller says, that "contract" is not extensively developed in Calvin and Perkins, and were it to have been, that it would not have followed the paths of seventeenth-century Puritanism. But I am by no means convinced that the Puritan emphasis upon the idea "does not derive from historic theology at all." One may, in fact, venture to say the important background for the term was not only legal but also theological. Second, Hill's judgment in *Puritanism and Revolution,* 129, on the relation of Calvinism and usury seems valid:

> Calvin came at the beginning of this reversal of values. He abandoned the traditional absolute prohibition of usury (which theologians had whittled away by allowing exceptions) and permitted it in principle (though restricting it very stringently in a great many particular instances). So revolutions in thought are initiated. This slight shift of emphasis, in the busy clothing centre of Geneva, was enough. Calvin-ism and lenience towards usury were henceforth regarded as synony-mous, however much individual ministers insisted on the distinction between legitimate interest and extortionate usury.

This against the extremely shortsighted observations of such writers as the Georges (*op. cit.,* 166-167) and Robertson (*op. cit.,* 111-112), who try to argue that Puritanism had a generally retarding effect upon the practice of usury. In line with our concern, Nelson (*Idea of Usury,* Princeton N.J., 1949) is certainly right in stressing the positive relation between Calvinism and the emergence of values favoring functional universalism, or what Nelson calls "Otherhood." In an important foot-note, Nelson remarks: " . . . We do not consider the modern temper to have arisen merely by a process of 'progressive stripping off of legal and moral restraints upon the anti-social greed of the individual.' We have adopted the word *Otherhood* precisely because we mean to imply that modern liberalism, at its best, looks, at the very least, to the advent of a certain kind of Brotherhood, a Brotherhood in which all are brothers in being equally others" (*op. cit.,* 81). Traditional status, rank, restrictions are broken down, and men become related on the basis of the func-tional contribution they can make to one another. It is not their inheritance that determines what they are, but their own willingness to labor. Incidentally, anyone who doubts the substantial threat to Elizabethan society posed by the Puritans should read the exciting accounts of the parliamentary activity of the Puritans, especially between 1584 and 1601, in J. E. Neale's classic work, *Elizabeth I and Her Parliaments* (2 vols., New York, 1958). Even though the Puritans never amounted to more than about 4 per cent of the population (see Ernest Barker, "Puritanism," *Church, State and Education* [Ann Arbor, Mich., 1957]), they were an extremely well-organized and influential group. Neale concludes his study with these significant words: "From the constitutional point of view, the most important theme in our story is the relationship of the Puritan Movement to parliamentary development" (II, 436). Had they won their way in Parliament, he claims, "stark revolution" (II, 149) would have transformed English political, social, and religious life.

INDEX